P9-DBY-078

People Will Talk

Also by John Whitfield

In the Beat of a Heart: Life, Energy, and the Unity of Nature

People Will Talk

The Surprising Science
of Reputation

JOHN WHITFIELD

WILEY

John Wiley & Sons, Inc.

Copyright © 2012 by John Whitfield. All rights reserved

Published by John Wiley & Sons, Inc., Hoboken, New Jersey
Published simultaneously in Canada

No part of this publication may be reproduced, stored in a retrieval system, or transmitted in any form or by any means, electronic, mechanical, photocopying, recording, scanning, or otherwise, except as permitted under Section 107 or 108 of the 1976 United States Copyright Act, without either the prior written permission of the Publisher, or authorization through payment of the appropriate per-copy fee to the Copyright Clearance Center, 222 Rosewood Drive, Danvers, MA 01923, (978) 750–8400, fax (978) 646–8600, or on the web at www.copyright.com. Requests to the Publisher for permission should be addressed to the Permissions Department, John Wiley & Sons, Inc., 111 River Street, Hoboken, NJ 07030, (201) 748–6011, fax (201) 748–6008, or online at http://www.wiley.com/go/permissions.

Limit of Liability/Disclaimer of Warranty: While the publisher and the author have used their best efforts in preparing this book, they make no representations or warranties with respect to the accuracy or completeness of the contents of this book and specifically disclaim any implied warranties of merchantability or fitness for a particular purpose. No warranty may be created or extended by sales representatives or written sales materials. The advice and strategies contained herein may not be suitable for your situation. You should consult with a professional where appropriate. Neither the publisher nor the author shall be liable for any loss of profit or any other commercial damages, including but not limited to special, incidental, consequential, or other damages.

For general information about our other products and services, please contact our Customer Care Department within the United States at (800) 762–2974, outside the United States at (317) 572–3993 or fax (317) 572–4002.

Wiley also publishes its books in a variety of electronic formats and by print-on-demand. Some content that appears in standard print versions of this book may not be available in other formats. For more information about Wiley products, visit us at www.wiley.com.

ISBN 978-0-470-91235-5 (cloth); ISBN 978-1-118-11464-3 (ebk);
ISBN 978-1-118-11465-0 (ebk); ISBN 978-1-118-11466-7 (ebk)

Printed in the United States of America

10 9 8 7 6 5 4 3 2 1

For Tom

CONTENTS

Introduction

Cassio: Reputation, reputation, reputation! O! I have lost my reputation. I have lost the immortal part of myself, and what remains is bestial.

Iago: As I am an honest man, I thought you had received some bodily wound; there is more sense in that than in reputation. Reputation is an idle and most false imposition: oft got without merit, and lost without deserving: you have lost no reputation at all, unless you repute yourself such a loser.
— *William Shakespeare*, Othello, *act II, scene III*

A s 1996 began, an increasing amount of Pierre Omidyar's time was taken up with a site called AuctionWeb, which he had launched a few months earlier as a hobby. One chore of Omidyar's was fielding about a dozen e-mails a day from buyers or sellers who were in dispute. AuctionWeb made no attempt to control its users, charged no fees, and gave no guarantees; it was simply a digital market, a place for buyers and sellers to meet. When complaints came in, Omidyar, who had a day job as a computer programmer, would forward the message to the other person

1

involved and ask the parties to resolve the matter between themselves. This usually worked, but Omidyar would have preferred not to get involved at all.[1]

AuctionWeb was possibly the least reassuring trading environment ever devised. Buyers were invited to bid on products they hadn't seen and then send money to people they didn't know, who were identified by usernames and virtual storefronts that had cost them nothing to set up and would cost them nothing to replace under different names. In such a situation, the obvious risk was that without someone in charge who had the power to punish bad behavior, AuctionWeb would become what economists call a market for lemons. Buyers, worried that their purchases would arrive in worse condition than advertised or not arrive at all, would bid low. High-quality sellers would take their goods elsewhere, and a race to the bottom would start, resulting in a yard sale where junk was sold for pennies.

Omidyar, and those who were using his site, had run up against the question of how to work out whom you can trust. AuctionWeb, because it seemed to demand blind faith from its users, highlighted the matter, but it's a question that we all face every day, just about every time we meet another human being, online or in the flesh, in business, romance, friendship, politics, or simply while listening to the morning weather report. When we decide to trust, we invest some combination of time, energy, and resources in other people, in the belief that they will keep their side of the bargain. The other guys do the same.

Omidyar could tell that blind faith was not getting the job done. He needed a machine for manufacturing trust that AuctionWeb's users could fuel and operate. The solution he came up with was to allow users to rate one another, awarding +1 as a reward, −1 as a punishment, and 0 as the neutral option. If users wanted, they could also leave a short written comment. What everyone said about everyone else would be on public display. By creating a record of past behavior, this feedback aimed to give honest sellers of high-quality merchandise an escape route from the market for lemons and give buyers a way to find these sellers.

In February 1996 Omidyar unveiled this system and posted a letter on the site:

> Most people are honest. And they mean well. Some people go out of their way to make things right. I've heard great stories about the honesty of people here. But some people are dishonest. Or deceptive. This is true here, in the newsgroups, in the classifieds, and right next door. It's a fact of life. But here, those people can't hide. We'll drive them away. Protect others from them. This grand hope depends on your active participation. Become a registered user. Use our feedback forum. Give praise where it is due; make complaints where appropriate.[2]

That month, Omidyar also began to charge sellers a percentage of the sale price to post listings on AuctionWeb, because the site was getting so much traffic that his Internet service provider had upped its fees. Fast-forward fourteen years, and in the first quarter of 2011 eBay, as AuctionWeb is now known, announced revenues of $2.5 billion.

EBay feedback is what's known as an online reputation system. If you like to measure a thing's significance in dollars, Omidyar's feat of alchemy proves the power of reputation. He used other people's willingness to gossip about one another and to act on that gossip to turn his hobby into a multibillion-dollar business.

As a summary of human nature, Omidyar's manifesto is hard to beat. But its common-sense assertions open out into a hall of wonders and mysteries. Most people really are honest and well-meaning—most of us, most of the time, can be trusted. Why, given the advantages of being otherwise, is that? Why, on the other hand, are some people dishonest and deceptive? And why could Omidyar count on his users to unmask and exclude such people? After all, even if I get a good deal, I may never buy anything from that seller again—so why bother to praise him? And if I get ripped off, I know not to deal with that person again—so why take the time to warn others about him?

This book is about the ways we work out how to trust people and how we persuade them to put their trust in us. As eBay users were among the first to discover, the digitized, often faceless, world in which we spend an increasing amount of our time and money has thrust these problems on us in new forms. Had our species not been able to answer them in the past, however, there would be no eBay on which to be defrauded or Internet, computers, books, shops, cities, civilization, or society. Our willingness to trust strangers and to be trustworthy is one of the most amazing and powerful things in the history of life and one of the hardest to explain.

Every time people interact, they create ripples of information that spread across their social ponds. People are consistent; how they've behaved in the past tends to be a good guide to how they'll behave in the future, so by detecting and interpreting these ripples, other people can decide to trust us or avoid us. Reputation, to put it another way, is indirect experience, a labor-saving device that allows us to sample other people before we buy into them.

Of course, reputation doesn't only report on behavior, it shapes it. The likelihood that how others treat us in the future will depend on what we do now negates the short-term benefits of sneakiness. The knowledge that others are watching and learning turns our every action into a message intended to show our character and inclinations in the best light. Reputation allows us to take fewer precautions and forces us to take fewer liberties. As Adam Smith, the father of modern economics, wrote in 1766, "A dealer is afraid of losing his character, and is scrupulous in observing every engagement. When a person makes perhaps 20 contracts in a day, he cannot gain so much by endeavouring to impose on his neighbours, as the very appearance of a cheat would make him lose."[3] We live in what the philosopher Robert Axelrod called the shadow of the future. In the 250 years since Smith put the power of reputation in a nutshell, economists have probably given the matter more thought than any other group (although novelists must come close). They respect reputation as a force that can make people honest and fair, even when they are driven only by self-interest; they have no morality beyond what they can get away with; and there is no external authority to enforce rules of conduct.

But reputation overshadows more than the dealings of merchants. A huge part of our nature, of who we are and what we do, is geared toward influencing and monitoring third parties. Without realizing it or meaning it, we run our lives so as to advertise our virtues, hide our vices, and uncover other people's abilities and intentions. Reputation has left its mark in our brains, our language, our emotions, our beliefs, our morals, and our best and worst instincts. And the study of reputation's influence on human behavior bridges evolutionary biology, economics, computing, psychology, neuroscience, and any other discipline that straddles the natural and social sciences. By bringing the insights of these fields together, I aim to show how deeply reputation is embedded in our biology. I also want to show that reputation's ability to encourage good behavior and deter bad, as well as deciding our success as individuals, is a vital part of a well-functioning society—which is why Omidyar needed to import it into AuctionWeb—and that when things go wrong, the ways in which people use or escape reputation is often part of the problem.

We'll begin by looking at what reputation is, where it comes from, and how you get one. Many other species have worked out that the best way to make a decision is to copy someone else. Many of the tools that reputation exploits were in place long before humans came on the scene. Birds, fish, apes, and insects pay close attention to their fellows and use that information to guide their own behavior. Once this starts happening, an animal being watched can begin to manipulate its audience: by showing how rich it is in physical, intellectual, or material resources, for example. This is one type of reputation, and humans, through their conspicuous acts of courage, strength, and generosity, pursue it as enthusiastically as any other species.

Not everyone can afford to advertise in this way, but everyone can do someone else a good turn. By helping another, we shape how everyone, not just the beneficiary, treats us in the future. Thus can reputation turn a group of selfish, boastful, gossipy, judgmental, and vengeful animals into a society of altruistic, generous, cooperative, and self-sacrificing humans.

Because reputation is a by-product of gossip, however, it depends on what other people say about us behind our backs. This has little to do with our behavior and a lot to do with other people's social connections and self-interest. Once you start thinking about reputation like this, a lot of its injustices start to make sense. You might be a great writer, like Herman Melville, but still die in obscurity for want of the right social network or skill for self-promotion. (Every society, whaling ship or not, has its Queequegs, quietly doing a brilliant job for a small reward, and its Ahabs, influential, charismatic, well-connected, and stark, staring mad.) We do, though, have a way to shape what other people think about us that is more reliable for being involuntary—the looks on our faces. Our most painful and most rewarding emotions send signals that tell the watching world what to think of us.

All of these deeds and instincts help us gain and defend a reputation for kindness and generosity. To evolutionary biologists, who seek to explain how selfishness can lead to altruism, such acts are the hardest to explain. Turn on the news, though, and you'll see that for the rest of us the terrible things that people do to one another are most noteworthy and troubling. One powerful aspect of reputation is that it can help to explain both the rage and disgust we feel at the news of a faraway atrocity, our desire to see the perpetrators brought to justice, and, conversely, the unconscious calculations that drive people to harm one another in ways that seem not just immoral but irrational and counterproductive. Understanding the environments that reward intimidation—where the best reputation to have is one that drives people away—makes sense of a good deal of the world's violence.

Reputation isn't just a way to encourage good deeds, it's also a way to prevent bad ones. It allows the control of behavior through surveillance. Again, other animals have these skills: to look at the tactics of species from chickadees to chimpanzees, you might think that back in the Precambrian, as soon as life got two neurons to rub together its first thought was "What's he/she/it up to over there?" followed quickly by "What does she/he/it think of me, and how can I manipulate that to my advantage?" You might also think that, having invented language, humans were not so interested in this. But in fact the reverse is true—the sense of being watched is one of the most powerful influences on human behavior, and we are uniquely specialized to control one another with our eyes. But, of course, gossip also plays a huge part in social control, both as a means of bringing offenders into line and as a means of bringing rivals down by attacking their reputations. Reputation is a way for societies to control their members: it is made in social connections and dies at social barriers. When people are isolated from one another, the selfish sides of our natures are uninhibited. This can happen through accidents of technology and economics, or it can be the deliberate strategy of the psychopath who must stay one step ahead of his reputation.

Finally, we'll look at two social situations that our species has never encountered before: the online world and the world of cooperation between groups and nations. In the first of these, reputation is everywhere, although we are still working out how to adapt, or curb, our ancient instincts to cope with the novelties of online social information. In the second, reputation has until now been largely absent—which is one reason global cooperation is so hard to obtain. Is there any hope for harnessing reputation on such a scale?

Reputation is uncomfortable because it gives other people power over us. In William Shakespeare's play *Othello*, when Cassio laments his lost reputation and Iago tells him to get a grip, each is half right. Our reputations, if not actually immortal, do outlive us, advancing or damaging our interests—influencing the way people treat our children, for example—just as they did during our lives. And Iago, although some way from being an honest man, is right to think that how a reputation is gained and lost often bears little relation to what we actually do. But both Cassio and Iago are wrong in thinking that a man can hold and control his own reputation. The reason our reputations survive our personal extinction is that they are not part of ourselves. This isn't how it feels—we hold our sense of worth and honor dear, and when they are injured it does feel like a bodily wound. Yet our reputations belong not to us but to those who know us or know of us. The information from which our reputations are made lives in others' minds.[4]

Another way to think of your reputation is as the part of you that lives inside other bodies. This distributed self is both an ambassador and a hostage, a point of influence and a point of weakness. It can make other people do your bidding, but it's also a remote control pointing back to you. It can be harmed by your own blunders or bad decisions or because it suits the captor's interests. It's not up to Cassio or anyone else to decide whether he has lost his reputation. That's what makes it one of the most powerful influences on human behavior. Reputation is not what humans use to measure one another; it's what they use to control one another. It might look like a yardstick, but it's really a cattle prod.

CHAPTER 1

Follow the Leader

I have in front of me the color magazine from my newspaper's Saturday edition. On the back cover, an improbably hairless Matthew McConaughey is advertising a Dolce and Gabbana scent. Inside, Diane Kruger is doing the same for Calvin Klein. Michael Owen, a famous soccer player, parades his taste in watches. Closer to the back, where the advertisements tend to be less glamorous, a seventy-something television presenter extols the virtues of a foot massager. Another week it might have been Nicole Kidman on the back cover, advertising Omega watches, or George Clooney pushing a coffee maker.

Companies pay a lot for someone famous to hold up their product and smile. Accenture, an accountancy firm, paid millions to be associated with Tiger Woods. They had second thoughts when his marriage fell apart. Such decisions, flying as they do in the face of golf and adultery's irrelevance to accountancy, show how deep-seated our interest is in what other people are up to.

Kevin Laland began working on nine-spined sticklebacks more than a decade ago, by accident. Britain's ponds and streams contain two species of this small fish: the nine-spined and the three-spined. Laland, who studies animal behavior at the University of St. Andrews in Scotland, sent a colleague out to collect some of the three-spined variety from a nearby pond. The colleague had just started working in the lab, however, and couldn't tell the difference between the two, so she came back with both. Since the team had both species, the researchers decided to experiment on them.

The team put seven fish into a tank split by clear plastic dividers into three compartments. Two of the compartments were feeding areas, each containing three fish. The final fish was confined in an observation area, where there was no food. One feeding area received a regular stream of bloodworms, which sticklebacks like to eat. The three fish in the other feeding area got either nothing or far fewer worms. After letting the fish in the observation compartment watch both areas for a few minutes, the researchers removed the other fish from the feeding areas, released the observer, and watched where it went.

The fish in the observation area could have spent its time monitoring its peers and learning which feeding station was the better bet. That's what the nine-spined stickleback did. Or the fish in the observation area could have spent its time minding its own business, learning nothing about where to eat. That's what the three-spined stickleback did, when it was its turn, heading to each feeding station at random.[1] Thanks to the mix-up in species, Laland's team had stumbled on a fish with social skills. Oddly, those skills were in a fish (the nine-spined stickleback) very similar to one lacking such skills (the three-spined stickleback).

Life is about decisions, for both humans and fish. Should I eat here or try somewhere else? Are there any predators about? Should I try to annex my neighbor's territory? Is this a good place to make my home? Would that male make a suitable father for my offspring? Such choices determine the difference between life and death, both in the space of a few seconds and in an evolutionary sense, between sending offspring into the next generation and being a genetic dead-end. One way to decide is through instinct alone, to have hardwired responses to the environment. This works well in stable environments: if the right thing to do goes on being the right thing to do for a long-enough time, there's a strong possibility that natural selection will inscribe that behavior in an animal's genes. Woodlice come into the world preferring cool, damp, dark places to warm, dry, brightly lit ones. This sends them scuttling to safety under rocks—it worked for their parents and grandparents and each preceding generation, and chances are it will go on working. When a woodlouse makes a decision, history does the heavy lifting.

This isn't always reliable. Caterpillars that once hatched from their eggs just as succulent young leaves were bursting out on the trees are finding, in a warming world with earlier springs, that the leaves are already old and tough when they most need them. Humans who evolved hearty appetites for fat and sugar in an environment where both were scarce are not well adapted to all-you-can-eat buffets. Hardwired behaviors are not much use in an unpredictable environment—if, for example, the best spots for prey change from day to day. Here, you need the capacity to learn.

One way to do this is by trial and error. This yields valuable firsthand experience, but it can also be expensive: spend too long in a barren feeding spot and it might be too late to try somewhere else. In addition, personal knowledge gives you a sample size of only one. A bird whose nest fails in one year doesn't know whether it really picked a bad spot or whether something else, perhaps bad weather or simply bad luck, was to blame for its barren year.

Yet an animal needn't rely solely on its own experience. It is surrounded by information, in the form of what others are doing. Animals suck that public information up and put it to their own ends. At its most basic, this means copying. One of the most powerful rules of thumb available to animals is that it's a good idea to do what others are doing. Most animals do not survive to adulthood, and many of those do not find a mate, breed, and raise offspring. So if they can see any animal that seems to be doing well, chances are it is doing something right, and other animals could do worse than to copy it.

This, then, is how the nine-spined stickleback decides where to feed—it copies its neighbors. It seems like such an obvious tactic that the puzzle becomes why its three-spined cousin trusts only in personal experience. The answer is that three-spined sticklebacks can better afford to make mistakes. They have hefty spines and armored plates on their bodies that make them an uncomfortable mouthful; several predatory fish such as pike have been seen to swallow and spit out a three-spined stickleback in rapid succession. Nine-spined stickle-backs are more delicate, with smaller spines and no armor. They hide in the weeds and peek out, watchful for signs of danger and safety, before committing to a feeding sortie. Spininess and social awareness, Laland's team found, are different solutions to the same problem.

This copying behavior is called social learning, and it's seen in all kinds of animals in all kinds of situations.[2] Some birds that nest in dense colonies won't start breeding in a site unless another bird is already there, however suitable that site may be. Conservationists who are trying to restore populations of colonial seabirds, such as puffins and terns, have used decoys to lend an empty site an air of popularity and so encourage birds to colonize a new area. Of course, hunters cottoned on to this long ago and use decoys to make the spot just in front of their guns seem more appealing to passing waterfowl.

Compared to most of the world's animal species, birds and even sticklebacks have pretty big brains. Yet you don't need much of a brain or a social life to tap into public information. The wood cricket has neither, yet it still takes notice of its neighbors' decisions. One of the main threats to crickets comes from wolf spiders, and if a cricket knows there are spiders about, it becomes cautious, spending more of its time hiding under leaves. If you then introduce a cricket that has never encountered a spider into a group of recently spooked insects, it will also hide under leaves, even if there are no spiders around.[3] This suggests that animals can evolve the ability to copy if such infor-mation is useful in their particular circumstances.

Sometimes, what an animal's neighbors are doing can make it go against the evidence of its own eyes. One of the most important choices any animal makes is whom to mate with. For most species, courtship is brief and the consequences costly and irreversible, so any piece of information they can get before committing is price-less. One such piece of information is whom others are choosing. If you, a female, see another female mating with a male, it's a vote in his favor (as long as you're not expecting him to provide any care for your offspring, which goes for most animal species), and you should be more likely to mate with him. This is called mate-choice copying, and the first species that was shown to behave this way in a controlled experiment was another small fish, the Trinidadian guppy, which lives in mountain streams on the eponymous Caribbean island.

Female guppies are functionally proportioned and colored. Males have larger and more brightly colored tails; under selective breeding by humans, this tail can become a garish fan, like a flamenco dancer's dress. As far as most females are concerned, the brighter a male is, the better. This preference passes from mother to daughter, and when Lee Dugatkin began working on guppies in the late 1980s, this was the beginning and the end of it—researchers thought that a female's taste in mates was genetically programmed. Dugatkin thought that it might be more complicated. There were already hints from studies of other species that females noticed both the attributes of males and the choices of other females when they picked a mate. The guppy, because it lives in shoals and because a lot was already known about how it chose a mate, was an ideal species in which to examine how peer pressure influences what females find attractive.

Dugatkin put two females—an observer and a demonstrator—and two males, one brightly colored, one drab, in an aquarium. Every fish was inside its own transparent container, preventing it from swimming freely around the tank. By putting the demonstrator's container nearest the drab male, Dugatkin could give the observer the impression that the other female had chosen to approach her less impressive suitor and snub his gaudy rival.

When Dugatkin allowed the observer to make her own choice, he saw that she, too, went for the drab male. The other female's example was enough to override her inbuilt preference for bright males.[4]

When a female sees a drab male succeed with the opposite sex, it's not simply that she prefers that male at that moment. Drab males become more attractive in general. This opens up another route besides genetic change by which an entire species' taste in mates can shift. Among wild guppies, there are some females who prefer drab males over brightly colored ones. How such choices arose and why they haven't disappeared are not known, but possibly this occurred through females copying one another, making it a trait that is passed on through culture, rather than through genes, and showing that when we take an animal out of its social world to study it, we may be getting only part of the picture and a distorted part at that. Dugatkin's experiment shows that even in fish, sexual desirability—beauty, you might say—is partly a social construct. Animals do not come into the world with an innate idea about what their perfect mate looks like. Or, rather, they do, but it is malleable and depends on what others around them are doing.

The benefits of taking a shortcut to a good decision by copying others apply just as much to human mate choice as to any other species. It would be surprising if our ideas of attractiveness weren't influenced by what people around us were doing. Not every study has found that men who are "taken" become more desirable in women's eyes: wearing a wedding or engagement ring does not seem to make men more attractive to women.[5] But there is much evidence that other people's opinions shape our tastes. If a woman sees another woman smiling at a photo of a man, for example, that man becomes more attractive to her. (For men—for whom the man is a potential rival—a woman's attentions make another man seem less attractive.)[6] Trying to investigate the question in as naturalistic a setting as possible, Skyler Place, a psychologist at Indiana University in Bloomington and his colleagues did an experiment in which observers could watch genuine human courtship behavior. First, they asked subjects in Indiana to look at photos of members of the opposite sex and decide how desirable they were. They then showed these subjects ten-second video snippets of the same people recorded at speed-dating sessions hosted by Humboldt University in Berlin. None of the American observers spoke German, so they could read body language and tone of voice but could not understand what was being said. Then the researchers asked the observers to decide whether the couple in the clip had been hitting it off or not and finally to re-rate the desirability of the person whose photo they had first seen.[7]

Speed-daters who seemed to be winning their partners' affections became more attractive to observers. Men, on average, rated all of the women they saw as more desirable after seeing a video clip, but the effect was much greater for women in whom another man showed an interest. Women, on the other hand, found a man less attractive if they saw him having no luck but more attractive if he was having some success.

Another study of speed-daters, this time using Harvard under-graduates, shows that mate-choice copying is actually more accurate than personal intuition. In this study, women's predictions of how much they would enjoy a five-minute encounter were more accurate when they were told simply how much another woman had enjoyed a date with the same man than when they were instead given informa-tion on that man's personality and tastes. Other people's experience, in other words, can be more useful than imagination (although, contrary to their own experience, the women in this study believed the opposite).[8]

It would be a mistake to suggest that human and animal social learning are just alike. We are far better at it and far more susceptible to its influence than any other species. Humans, for example, can copy not only what a person achieves—using a rod to catch a fish, say—but also how he or she achieves it, through the position of the arm, the casting technique, and so on. No other species can copy technique so well; instead, they focus more on achieving the same goal. We use social learning all the time, in every area of life, and at every level of our intellect. It's what makes and destroys brands and businesses: I notice that Hamax child seats are the most common on bicycles, so I go out and get one myself; looking for somewhere to eat, I walk past the empty restaurant and go into the crowded one next door, just as a nine-spined stickleback would do. We get our language, religion, customs, and politics, not by sampling every option and picking the best one, but by copying people around us. The same goes for decisions we don't even realize we're making: as infants, for example, we learn what to fear partly by seeing what scares our parents.[9] Learning from others, rather than by trial and error, gives us access to vast quanti-ties of knowledge and expertise that no individual would be able to discover independently. Once the wheel and the atomic bomb were invented, it became much easier to copy them than reinvent them.

Some psychologists have described humans as default social learners, turning to copying before trial and error or innovation.[10]

Another study, by Kevin Laland and his colleagues, hints at why this might be the best policy.[11] It's easy to guess at the advantages of a particular learning strategy but much harder to work out how it will fare when thrown into competition with other possible strategies. To tackle this question, Laland staged a gambling tournament for computer programs, with a 10,000 euro prize for the winner. He put out a call for anyone who was interested to write and submit a program to play a sort of experimental gambling machine called a multiarmed bandit. (A one-armed bandit is a primitive slot-machine with one lever and a fixed probability of winning.) In Laland's tournament, the programs faced a bandit with a hundred arms, each with a certain probability or returning a certain reward. A program's goal was to work out which was the most profitable arm to pull. To make things more difficult, every so often the payoffs of each arm of the bandit changed, so the competing programs also needed to be able to adapt on the fly.

To learn which arm to pull, programs had two options. They could obtain information directly about any given arm—as the equivalent of a free pull of that arm, which cost nothing but returned nothing. This move was called "innovate." Or they could take the social route and receive some information about how other programs were doing at that moment, a move called "observe." The third option was for the program to put its money where its mouth was and pull an arm, which was called "exploit."

The tournament attracted 104 entries from 16 countries, devised by researchers who specialized in everything from primatology to computer science, management, and philosophy. The top programs, including the winner, which was called "discountmachine" and was the work of a team consisting of a Canadian mathematician and a neuroscientist, almost all relied on alternating bursts of observation and exploitation. Discountmachine hardly ever bothered to find anything out for itself, opting to innovate in fewer than one in every twenty moves. It won even though direct learning took no more time or effort than copying, and even though more than half of the time a program choosing to observe saw another program pulling an arm of the bandit that it already knew about. The strongly social programs won even when Laland made copying less accurate, increasing the probability that instead of pulling the arm it had seen another program pull, a program using copying made a mistake and pulled an arm at random. It seems that if you can trust that others are doing what's best for themselves, then parasitizing their experience is by far the best way to acquire information.

The benefits of this are obvious, but copying isn't free. It takes time and energy that you could be using to find out something for yourself. In addition, it has its risks. Copying is a basic form of trust—trust that the other guy has got it right. This trust might be misplaced: he might be mistaken, or things might have changed since he made his decision. Things get particularly volatile when decision makers can see the choices that their neighbors are making but not the information that they're using to make those decisions.[12] In such a situation, once a few individuals have chosen a certain option, any animal susceptible to social learning is going to copy them, even, perhaps, against its own judgment. We feel vindicated in our own choices when we see a large crowd of people jumping the same way—investing in a particular stock, for example—but if we're all following one another, without making any independent assessment, then even though a new recruit might make the herd look more impressive, she brings no more knowledge and makes the decision no more reliable. In such situations, a pebble of information can start a landslide of decisions; economists call it an information cascade. Often, the initial decision was a good one; we wouldn't copy one another if it didn't work more often than not. The consequences are frequently harmless fads and crazes. Yet sometimes rational individuals copying one another can create social disasters, such as a bank run or a stock market crash.

Sometimes it pays to find out things for oneself. The challenge is to work out whether your own information is better than the herd's, particularly when what your personal experience tells you is at odds with what everyone else is doing. Again, sticklebacks show the way. Laland's team found that before the nine-spined stickleback decides where to feed, it compares the available public information—that is, where its neighbors are eating—with its own knowledge of the environment. If, in its compartmentalized tank, a fish has to choose between copying six fish feeding at a poorly supplied feeding station and two fish feeding at a richly supplied one, it is likely to ignore the majority and go for the better meal, thus avoiding falling into an information cascade.[13] If a fish can sample both feeding areas for itself before seeing other fish feed, it is likely to go back to the one it has personally found more productive, even if in the meantime the researchers have swapped the good and the bad patches and let the fish watch others feeding under the new arrangement. At least, this is what happens if the second feeding bout follows soon after the first. If the fish has to wait a week before returning to the same environment, it disregards its prior experience and becomes a copier. This might be simple forgetfulness, but it also may reflect the deteriorating quality of the fish's private information. There's little to guarantee that last week's hot spot for bloodworms will still be the best place to feed.[14]

Like sticklebacks, birds that choose a nesting site compare private and common knowledge. A colonial seabird, the kittiwake, a dainty gull of the northern oceans that nests on cliffs in raucous groups thousands strong, moves its nest site after a failed year only if others around it have also failed. If an unsuccessful pair's neighbors breed successfully, the failures are likely to try again in the same spot.[15] Failed breeders aren't the only animals in need of pointers from others. Once you get past thirty, young folk start to seem ridiculously impressionable, mindlessly aping whatever is fashionable. Yet being impressionable can make perfect sense, because if your own experience is limited, what others are doing may be the best source of information you have. (One highly placed entry to Laland's tournament was called "CopyWhenYoungThenLearnWhenPayoffsDrop," which says it all.) First-time breeders are in the same position as failed breeders—they've yet to figure out what works. Wrens and budgerigars are two species in which young birds choosing a nesting site for the first time are more likely to set up home near other birds' nests, while more experienced breeders tend to seek out a more isolated spot. The worse your private information is, the better the public information looks. This is also why it so often seems as if "all the good ones are taken." The mere fact that they're taken makes them seem like good ones.

Similarly, as Dugatkin probed deeper into how female guppies choose mates, he showed that the fish do not copy blindly but rather balance many factors, including male appearance, female preference, the range of options available, and what everyone else is doing. For example, social influences do not make a female blind to a male's charms: if one potential mate is much brighter than another, a female will follow her genes and ignore another's lead. Yet a drab male attended by more than one female or by a single female for a lengthy period becomes more attractive to onlookers, swaying the balance back from innate taste toward social influences.[16] It's as if a female awards points in various categories and then mates with whomever scores highest.

When an animal is deciding whether to follow another, it also bases its decision on the quality of the leader. If a stickleback does choose to imitate others, it does not pick its models at random. Instead, it will prefer to copy a big stickleback rather than a small one.[17] As well as being a sign that a fish has a knack for finding food, large size is a sign of advanced age, because fish keep growing throughout their lives. A big fish is the living embodiment of its own good decisions; its neighbors know this and pay heed. If chimpanzees are shown the solutions to two equally difficult problems, each returning an equally valuable food reward, they tend to copy the solution demonstrated by the older, higher-ranking animal. This suggests that a bias toward copying the top animals in our group is older than our own species and evolved before the lineages of humans and chimpanzees split about six million years ago.[18] The same goes for mate choice. Young female guppies are most susceptible to the influence of other females and are most likely to copy the decisions of large, old fish. These older fish will copy other old females but are immune to the younger generation's fads.[19]

The human urge to copy another's mate choice is similarly swayed by the quality of the demonstrator, except it's not the old or large whose tastes we follow, it's the beautiful. The study of Berlin speed-daters found that male observers' opinions of a woman rose more when they watched her win over an attractive man, particularly when observers rated that man as more handsome than themselves. There was no such effect on female observers in this study, but other experiments have found that the attentions of a beautiful woman make a man more desirable to other women.[20] One study found that having good-looking friends on Facebook makes you more physically attractive to those viewing your profile.[21] The same rules, then, seem to apply to both human and guppy romance. Attraction may be biological, but sometimes biology tells us to copy Angelina Jolie.

This brings us back to celebrity endorsements. When I see George Clooney endorsing Nespresso, I'm tempted to follow his lead not so much because I enjoyed *O Brother, Where Art Thou?* or because I think that consuming a capsule-based coffee beverage is going to make me more like Clooney. It's rather that I recognize Clooney as a successful, high-status individual and so assume he's doing the right thing. That reasoning doesn't apply only to celebrities. My magazine carries an advertisement for the Panasonic Eco-Max vacuum cleaner that boasts of its unrivaled suction and maximum efficiency. Before you see these claims, however, you see an attractive, well-dressed woman wearing an ecstatic look while pushing the thing. We are all alert to the signs of biological, social, and financial success, and we are all more likely to be swayed by those who display them, as the speed-dating study found.

You rarely, on the other hand, see an old person advertising a product that isn't aimed at old people. Western culture no longer honors old people to the extent that, in common with almost every society studied, it once did. Perhaps this is because old age is less unusual than it used to be and thus less of a marker of success, and also because the pace of social and technological change has increased to such an extent that being old is taken more as a sign of obsolescence than status. Change makes social learning less reliable, because you risk copying someone who has outdated information. So when you see a senior citizen in a laptop advertisement, the message isn't

"This computer is chosen by the wise," it's "This computer is so simple, even granny can use it."

Sometimes it's easy to spot the link between a product's properties and the celebrity chosen to promote it. Easy-on-the-eye film stars advertise perfumes and cosmetics because these products are intended to make their users sexier. Breakfast cereals, sports drinks, and sneakers tend to be advertised by sports stars, to give the impression that the products will make us healthier and more athletic. For items that are more like status symbols than functional objects, almost anyone famous enough will do: no one buys an Omega watch (advertised by George Clooney and Nicole Kidman) because they want to know the time or a Louis Vuitton suitcase (advertised by everyone from the Argentinian soccer player Diego Maradona to Mikhail Gorbachev, via Bono) because they need something to carry their socks in. They do so to advertise their own wealth and taste. Of course, we have ideas about a product's desirability independent of who's plugging it, so celebrities need to be careful about what they let themselves be associated with. That's why you're unlikely to see Nicole Kidman ecstatically pushing a vacuum cleaner anytime soon.

A guppy could grasp what's going on here, but it might struggle with the idea that an accountancy firm would want to hitch itself to Tiger Woods's image. Humans, however, are promiscuous copiers, and when we see that a person is a success in one area of life, we become more likely to copy that person in other areas. Accenture wasn't paying Woods so that the company could be associated with his deft touch with a sand wedge. It was using him as a model of more general skills and abilities, such as dedication, competitiveness, and attention to detail. Accenture was hoping to tap into what psychologists call prestige bias.

Prestige bias has been seen in many different societies—among hunter-gatherers, for example, the best hunters' opinions on all matters carry more weight—and in many different experiments. A 1972 study showed that students' views on campus activism were swayed equally by listening to a talk from an expert on the subject and by one on the same topic by an expert on the Ming dynasty.[22] We prefer to copy professional-looking people to scruffy ones, even, experimenters have found, if they're rolling a marble through a maze.[23] Prestigious people—what are called local opinion leaders—shape their community's uptake of technologies, products, customs, and even words and pronunciation. (The London suburb of New Malden, for example, now contains the largest Korean community in Europe, because the South Korean ambassador moved to the neighborhood in the 1960s.) In humans, the power of prestige depends not only on how highly we rate the other person's knowledge but on how poorly we rate our own. The less we know about the subject at hand, the more complicated and difficult it is to grasp, and the harder it is to find out things for ourselves, the more susceptible to prestige we become.

Why do we generalize expertise in this way? In a persuasive hypothesis about the origin and function of prestige in humans, the anthropologists Joseph Henrich and Francisco Gil-White argue that it's because to do any difficult task successfully, you have to combine many separate skills into a complicated whole. For example, to be a good hunter you need to know where to find your prey, how to track and stalk it, and how to bring it down. Anyone trying to copy a successful hunter will struggle to work out which particular thing is the key to success—you can see that the hunter is good, but you're not sure what's making him so good. The safest thing to do is to buy into the whole package. This tendency to generalize means that prestige bias cuts both ways, and if someone trips up in one area of life, we are apt to see him as an all-around screw-up. (Although what constitutes tripping up also depends on the norms of a person's community. What's outrageous for a golfer is unremarkable for a rock star.) The judgment then becomes whether someone's failings outweigh his or her successes and how much to connect the different areas of life. So when Tiger Woods's marital difficulties became public knowledge, Accenture ended its association with him. Nike, though, stood by Woods, perhaps because it pays primarily to be associated with his golf game and has less interest in his all-around qualities.

What's in it for those being copied? For most animals, not much. A stickleback eating bloodworms doesn't benefit if other sticklebacks follow its lead. It may even do better if it can keep the food source secret. That certainly goes for mate choice, where you risk making your partner desirable to someone more attractive than yourself—what you might call the "Jolene" effect, after the Dolly Parton song. Sexual jealousy is one way to deal with this, whereas Parton opts for groveling. The Atlantic molly, a fish in the same family as the guppy, has evolved a more cunning strategy.

In this species, males copy other male's mate choices, possibly because females are fertile for only a few days of each month and a male can't tell whether a female is receptive unless he courts her. So a male molly can work out where to focus his efforts by watching the other males around him. The last thing a male fish wants, however, is another male copying his moves. If a female mates with multiple males in quick succession, their sperm must race to fertilize her eggs. This is called sperm competition.

Martin Plath and his colleagues found that a male molly's taste in females depends on who's looking.[24] In private, a male will direct his attention toward the larger, and therefore probably more fecund, of two females. Yet if you put another male in the tank, the first male's choices will sometimes become random: he's just as likely to attempt to mate with the smaller female. This effect is particularly strong if the observer male is large and thus more attractive to female mollies. Take the observer away, and the first male reverts to his earlier type.

It seems, then, that if a male molly thinks another male is a rival, he tries to jam any attempts to eavesdrop on his mate choices. If the observer isn't perceived as a threat—if the two males have previously shared an aquarium, for example, and if the first male has never seen the observer court a female—he doesn't bother trying to hide his choices, and observers make no difference. It's not known how often deceit works or whether observers try to conceal their interest to get a better chance of eavesdropping accurately. For the male under observation, though, concealing his preferred mate presumably has some benefits; otherwise, it's unlikely that he'd bother with the trick. It presumably must not work all of the time, either, or observer males wouldn't bother to copy.

Humans, unlike other species, have something to offer those they copy. The prestige we give to people who excel at something, argue

Henrich and Gil-White, is a payment for getting up close to excellence, so that we can observe it in detail and copy it more accurately. By honoring the model, you help yourself. In a world of social learning, the skillful have a valuable resource. In return for sharing their skill, they get deference, influence, preferential treatment, and a degree of license to break rules and avoid obligations that would not be tolerated in the less talented. In animals, status and hierarchy are created by force. Chimpanzees copy high-status individuals, but they don't get to the top by being good problem-solvers. They get there by winning fights. The same is true across the animal kingdom. Dominant individuals can take what they want and coerce others into doing what they want. High status repels other animals—the weak keep their distance from the strong and glance at them hastily and sidelong. Humans have this in their repertoire, of course, but in our species, status is also an attractive force. We will give attention freely to those we seek to emulate, and most of the top people in our societies— politicians, artists, scientists, business people, and even soldiers and sports stars—get there because they have skills that other people want, not because they dominate those beneath them. In fact, as Henrich and Gil-White point out, in many societies high-status people self-deprecate, showing that whatever their prestige they are not seeking dominance. This is both good manners and a smart move, because, as we'll see in later chapters, there are few quicker routes to unpopularity than trying to dominate other people.

Social learning is only the beginning of our story. Reputation, as humans use it, is much more than simply copying what other people do and honoring those who do it best. The shadow of the future does not fall over social learning: we copy people because it pays in the here and now. Reputation building, in contrast, is about doing things that are expensive as a way of reaping a benefit in the long term. Social learning is used to plan behavior in general, whereas we use a person's reputation to plan our behavior toward that person, which may not involve imitation.

The uses of copying do, however, provide two pillars of reputation. The benefits of social learning—which is widespread across the animal kingdom and doesn't require a great deal of what we would regard as intelligence or self-awareness—give us a reason to care about what those around us are doing. The economy of prestige, which is, as far as we know, unique to humans, gives us a reason to care about what others think of us. We can begin to see another vital facet of reputation here—that the audience shapes the performance. People would still need to gather food even if there was no one to admire them for it, but the prospect of admiration gives an additional reason to gather food and may sway the types of food that we decide to pursue. It might even make us give that food away.

CHAPTER 2

An Introductory Offer

Murray Island lies at the northern end of the Great Barrier Reef, in the Torres Strait that runs between Australia and Papua New Guinea. The indigenous people, who currently number about 450, call it Mer, and so are known as the Meriam. When they celebrate, they eat turtle meat, and when a feast is planned—when a tombstone to a dead relative is unveiled, for example—the person organizing the celebration commissions one of the island's half-dozen turtle hunters to go to work.

The hunt leader organizes a crew, typically two other men. The day before the feast, they set sail in a small open boat with an outboard motor and look for turtles among the channels and lagoons of the reef. The leader stands in the bow of the boat, reading the tides and the currents, working out where the animals might be, and scanning the water for any sign of them. When he spots one, he decides whether it's large enough to be worth pursuing and, if so, directs the chase, instructing the crewman at the tiller. When the animal is tired and cornered, the hunters pull close, and the other crewman, the jumper, leaps from the boat onto the turtle's back. When turtle were hunted from sailing canoes, the crewman would tether the animal using a sucker fish tied to a line, like a living harpoon. Now jumpers drive a metal hook into the turtle's shell and use it to wrestle the beast, perhaps weighing three hundred pounds and capable of breaking a limb with its flippers, into the boat. The hunt might last twelve hours or more, and the group will return with two or three turtles, which will be delivered live to the feast organizer.

In return, the hunters get nothing. They're not paid in cash or anything else for the turtle. They don't get any of the turtle meat, unless they attend the feast, in which case they still get no more than any other guest. They're not made guests of honor. They're not even given expenses—they have to pay for the upkeep of their boats and for the gasoline they use on the hunt.

In chapter 1 we found the place where reputation starts, with success. If you are really good at one thing, people will think you excel at everything (or vice versa). Still, they have to know that you are successful, and that's where the expensive and seemingly selfless acts of the Meriam turtle hunters come in.

In the late 1990s, anthropologist Eric Smith, of the University of Washington in Seattle, traveled to Murray Island with two members of his research group who were experts in Meriam culture, Rebecca Bliege Bird and Douglas Bird, to try to find out what hunters might get in return for the meat they provide and to learn about the trouble they go through to get it. Even though the hunters' achievements weren't publicly honored, it soon became clear that their work didn't go unnoticed. Asking around revealed that pretty much everyone knew and agreed about who the best hunters were, both now and among the elders. (Meriam men become jumpers in their teens, and about half of the crewmen graduate to lead hunts in their late twenties; hunters usually retire in their forties.) From interviews, the researchers also constructed family trees, to see who had been mating with whom and how productive the unions had been.

These genealogical studies revealed that hunters began reproducing earlier than nonhunters—about one in five hunters fathered a child while still in his teens, compared with one in fourteen non-hunters. Hunters were only half as likely to go through life childless as nonhunters, and they averaged a total of about five children, compared to slightly more than two for everybody else. To compare the rewards of excellence in different areas, Smith and his colleagues also asked the Mer to name who among them excelled at other skills, such as fishing and political leadership. Turtle hunters' reproductive success, they found, surpassed that of every other group of men, be they fishers, farmers, or even well-known lotharios.

Turtle hunters father children by a greater number of women than other men do, and their partners tend to be younger women and thus more fertile. Yet the biggest effect on their reproductive success seems to lie in the quality of the mates they attract. The Meriam describe some women as *au dorge dorge koskir*, the closest translation of which is "hard working." Such women are tough, resourceful, and inventive and are so good at fishing, gardening, and collecting shellfish that they produce a surplus of food to share with their neighbors. Turtle hunters were especially likely to be partnered with hard-working women. When asked to name what they looked for in a man, women mentioned his being a good provider, but none of them said they had a thing for turtle hunters. Smith thinks that hunting turtles is a route to high status among other men—jumpers, he says, are the jocks of their group, and hunt leaders are seen as the aces—and that women pick up on this male hierarchy when choosing their mates. People notice the abilities of those around them and reward the best with prestige. Smith's study reveals the tangible evolutionary benefits that prestige brings and shows why it pays to be a good hunter.[1]

Social learning means that skillful, smart, and athletic people attract followers who want to learn from them. Yet copying can get you only so far. There's a limit to the number of people who can, say, accompany a skilled hunter on his business and a limit to the number of people who can or want to be hunters. We all need to cast our social nets wider than this, to find allies, mates, and friends. We need people to trust in our abilities and intentions.

As in every human interaction, ignorance and unfamiliarity form barriers to trust. There are not many greater investments in another person than allowing him to father your children and few decisions more important. It's hard to tell who will be a good mate, though, just by looking at him. So a woman seeking a mate wants some indicator that reveals whether a man is strong, healthy, and clever. The same goes for anyone choosing a partner for a risky but potentially rewarding joint project, such as a political allegiance, a business venture, or a bank job.

There is, however, a problem. Deceit pays, and trust can be misplaced. The man spinning stories about his ability to feed a family might be weak and lazy. The inventor wowing a millionaire investor with his perpetual-motion machine might have no more than a box with some wires sticking out of it and a mail-order diploma. That savvy-sounding young criminal might have learned everything he knows from playing *Grand Theft Auto*. Bluffing becomes a temptation and a risk any time that partners' interests conflict, which goes for just about any interaction with a potential for one party to exploit another—and that means almost any interaction with the potential to create something worthwhile.

There is a way to make information reliable. You make it expensive to send. Cheap communication is untrustworthy, because messages can be faked. It's a lot easier to buy a mug that reads "World's Best Dad" than it is to be a good dad. Smart women learn to ignore untrustworthy signals and to look for things that are difficult to acquire, such as a well-paid job. The tougher a task is to do, the fewer people can do it, so it becomes a more reliable sign of quality and more powerful as a creator of trust.

Costly signaling, as it's called, occurs in conflicts across the animal kingdom. Before stags lock antlers, they bellow at each other. Bellowing is a proxy for brawn: the biggest, fittest stags have the loudest, deepest bellows, and because the listening stag knows that its rival's voice is a good guide to its fighting ability, the stag benefits from heeding the signal and avoiding a potentially fatal fight. (Humans also take a deep voice as a sign of fighting ability.)[2] Males and females often have differing interests when they seek mates. To oversimplify a bit, a male's path to evolutionary success involves mating with as many females as he can, whereas for females quality is more important than quantity, and they typically want to choose the male who will provide them with the best offspring. As a result, sexual displays—such as the plumage of birds of paradise or the croaks of frogs—are expensive, and only top-quality males can afford them. There's a parallel body of theory in economics, which argues that employees signal their worth by acquiring a costly education and that employers reward this with higher wages. If any of these signals, animal or human, were cheap, they'd be an unreliable measure of quality, so their intended targets would ignore them.

Smith and his colleagues believe that turtle hunting among the Meriam is a costly signal. By providing the meat for feasts, hunters show that they are among the few on the island with either the physical prowess to subdue a large and uncooperative marine reptile or the intellect and the leadership skills to organize and execute a hunt. The ritualized meat sharing on Mer is particularly suited for sending a signal, but sharing of one kind or another is common wherever there is big-game hunting. In every society where the link between hunting and reproduction has been studied, which is about half a dozen so far, the best hunters have more offspring. You can't eat your way to dynastic glory, but you can feed your way to it.

In societies where we buy our meat at the supermarket, people find other ways to send costly signals. You could, for example, buy organic meat at the farmers' market and show that you care about the environment and the welfare of farmers and their animals, and you have the money to pay for it. In general, people can wring opportunities to show off from the most unlikely situations.

Henry Lyle, a graduate student of Eric Smith's, applied the same approaches that had worked so well among the Meriam to the study of a behavior closer to home and more recent in origin: illegal file-sharing among the undergraduates at two colleges in Sacramento, California.[3] Downloading, he found, is an equal-opportunity crime: seven out of every ten students confessed to doing it, and just as many of them were women as men. Yet creating the resource—uploading music and video files to peer-to-peer networks—is a boys' game. Three-quarters of those who did it were male. This male bias doesn't merely reflect general geekiness, because uploaders were no more computer literate than the average member of either sex.

Like turtle hunters, uploaders provide resources valued by other members of their community, in the form of both the files and the computer gear needed to host them. Like Meriam feasts, a few creators provide for a large number of consumers. Like turtle hunters, creators pay a price for doing so. By opening up their machines to the network, uploaders expose themselves to viruses and hackers, and they risk prosecution by vengeful media companies, which could result in a six-figure fine.

What do uploaders want in return for their risk-taking? To Lyle's surprise, they weren't concerned with their reputations online, and downloaders weren't interested in where their files came from or the technical specifications of their delivery. So uploading is not a way to become known and admired online. Instead, file sharers seem to be seeking prestige among their real-world peers. The few women who uploaded files tended to keep quiet about it, but men knew who among their friends was providing files, were more likely to talk about it, and were more likely to upload while someone else was with them.

Sharing media online, Lyle discovered, seems to be the latest version of braggadocio. When he got groups of students together to talk about their file-sharing behavior, he found that twenty-first-century young men discuss the speed of their processors and the fatness of their hard drives just as their mid-twentieth-century counterparts would preen over the horsepower and acceleration of a souped-up Ford Mustang. "What's your pipe size?" (referring to the speed of Internet connection) was a popular conversational gambit among the Sacramento students. Unlike a car, displays of largesse such as digital uploading and turtle hunting are signals that benefit those who receive them. When you get your friend's message that he is a broadband Robin Hood with top-of-the-range equipment, you also get the latest episode of *Glee* and the new Foo Fighters album. Conspicuous production is an even better means of broadcasting your wealth and skill than conspicuous consumption is, and the Web makes it so easy to spread and share resources that it might have been designed to harness the power of generosity as a signal. If you put a file online, it becomes accessible to a vast audience, and, even better, it is not depleted by those who consume it, so there is no limit to that audience. An MP3 file is like a supply of turtles that never runs out.

Costly signaling adds a new dimension to the economy of prestige created by social learning. Giving stuff away, be it meat or music, is a good way to publicize your skills and attributes, which might be especially important if, like the Meriam hunters, no one can observe you in action. You also show that you're so good that you have resources to spare. It's like an introductory offer, a way of buying your way into a relationship that you hope will pay off in the long run.

For the targets of these offers, there's the added benefit of being in a buyers' market. Costly signalers don't simply have to show that they're good at what they do. They have to prove that they're better than other potential partners who are available. This provides an incentive to invest as much as possible in signaling—because you don't want someone less capable than yourself sending a better signal—and this might create a kind of arms race, as people vie to attract the highest-quality partners (the hardest-working women, for example) by outdoing one another with their generosity.

Karolina Sylwester and Gilbert Roberts, evolutionary psychologists working at Newcastle University, tested the idea that people choose partners on the basis of who gives the most, and that when people must compete for colleagues they increase their generosity accordingly.[4] First, they got a group of subjects to work through an experimental social dilemma called the public goods game. (This and other games will be popping up repeatedly in the course of the book.) In Sylwester and Roberts's version of the game, players, working in groups of four, were given some money and then given the option of putting all, some, or none of it in a common pot. The experimenters then doubled the amount in the pot and divided it equally among the four players, regardless of how much they contributed. This creates a tension between group and individual benefit. If everyone starts with $10 and puts it all in the pot, everyone ends up with $20. But if only three players do this, and one puts in nothing, he nevertheless gets a quarter of the common pot, in this case $15, and so ends up with $25 to everyone else's $15.

The temptation is to exploit other people's efforts; when public goods games are played in the lab, most people start off generous, but when they notice that certain individuals are free riding, they stop cooperating, and the common resources dwindle to nothing. Field studies have found the same thing: Nichola Raihani and Tom Hart manipulated the number of dirty dishes left in the sink of the Zoology Society of London's tea room and measured how that affected the probability that their colleagues would clean up after themselves. The dirtier the communal sink, they found—the more evidence there was that others were free riding—the more likely people were to leave their own mugs and plates unwashed.[5]

Sylwester and Roberts, though, added another game to the mix. After the public goods game, they allowed players to pick a member of their group to play a two-player game. Again, players put their money into a pot, which was then multiplied and divided, but here there was no social dilemma. The pot was multiplied by either two or eight, before being split between the two players, so each player was guaranteed to get back at least what he or she put in. There was a catch, though. You were allowed to play this second game with your chosen partner only if he or she chose you, too. If the person didn't choose you, you were paired with someone picked at random.

Those who gave the most to the public pot, the researchers found, were most likely to be chosen by other group members. By giving more, they advertised their virtues to other players who were looking for someone generous to cooperate with. When the common pot in the two-player round was multiplied by eight, thus increasing the benefits of finding a cooperative partner, the most generous players in the public goods game became even more popular. Generous players were most likely to end up with their preferred partners, and they had more money when the experiment was over. In effect, the most public-spirited people eventually generated private wealth with one another. More cooperative people attract more cooperative partners and thus forge more profitable relationships with them. This seems to apply on Mer, for example: turtle meat is a public good, shared among everyone. But the hunters who provide it are chosen by the hardest-working women, and they raise the largest families.

The key feature of the public goods game is that players get the same out of the common pot regardless of how much they put in. This creates what is known as a collective action problem. Such problems arise anywhere you have a resource that everyone can exploit, regardless of whether they contribute to its creation and upkeep. In such a situation, everyone does best if all people do their bit, but any individual does better by taking as much as he or she can and putting back as little as possible. Without some force counteracting this logic, natural resources—such as forests, fisheries, clean water, and the climate—are destroyed in a tragedy of the commons.

Solving collective action problems is a key challenge of human society, and reputation's role in solving them is a major theme of this book. Making public resources an arena where people can display their generosity and thus become more attractive to those they need in other areas of life seems to be one way in which collective action problems can be solved. Many good deeds seem best explained as a form of what's become known as competitive altruism, a means of showing off one's positive traits and buying a good reputation.

Competitive altruism can help explain some paradoxical acts of generosity. Another pair of evolutionary psychologists, Mark Van Vugt and Charlotte Hardy, did an experiment in which subjects played a variant of the public goods game where the participants got an additional private bonus if the amount in the common pot exceeded a certain threshold.[6] Giving players an incentive to build a reputation— telling them that they would be playing a second game with people who knew how much they had put in the pot—significantly increased the size of public contributions. It did so even when players knew that the bonus threshold had already been passed, and thus their contribution made no difference to whether the public good was obtained. The same result occurred when the researchers set the threshold so high that it became unattainable, even if a player put in all of his money. People still increased their public contributions when they were given a chance to build their reputations. This apparently wasteful generosity seemed to pay off—players accorded the highest status to the most generous members of their groups, even when that generosity was unnecessary or useless. This, Van Vugt and Hardy suggest, might explain why we contribute to causes even when our individual effort is unlikely to make much difference, such as voting in elections, and why people continued to give to the appeal following the Asian tsunami of 2004 even when aid agencies let it be known that they already had more money than they could spend.

This isn't to say that good deeds are driven by ego and self-aggrandizement, but the emotions and reasons that motivate an act aren't the same as the forces that might cause such behaviors to evolve. The glow we get from doing and seeing good is like the pleasure we take from warmth or food, a prompt toward doing the things that will serve us best, in this case, perhaps, seeking and attracting the most generous and powerful people around us.

Take blood donation. This is another resource created by the few for the benefit of the many. Only 5 percent of the U.S. population gives blood, but many people will need a transfusion at some point in their lives. If you've ever given blood, you'll know that it takes at least a small amount of time, may involve some discomfort, and might leave you feeling a bit feeble. There's no direct reward: donors in most countries are not paid, nor do they get preferential access to stored blood for themselves or their families.

About the only reward that blood donors get is a badge or a sticker letting others know of their good deed. Here's a clue about what donors might get out of their generosity. Anyone who sees such a badge knows that the person wearing it is healthy enough to be accepted as a blood donor (in the United States, about one in three prospective donors is turned down for health reasons) and brave enough to have a needle stuck in his or her arm. A study conducted by Henry Lyle, who led the analysis of file-sharing described earlier, found that people do see blood donors as healthy and generous, and that they view giving blood as something with costs, particularly anxiety. Blood donation, Lyle argues, could be another costly signal.[7]

Blood donation and other philanthropic acts, such as the $21 billion that Bill and Melinda Gates have given to their charitable foundation, are not intended as displays of wealth or power. The inconvenience of giving blood or the cost of developing a malaria vaccine seems like a worthwhile price to pay for the possibility of saving a stranger's life. Even if people aren't driven to do good by the thought of the rewards, however, that doesn't mean there are no rewards. The good work of the Gates Foundation gives Windows users something else to think about besides downloading the latest security patch, and a 2010 survey rated Microsoft as America's most inspiring company.[8]

Generosity, then, brings a benefit not because it makes the recipient of your gifts grateful. Rather, it creates word-of-mouth advertising that makes you more attractive to others who, although they might not have benefited from the act itself, know your reputation for generosity.

Yet anyone who tries too hard to show the world that he's a good guy is likely to provoke cynicism. When we see someone parading his or her virtue as a peacock does its tail, we sense that the person is buying something, rather than giving something. Anonymous good deeds seem particularly noble because the benefactors are passing up the opportunity for self-promotion. In Matthew 6:1–4, Jesus says,

> Therefore when thou doest [thine] alms, do not sound a trumpet before thee, as the hypocrites do in the synagogues and in the streets, that they may have glory of men. Verily I say unto you, They have their reward. But when thou doest alms, let not thy left hand know what thy right hand doeth: That thine alms may be in secret: and thy Father which seeth in secret himself shall reward thee openly.

By warning his followers that God ignores public generosity, Jesus is urging them toward a higher nobility but also advising them to distrust the motives of conspicuous do-gooders.

Again, experiments with economic games can help reveal our intuitive mistrust of public generosity. Yet another pair of evolutionary psychologists, Pat Barclay and Rob Willer, conducted a two-game experiment similar to Sylwester and Roberts's study of competitive parties choice described earlier. First, their subjects played a game called the continuous prisoner's dilemma. In this two-player game, participants were handed $10 and given the option of sending any amount to the other player. ("Continuous" refers to the fact that a player can choose to hand over any portion of his or her endowment, not, say, only $0, $5, or $10.) The experimenters doubled whatever the players gave throughout the game, so, as with the public goods game, group profits were greatest if both players handed over all of their cash, and each ended up with $20. For any individual, however, the best thing to do was to hand over nothing and take the other player for a sucker.

After this, one player from the first game played another round of continuous prisoner's dilemma with a third player. Sometimes, the players were paired at random, and what had happened in the first round was kept secret. Other times, the players were paired at random, and the first-round decisions were made public. In other games, the third player got to choose which of the first two players he wanted to be paired off with.

When players gave in private and were paired off at random, they gave one another almost nothing. When their decisions were made public but the partnerships were random, so that players could not influence the third player's choice, they were a bit more generous. Yet when they felt that they were competing for the opportunity to play again with someone else and thus make more money, they gave about half of their $10 to the other player. Again this shows that requiring people to compete for partners makes them more generous.[9]

The experiment also showed that people devalue generosity when they know it can be used as a signal. In the second game, players who had given generously in the random condition, when they were unable to advertise their altruism to the observing third player, received more from that player than those in games where the third player could choose whom to play with. It seems that even though the observers chose generous players, they knew that the generosity they saw was also a bait, to try to tempt them to hand over their money, and thus were unwilling to invest much trust in people who displayed it. Barclay and Willer argue that increasing the reputational benefits of a signal—making it available to a larger audience, for example—without changing the signal is the equivalent of decreasing the signal's cost. It makes it less trustworthy.

Our aversion to altruistic grandstanding is another example of the social cattle prod. By rewarding altruism with prestige, we encourage the rich and the strong to reveal their greatness by displaying their goodness. Yet we also need to prevent prestige from becoming dominance and stop enticement from becoming coercion. In his book *Hierarchy in the Forest*, the primatologist Christopher Boehm describes how hunter-gatherer groups use gossip and mockery to prevent any one individual from becoming dominant.[10] Even truly exceptional hunters or warriors are prevented from attaining a higher status than the rest of the group, because they might then begin to oppress their fellows. Boehm quotes a Kalahari bushman: "We refuse one who boasts, as one day his pride will make him kill somebody." (Nevertheless, even if high achievement does not lead to political power, this is another society where the best hunters have the most children.)

The bushman's remark hints at why the urge to bring people down should be so strong, and why there's more of a market for gossip about celebrities' failings than there is for news of their successes. "Goody Two-shoes" and "holier than thou" aren't terms of praise. The English like to mock celebrity do-gooders and talk about the "tall-poppy syndrome"—the urge to cut down anyone who rises too high—whereas the Dutch speak of *maaiveldcultur*, where *maaiveld* refers to a pasture where everything is mown down to the same level. The powerful, of course, don't like this at all. "You cannot add to the stature of a dwarf by cutting off the legs of a giant," Benjamin Franklin Fairless, the president of the United States Steel Corporation, told a 1950 House of Representatives' investigation into industrial monopolies. No, but it makes it harder for the giant to trample you. Tall-poppy syndrome is another illustration that reputation is not a measure of our social worth but a means for people to control one another.

Anyone who wants to encourage public-spirited behavior—governments in their citizens, companies in their employees, or schools in their pupils, for example—should think about how they can channel people's urge to show off in a direction where it will do others some good (tax breaks for charitable giving, for example), and how they can create the social conditions where altruism can earn a healthy prestige but does not raise people to dominance, thus provoking a cynical mistrust of good deeds.

For researchers trying to explain human generosity, the important thing about public displays of generosity and the theory of competitive altruism and costly signaling that seeks to explain them is that the giver's actions are unconditional. Turtle hunters, file-sharers, blood donors, and philanthropists don't target their generosity toward specific individuals, and they don't expect to be repaid in kind. Rather, they are investing in their reputations. This might make them especially powerful as a means of creating and preserving public goods, because whether other people are contributing does not matter to the givers—indeed, the less other people contribute, the more they stand out. In this situation, generosity is an advertisement, not a swap, and the problem of free riders is irrelevant.

Of course, in many situations we care very much whether the recipients of our cooperation deserve it. There are other reasons for altruism besides showing off and other forms of reputation besides physical or financial health. All of us use and care about these forms of reputation, and they are a crucial part of every person's makeup and every society's collective well-being.

CHAPTER 3

You Scratch His Back, and I'll Scratch Yours

W hile I was writing this chapter, my mother went on a walking holiday to Montenegro, in the former Yugoslavia. A couple of weeks later, we received in the mail an envelope with a British stamp. Inside was a postcard that my mother had sent, a little stained and creased, and a note from someone that said, "This postcard arrived stuck to a postcard from my brother, who had been on a walking holiday in Budva" (a town on the Adriatic). There was no name or address from whoever sent the card on.

I was reminded of an incident from about a decade ago, when I found a daily planner lying in the street. After checking for anything scandalous, I mailed it to what seemed like the most prominent name in the planner's address book, in the hope that it might find its way back to its owner. Like my own benefactor, I did so anonymously and gave up a stamp, an envelope, and a small amount of time.

When we think of human altruism, it's usually grand and outstanding examples that spring to mind, acts of life-saving heroism and life-changing generosity. But our cooperative nature manifests in ways so commonplace as to be invisible. The postcard and the daily planner were memorable, but every day people I don't know and will never see again are kind and helpful to me in ways that I won't remember, and I try to show politeness and consideration to others. We open doors for one another and wait in line, pass the salt, and "hold that for a second." In their second year, children, about as soon as they are physically able, will go out of their way to help, putting down a toy to pick up something that another person has dropped and hand it to him or her, or opening a door for someone whose hands are full. They do this without being asked and without expecting a reward. Children also share resources, such as food or toys, and information—pointing to help a searcher find an object, for example—from a young age.[1] We are a very helpful bunch.

Yet at any moment there's more to be gained from selfishness than from cooperating, and any person who can take the benefits of social life without paying the costs gains an immediate advantage. Every time we help, we aid people who might be our competitors, making our own lives ever so slightly more difficult and theirs ever so slightly easier. If you let the door slam in a person's face, you'd get where you were going a little bit quicker. If you could sneak or shove your way up that queue, it might be the difference between getting a ticket to see *Inception* and having to settle for something with Vin Diesel in it.

In the 1960s and the 1970s, evolutionary biologists erected two pillars to hold up a theory that explained why the living world contains altruism and cooperation. The first of these was nepotism. In a paper published in 1964, the late Bill Hamilton, an Englishman often described as the most important evolutionary biologist since Darwin, showed that one currency in which altruism can yield a profit is your relative's genes. The care that parents take of their offspring is an obvious example of this; Hamilton's insight was to realize that the same forces might work between siblings, cousins, and so on. The closer the family tie between two organisms, the more genes they share, and so the greater their shared evolutionary interests and the lower the hurdle to cooperative behavior. For my PhD, for example, I studied aphid species that produce soldiers. These soldiers use their powerful legs and tough claws to fight off predators and are often killed doing so. But as long as their sacrifice saves one family member it is worthwhile—aphids reproduce by cloning themselves, so a soldier is genetically identical to all of her sisters and should value each of their lives as highly as her own. (That only about one percent of the four thousand known aphid species produce soldiers shows that having unusually close relatives is not sufficient for social behavior to evolve, but that's a subject for another day.) Kin selection, as Hamilton's theory is known, can help explain many other examples of cooperation, such as the birds that remain as helpers at their parents' nest instead of setting up on their own, and the group solidarity of species such as meerkats and wolves.

People are certainly nepotistic. We put relatives at the head of the queue for favors, both consciously and unconsciously. If people die childless, they tend to leave their estates to siblings, nephews, nieces, and so on. A Bedouin proverb states, "Me against my brother, my brothers and me against my cousins, then my cousins and me against strangers." In experiments, people are more generous toward others who share their surname and, as studies using manipulated photos have shown, toward people who look similar to themselves.[2] This doesn't explain why we should help people who aren't related to us, however, thus opening ourselves up to being cheated, or why we should resist the temptation to cheat such people.

In 1971, the American biologist Robert Trivers, who has a good claim to being the most important evolutionary thinker since Bill Hamilton, suggested something besides genetic ties that could drive the evolution of altruism. It can pay to help, he said, if the beneficiary returns the favor. If you can be confident of meeting the same individual in the future, it's worth helping the person when he or she needs it, so that this person will help you in your time of need. Trivers called this reciprocal altruism, and it became the second pillar of animal cooperation.[3]

To illustrate his idea mathematically, Trivers turned to the prisoner's dilemma, the economic game that we discussed in chapter 2, in which two players must, without knowing the other's mind, choose whether to cooperate or cheat. The name comes from a scenario in which criminal conspirators are deciding whether to inform on each other. If both prisoners keep quiet (cooperate), the case against them will be weak, and each is looking at a short sentence, say, two years. The problem is, if one sings and the other guy keeps quiet, the stool pigeon does really well (getting only a year's jail time), and the tight-lipped fellow does really badly (is put away for four years). If both talk, defecting on each other, neither does quite as badly, but the court has enough to put them away for three years.

The dilemma is that cooperation pays more than mutual cheating but less than unilateral cheating. This creates the maddening situation that you do best if you cheat, regardless of what the other player does, and the same goes for him. The logic of cheating is unanswerable. Yet you'd do better as an individual if you could only both cooperate. Most important, if there are other pairs of prisoners in the same situation who do cooperate, they'll be back on the street before you and will probably take over your business.

If you play the prisoner's dilemma with a partner only once, there's no incentive to do anything but defect. Life, however, is not necessarily like that. Two animals living in the same place have a chance to interact repeatedly with each other. There's a chance for trust to develop and, with it, mutually beneficial cooperation. But the temptation to cheat never goes away, so trust needs teeth—any animal that cooperates indiscriminately makes itself a sucker. For example, one powerful strategy for playing the prisoner's dilemma is called tit for tat. This means cooperating on the first move and then copying whatever your opponent did previously. So if you should meet a cooperative player, you can get into a run of cooperation; if you meet a cheater, you won't get fooled twice; and if the sinner repents, you return the favor.

Much of human morality and psychology, Trivers wrote, could be explained as adaptations to promote and enforce reciprocal altruism, such as the gratitude, friendship, and trust we feel toward those who help us and the suspicion, anger, and desire for revenge against those who take without returning.

Reciprocal altruism sounds obvious—and no one doubts it is an important factor in human cooperation—but it's a harder thing to achieve than you might think. Many primates and some antelope seem to trade grooming sessions, but this happens during the space of a few minutes. For anything longer term, you'd need a life long enough and a social world stable enough to make it likely that you'll meet the same animal time and again. That counts out short-lived and very mobile species. You also need the smarts to recognize individuals; remember how they treated you, and you them, in the past; and use that information to implement the appropriate behavior at your next meeting. That requires a big and expensive brain. Very few species besides humans meet these criteria, and most of the animal behaviors suggested as examples of long-term, complex reciprocal altruism have turned out to have other possible explanations—the animal being helped might be related, for example, or the helper might be getting some other benefit. Even the best-known example of reciprocal altruism in animals, when well-fed vampire bats regurgitate blood for hungry roost mates, has come under suspicion—the female bats that share blood, for example, tend to roost with relatives, so kin selection might be a better explanation for food sharing.[4]

But reciprocal altruism can't explain why we help strangers we are unlikely ever to meet again—why, for example, someone would think to send on a misdirected postcard. One possibility is that this is all a mistake. People evolved around relatives, in small groups where you met the same people over and over. It paid to be helpful and didn't pay to be too discriminating. Now, even though we live in vast crowds of strangers, perhaps our psychology has not caught up with our circumstances, and we treat people well because we subconsciously assume that they're either related or that we're bound to see them again.

Besides being unsatisfying, however, this idea seems not to fit the evidence. People are cooperative, but they're not blindly cooperative. We separate kith from kin, we are sensitive to whether our favors are returned or not, and we are judgmental of bad behavior, whether it's directed toward us or others. If altruism isn't a mistake, being kind to strangers becomes a riddle worth solving. Surely, there must be something to gain by helping someone you've never met before and might never meet again. Overcoming the reasonable fear that a person might exploit you requires a powerful force, and that force is reputation.

• • •

In the late 1960s, Richard Alexander attended a symposium in the University of Michigan's biology department, where he was a professor, at which a paleoanthropologist put up a diagram showing how human brain size had increased massively through time. *Homo habilis*, for example, lived about two million years ago and had a brain of about five hundred cubic centimeters, a bit bigger than a chimpanzee's. *Homo erectus*, who came about half a million years later, had a brain roughly twice as large, and the genus's reigning champion, *Homo sapiens*, has a brain roughly half as large again, around fourteen hundred cubic centimeters. This is too expensive to be a luxury: it takes up only one-fiftieth of our body weight but consumes one-fifth of our energy budgets. Why, Alexander wondered, did brains get bigger and then, even when they were bigger than those of any other primate around, keep on getting bigger? What hostile force could have driven this change?

At the time, it was uncommon for evolutionary biologists to think about human behavior. Alexander had built his career studying crickets, making tens of thousands of tapes of the calls of thousands of species and discovering more than four hundred species new to science. But back as a grad student in the 1950s, when the study of evolution barely existed as a specialty, he had also pledged to himself to seek out and tackle what struck him as the hardest problems. Humans seemed the most complicated subject available, and human behavior the most difficult aspect of our biology to explain. The puzzle of the ever-expanding hominid brain reawakened that urge, and he pitched himself into the anthropology literature.

A big brain, he decided, was a social tool. The only reason for humans to invest in intelligence was the challenge of dealing with other humans. Operating in a group offers a huge advantage, most especially in the struggle against other groups—but so does exploiting the members of your own group. So people need to avoid being exploited by those around them and also need to be alert to opportunities to sneak an advantage. The key is that in most social situations, people's interests are partially aligned. A group's members seldom want exactly the same thing, but they rarely want completely different things—they might agree about the need to dig an irrigation system, say, which is something that no individual could achieve single-handed, but disagree about how the work should be divided up, or where the water should go. To Alexander, most moral problems seemed to flow from the interplay of these conflicts and confluences of interest, from situations where one person's gain is another's loss, and where the benefits of cooperation rub against the benefits of cheating. Morality is a way to resolve these conflicts, and the reward for solving them is group cohesion. People, Alexander reasoned, are one another's greatest resource and greatest menace. We cooperate within our groups so as to compete more effectively with other groups.

Alexander knew of Robert Trivers's paper on reciprocal altruism and thought it one of the best pieces of work he'd ever come across. After dealing with reciprocal help between two animals, Trivers went on to discuss what he calls multiparty interactions. In a close-knit human group, he wrote, there could be an advantage in knowing who has helped and who has cheated in the past. If people learn from one another's experience, you should care about the opinions of everyone who knows what you are doing and not only about the opinion of whomever you are doing it to. It might even pay to be generally altruistic, giving help freely to everyone within your group, so that everyone gives back to you in turn.

This seemed particularly relevant to human behavior. We don't just take note of and care about how other people treat us. We care about how they behave toward one another, and we reward and punish them even if their actions don't affect us. This, Alexander reasoned, is a powerful extra incentive to cooperate besides kin ties and swapping favors and a way for groups to remain cohesive and police conflicts of interest. It can pay to try to reunite someone with his lost mail not because you expect the person to do the same for you, but because someone else will observe your helpfulness and will trust you when you need help. Tossing that mail is a bad idea, because then this judgmental audience will refuse you help when you need it.

Alexander's idea was that following the golden rule is a form of self-help: you treat others as you would like to be treated and don't do to others what you wouldn't want done to yourself. (Versions of this rule are found in all of the world's major religions.) He called his notion indirect reciprocity, to contrast it with Trivers's reciprocal altruism, and extended it into philosophy and beyond. In 1986, he wrote:

> Indirect reciprocity is the foundation of moral, ethical and legal systems. Its existence and pervasiveness in human social life, I believe, are the most important factors to consider in an analysis of the nature and complexity of the human psyche. I think they account for human interest in theatre in all of its guises, from soap operas to Shakespeare, poetry to sociology, neighbourhood parties to the Olympic games.[5]

Self-awareness allows us to see ourselves as others see us, with a view to manipulating their opinions. Our consciences tell us what we can get away with without doing excessive harm to our future prospects. Our ethics revolve around questions of what we owe to people and how we should treat them, based on how they have treated both us and others in the past. All, says Alexander, flow from indirect reciprocity, the urge to do to people as they have done to others.[6]

In these views of cooperation, be they Hamilton's, Trivers's, or Alexander's, morality becomes self-serving and altruism becomes an investment, an outlay in the expectation of a greater future return. You could even think of altruism as "social hustling," Alexander wrote, with the benefactor, through his behavior, setting up the observer, who will later more than repay the original good deed. Again, that's not to suggest that social hustling is deceitful or that people actually make decisions by calculating costs and benefits or that they are driven solely by self-interest. They are driven by emotions such as anger, empathy, and pity and by a desire to uphold morals such as equity and justice. But these motives do not contradict the view that our behaviors, emotions, and morals arose because our ancestors got some personal benefit from them. People do not eat food or have sex because they calculate that doing so will increase their genetic contribution to the next generation. They are driven by appetites. Similarly, morality is an appetite for certain kinds of behavior in ourselves and others.

Finding an evolutionary explanation for morality, Alexander says now, was not nearly as difficult as he'd thought it would be. Having cracked that, he went on to what he then saw as the really tough problem—the arts, and particularly humor. Jokes, he began to think, are all about the manipulation of social status and group identity. By telling jokes, we boost our own status. By making jokes against other people, we lower their status, and by telling jokes to our own group about other religions, races, or nationalities, we draw our team closer together.

Alexander made his arguments verbally, but these days, biological theories tend to gain credibility and momentum only when expressed in mathematical terms—as Hamilton had done for kin selection and Trivers for reciprocal (although not generalized) altruism. In the decade after Alexander's book on the evolution of morality was published, there was little interest in indirect reciprocity, and for most of the last three decades of the twentieth century, evolutionary biologists focused on explaining altruistic behavior with kin selection and reciprocal altruism, believing that these two pillars were probably all that was needed. This included a vast number of studies testing different wrinkles on the prisoner's dilemma. In the late 1980s, Robert Boyd and Peter Richerson, two of the world's leading experts on cultural evolution, showed how indirect reciprocity could work if help went in a circle, with A helping B, who helped C, who helped A.[7] Yet this seemed to work only in very small groups—it seems unlikely, for example, that in the intervening decade the person to whom I sent the daily planner sent a lost item of mail to the person who would go on to send me the postcard. In 1992, Lee Dugatkin coauthored a study analyzing a strategy for playing the prisoner's dilemma called "observer tit for tat," which, unlike regular tit for tat, defected on its first move if it had seen its opponent defect previously. Observer tit for tat did well—better than tit for tat—if two players had little chance of meeting repeatedly.[8] In general, however, there was little confidence that such a mechanism could evolve—getting simple reciprocity to work seemed hard enough; indirect reciprocity seemed to place even greater intellectual demands on its users and to require an even more specialized social environment.

The breakthrough came courtesy of two Austrian scientists in 1998. Karl Sigmund, a mathematician at the University of Vienna, is one of the leaders in evolutionary game theory. Together with his student Martin Nowak, who now works at Harvard, he had already spent several years investigating the dynamics of reciprocal altruism and the prisoner's dilemma, to see under what conditions cooperation emerged and what tended to work against it. The two of them began to discuss indirect reciprocity. Sigmund knew of Alexander's work and of its discouraging lack of theoretical support, but Nowak was undeterred and within the space of a few days had come up with a model that showed how indirect reciprocity could work.

The model took the form of a computer simulation of a group of a hundred individuals—chosen because it's approximately the same size as the hunter-gatherer groups in which human social behavior emerged.[9] Individuals in the group pair up at random. In every pair, one, again chosen at random, must choose whether to help the other. If he does, his evolutionary fitness drops by a certain amount, and the recipient's rises by a larger amount. (All theories of cooperation work only if the benefit of being helped is greater than the cost of helping.) If the potential donor decides not to help, both players remain unchanged. Then they go their separate ways, never to meet again. After a few such encounters, so that everyone gets a chance to be both donor and recipient, there is breeding. Those with the highest fitness become more common in the next generation, while those with the lowest are edged out.

The best thing to do in this world is nothing—hold on to your chips when you play donor and hope that some sucker helps you. After a few generations, suckers and social interaction will soon disappear, even though, if everybody cooperated, the benefits of being helped would outweigh the cost of helping. But Nowak and Sigmund came up with a way to add reputation to their simulation.

They did this by giving everybody in their world something they called an image score. This is a lot like eBay feedback. Everyone's score starts at zero. A deity watches over social encounters and updates the participants' image scores accordingly, as if chalking or erasing tally marks on their foreheads. Every time a donor helps a recipient, the donor's score goes up by one. Every time a potential donor refuses to help, his image score drops by one. This lets you know how your partner behaved in the past: if he has a positive image score, he's been mostly helpful; if negative, mostly unhelpful.

The hundred individuals began with a variety of rules about how to use image scores to decide whether to help one another. Some picky types, for example, gave only to recipients with image scores of +3 or better, others less discriminating helped everyone whose score was above –3, and so on. As the generations rolled by, one strategy came to beat out all of the others. This was to help everyone with a score better than zero. This strategy allows helpful people to form networks of mutual aid, even though that aid isn't exchanged directly, and it allows people to avoid wasting their help on others who will not pay into the network.

No one, least of all Nowak and Sigmund, would claim that this simulation is an accurate picture of human society and behavior. It's an attempt to pick a few aspects of the world that might be important and study how they play out in a simplified world. Yet it's easy to see how the model might capture some aspects of how we make social decisions. Most important, it worked. If their simulated group had remained resolutely antisocial, despite the benefits of cooperation, no one would have been interested in Nowak and Sigmund's analysis. But by showing how reputation could make cooperators prosper and cheats perish, their study shone a light on helpful acts that kin selection and reciprocal altruism can't explain, and it suggested that being nice to strangers might be a behavior honed by natural selection, not a hangover from a less anonymous world.

Nowak and Sigmund's study began a decade, and counting, of intense study of indirect reciprocity, during which theorists and experimenters have knocked the ball between each others' courts. More often than not, the German biologist Manfred Milinski has been on the experimental side of the net. Milinski began his career working on sticklebacks. Through the 1980s and the 1990s, he studied how the fish decide where to eat and whom to mate with and how distractions such as predators and parasite infestations affect those decisions. He also considered how sticklebacks play the prisoner's dilemma. This occurs when two fish swim close to a predator, such as a pike, to check whether it's in hunting mode. Using cleverly placed mirrors, Milinski gave a lone fish the impression that its reflection was either cooperating, swimming alongside to check out the danger, or defecting, hanging back to get the information but avoiding the risk. In such situations, he found, sticklebacks play tit for tat and refuse to face danger if paired with a laggard.

In the 1990s, Milinski began to apply his knack for devising an ingenious experiment to investigate human cooperation and reciprocal altruism, looking at the kinds of strategies real people used when they played the prisoner's dilemma. Around this time, a pre-publication copy of Nowak and Sigmund's analysis came his way. For the first time in a quarter of a century, he realized, there was a new idea about the evolution of altruism on the scene. But did the model really capture how people behaved? Working with his student Claus Wedekind at the University of Bern in Switzerland, Milinski set about finding out.

Milinski and Wedekind divided seventy-nine first-year undergraduates into eight groups of nine or ten players and gave each person a few Swiss francs. As in Nowak and Sigmund's simulation, two players in each group were paired at random, and one was given the option to either part with one franc so that the receiver could get four, with Milinski's research funders making up the difference, or to hold onto her money, with the receiver getting nothing. Players were identified only by numbers and made their decisions by pushing a concealed button, so that who was doing what was hidden both from the experimenters and from the other members of the group.

There was no opportunity for payback—no two players ever met as both donor and receiver. As the rounds went by, though, the players learned something about how their partners had treated the rest of the group. Each time a player's number came up, all of her past decisions—to give or not to give—were displayed on a board for all to see. In this way, an image score emerged.

One player in this experiment never gave anything. On average, however, donors chose the generous option more than half of the time. But they did not give willy-nilly.

Players who had given in past rounds and so built up a positive image score were much more likely to receive help than were those who hadn't.[10] Counting every "yes" decision as a +1 image score and every "no" as –1 showed that those who received help had an image score of about +0.5, and those who didn't had an average image score of about –0.5—quite close to Nowak and Sigmund's theoretical result. In other words, when players decided whether to help, they based their decisions on how their partners had treated the rest of the group. They rewarded good behavior and, whether consciously or not, tried to maintain a good image in the eyes of their fellows.

Several other experiments have confirmed that we channel our help toward those who have helped others. Two Harvard psychologists, Kristina Olson and Elizabeth Spelke, studied image scoring in three-year-old children, asking them to divide a reward (some shells) among a group of dolls.[11] Told that the day before, some of the dolls had given another doll a penny whereas others hadn't, the children gave the shells to the generous dolls. Like cooperative behavior in general, the urge to reciprocate indirectly emerges early in life. In fact, it might even be there when we are born.

Kiley Hamlin's experiment has the flavor and production values of a puppet show from 1970s kids' TV. The actors are wooden blocks with cartoon eyes glued on them, and the set is a green hill standing out slightly from a flat white background. A round red block starts off at the bottom of a hill. It tries to get over but falters, making it halfway and sliding back. In some scenes, a yellow triangle enters stage right and, coming up the hill behind the red block, pushes it up to the top. In others, a blue square appears at the crest of the hill and bears down on the round block, knocking it back to where it came from.

Hamlin and her colleagues presented their scenes of help and hindrance to six- and ten-month-old babies. Then they offered the infants the helper and hinderer blocks on a tray and invited them to choose one. Fourteen out of sixteen ten-month-olds reached for the helper, as did all of the dozen six-month-olds.

Next, the researchers staged more ambiguous scenes. In these, they paired the round block with either a helper, a blocker, or a neutral character that scooted about while the round block sat and watched, making no attempt on the hill. Then the babies were given a choice between a helper and a neutral, or between a hinderer and a neutral. They rose to the challenge: in each age group, seven of eight chose the helper above the neutral block, and the same number chose the neutral above the hinderer.[17] Babies are not the most consistent strategists, and infant psychologists seldom find more than about two-thirds of their subjects behaving the same way in any experiment. This near-unanimity is rare indeed.

Before humans can walk or talk, then, they are watching those around them, working out who's nice and who isn't. They can already deduce what other entities want, and they know that it's better to help them get it than not. They can also understand that ignoring someone is better than thwarting him. Babies use this knowledge to plan their social behavior, reaching out or shunning accordingly. This need not mean that their decisions are purely innate and owe nothing to learning and experience, because by the time babies are six months old, they have already seen a lot of social interactions. Yet it does strongly suggest that at least some of our ability to size people up and work out how to treat them is hardwired. So the next time you meet a baby, be nice. It's judging you.

Theory, then, describes how reputation can make being kind to strangers a winning strategy, with image scoring serving as a way to separate the helpful from the undeserving. Experiments show that people do indeed seem to plan their behavior by forming image scores for those around them. So, is that why we cooperate and why we care about reputation? It's almost certainly part of the answer, but it's almost certainly not the whole answer.

Other theorists soon began to tinker with the model and found that if you made it more realistic, it didn't work so well. Suppose, for example, you meet someone with a terrible image. You shouldn't help this person. But in the Nowak and Sigmund world, the deity will then swoop down and scratch a point off your own score. By being a good citizen, you've given anyone watching the impression that *you're* the unhelpful one. Nowak and Sigmund peopled their virtual world with individuals who based their behavior on the image scores of those they met. Yet two evolutionary biologists, Olof Leimar and Peter Hammerstein, repeated the computer simulation and included a strategy that cared only about its own score and not about anyone else's. This strategy did just enough helping to keep its own image positive. It bought a good reputation, in effect, but it didn't care who it bought it from—if its score needed a top-up, it would help the first individual it met, regardless of how he'd behaved in the past. The interloper thrived, quickly driving out the strategy that based its behavior on others' image scores, rather than on its own.[13]

It doesn't seem fair that an upstanding strategy should lose out to a sneaky one. From a few lines of computer code bumping into another few lines of code, there has sprung a question of ethics, a hint at the kind of rules that might form the foundations of morality. What is a good deed? The observers living in Nowak and Sigmund's world take a simple view—that it's nice to be nice, even if you're seen to be nice to someone nasty. Leimar and Hammerstein showed that this is a shaky foundation on which to build a reputation. They also suggested a way to fix the problem, showing that things become different if you add motive to the mix and fill the world with individuals who care not only about what others do, but also about why they do it.

Acts certainly look very different depending on what you know about them. A famous commercial for a British newspaper shows a threatening-looking skinhead sprinting down a street to grab a middle-aged man in a suit, who lifts his briefcase in defense. It looks like a mugging, but a shift in camera angle reveals the youth as an altruist—he pulls the man out from under a load of falling bricks.[14] In the real world, mistaking an altruist for an assailant can have terrible consequences. One Friday night in September 2009, three teenagers, two of them girls, fatally injured Ian Baynham, a sixty-two-year-old civil servant, in a homophobic attack in London's Trafalgar Square. Baynham was with a friend, who grabbed one of the girls, but a passer-by thought he was assaulting her and intervened, allowing her to get away.[15]

Baynham's killing is both an example of how bystanders are moved to go to a stranger's aid and horrible proof of how image scoring can misfire. Yet there are other ways to judge a deed. Instead of, for example, labeling someone who refuses to help another as "bad," you might label him "good" if you know that the other guy had it coming.[16] Replacing simple image scoring with these sterner rules takes away the incentive to help someone with a bad reputation and replaces it with one to snub the person. In computer-simulated tournaments between different strategies, those that label anyone who helps someone with a bad reputation as "bad" and label someone who refuses such help as "good" do well—better than simple image scoring—and allow cooperators to keep cheats at bay. Forgiveness, where a single good deed is enough to restore a good reputation, also does well in these virtual worlds.[17]

This seems like a more rational way to behave. So given the chance to judge motive, do people take it? The evidence is mixed. Manfred Milinski and his colleagues did an experiment that found that players who refused to help an uncooperative player were in turn refused help, even when everyone knew enough about past behavior to work out whether the initial refusal was justified. The results were almost identical to a system driven purely by image scoring, and players who snubbed an uncooperative player became more generous in subsequent encounters, as if they knew they had damaged their reputations and were trying to repair their image scores.[18]

Similarly, when we decide how to deal with someone who has a bad reputation, we consider how it will affect our own images. When we start a new job or relationship or move onto a new street, we may well be more worried about building our own reputations than about reacting to the reputations of our new acquaintances. We tend to make a special effort to be nice, even to people we have our doubts about or have heard bad things about. When you have little reputation yourself, it might pay more to build up your own good name than to punish others for their bad names. When your image score is large enough, you can refuse cooperation without jeopardizing your own good name even if others will mark it against you.

Kiley Hamlin and her colleagues, on the other hand, conducted an experiment that looked at similar behavior in infants. This was a lot like their study with the hill-climbing shapes, except instead of watching a block climb a slope, the babies watched a duck hand-puppet struggling to open a box and either being helped or hindered by an elephant puppet. Then both elephants, the helper and the hinderer, performed another scene in which they were playing with a ball and dropped it. Two moose puppets watched this scene. One moose was a rewarder—it picked up the ball and gave it back. Another was a punisher—it took the ball away. So the babies got a chance to watch a nice elephant or a nasty elephant be either rewarded or punished. The researchers then gave the babies a choice between the rewarding moose and the punishing moose.

Image-scorers would prefer a rewarding moose regardless, even if it gave the ball back to an elephant that had treated the duck badly. This is what five-month old babies did. Yet eight-month-olds were different: thirteen out of sixteen in the experiment preferred a moose that punished a naughty elephant to one that gave it a reward it didn't deserve. This suggests that our understanding of who deserves punishment emerges a few months later than our ideas about who deserves cooperation, but still that it requires little, if any, social experience or moral training.[19]

Why did babies succeed in Hamlin's experiment where adults failed in Milinski's? One possibility is that in Milinski's study, where past decisions were presented as a list of Y's and N's on a screen, it was just too difficult to calculate who deserved what. That's a lot of information in an unfamiliar format to swallow at once. Suppose you see that your partner refused to give in the previous round. That's okay, however, because he was up against a player who'd been stingy in his previous round. In making this judgment, you trust that your current partner made the right call—that he looked at that person's past behavior and saw that *his* meanness was not justified by his previous partners' behavior, and so on. If anyone makes a mistake anywhere along the line, withholding help from someone who actually deserves it, the whole system can snarl up with unjustified punishment. To use this kind of strategy in planning your behavior, you've got to get your head around all of this information and assume that everyone in the past did the same. In the real world, working out motive is a challenge even for police and courts, which are specialized to do just that. For the rest of us, observing the last link in the chain might not be perfect, but it's a lot simpler.

The babies in Hamlin's experiment, though, saw a much more elementary interaction expressed in a direct and natural fashion, so it was easier to see the motive behind the deed. I would guess that people in the real world are the same, and that we go by what we can see if we don't have any other information or if that information is too complex or unreliable, but that we will take motive into account if we can.

Indirect reciprocity seems like a panacea, a universal guarantee of good behavior, but there are lots of types of cooperation that indirect reciprocity alone cannot protect. This is because the options it gives for dealing with bad behavior are effective only in one-on-one situations. In Nowak and Sigmund's model and in Milinski's experiments, those who refused to help someone else paid no material cost to do so (although their reputations suffered), and the person on the receiving end couldn't go elsewhere. Yet many of the most spectacular examples of human cooperation, such as irrigation systems or warfare, involve large groups working together. Refusing to help is not a good way to solve collective action problems. Suppose you're digging a well, and you notice that someone in the group isn't pulling his or her weight. If it was just the two of you, you could throw down your tools, and the person would have an incentive to work harder. If you withdraw from a group, however, you join the free riders, and everyone suffers, even those who were doing their bit. They in turn have less incentive to carry on, and the effort collapses, leaving a half-dug well.

We saw in the previous chapter that collective action problems can be solved if people use the public realm to show off their abilities and resources. Indirect reciprocity can be used to solve these problems in a similar way, allowing us to broadcast our trustworthiness by contributing to the public good and so reap the benefits in other situations. Social life is a patchwork. We move between many different situations, from pairs to groups large and small. Sometimes we are anonymous, other times we are exposed. We are all asked for help, and we all need it. You can't capture this complexity with a game played in the lab for a handful of cash, but you can take a step toward it by combining games.

For the last few years, this has been the focus of Milinski's research. In one experiment, he and his colleagues alternated the public goods game (do you want to give to the common pot?) with an indirect reciprocity game (do you want to give to one other player?). Those who gave generously to the group were nearly always rewarded in one-on-one interactions; those who gave nothing to the public good usually received nothing from their fellow players.[20] Alternating the games in this way kept group cooperation high. When Milinski took away one-on-one interaction and made people play the public goods game in isolation, or when he gave people different identities in each game and so took away the ability to transfer reputation from one situation to another, contributions to the public good dropped away to nothing, and everyone lost out.[21] Concern for individual reputation can also enhance collective action when there's no monetary reward. Milinski's team found that revealing either the two meanest or the two most generous players after each round was enough to boost group contributions, as people invested more in a bid to avoid shame and win honor.[22]

Despite the incentive to be selfish, the public goods game still offers the opportunity to get back more than you put in. In another experiment, however, Milinski's team took away even this and alternated the indirect reciprocity game with rounds of donations to UNICEF, the United Nations' charity for children. Giving to needy, unknown people on the other side of the world is unlikely to be repaid directly. The researchers found, though, that the more people gave away, the more other players gave them, so much so that they emerged with a net profit. Charitable donations also brought political benefits. At the end of the experiment, the researchers gave their subjects a ballot paper listing the pseudonyms of their group members and asked them to imagine that they were electing a delegate to a student council. Those who gave UNICEF the most money got the most votes, whereas generosity toward other players had no effect on political popularity.[23]

The lesson of half a century of research is that none of the different pillars of cooperation can support the entire edifice on its own; none is a complete answer or applies in every situation. Perhaps someone saw whoever sent my postcard on and thought more kindly of the person because of it, or perhaps no one did—our cooperative instincts need not turn a profit every time, just often enough to outweigh their cost. Yet cooperation is so pervasive and so woven into the way we behave that it cannot be a hindrance or an aberration. Quite the reverse, our better instincts and behaviors have emerged because of, not despite, natural selection. They are strategies that pay off in many different ways but that need to be protected from the ever-present temptation to cheat and free ride.

Caring about reputation and basing our treatment of people on how they have treated others are powerful protectors of cooperation— perhaps, in large, relatively anonymous societies, the most powerful— and a strong force for keeping groups together and curbing cheating. Reputation has enabled human cooperation to attain a breadth and a complexity that no other species has managed, and it doesn't need any higher power to enforce rules and dish out punishments.

You'll have noticed, however, that people don't have image scores marked on their foreheads. Our means of spreading the information from which reputations are made are more complex, more fun, less direct, and much less reliable than that.

CHAPTER 4

Casting a Shadow

For several weeks at seven-thirty each evening, Henry Moore took a walk through midtown Manhattan. He started at Broadway and 33rd Street, a block from where the Empire State Building rose, and ambled up Broadway to 55th Street, four blocks south of Central Park. As he did so, he recorded every bit of conversation he could overhear. He eventually collected 174 snatches of chat—enough, he wrote in a paper published in 1922, to "secure an exact comparison of masculine and feminine leitmotifs in conversation."[1]

When men spoke with one another, Moore found, their subject was most often money—this was, after all, New York City at the beginning of a boom. "I sold it for three times what I paid for it," "I had only five and a half bucks when I hit town," and "He's insolvent, this is no place for him," were some of the remarks he jotted down. When two women spoke, they talked most often about men, for example: "She was just as glad to see him as he was to see her," "What's the use talking to that man?" and "But the other fellow wouldn't salute."

While I was writing this book, I, too, listened in on conversations in public places when and where I could. These are some of the things I heard:

"Jules has got a PS3, but he's stingy with it." (Two students on a bus in London.)

"When it comes down to it, she's just stealing from her friends." (A man to a woman in a park.)

". . . and out came a trio led by some chap I'd never heard of, called Nat King Cole." (Two men on a bus in Brighton.)

"I'm going to tell you something about your mother." (Two elderly men in the café at the National Gallery.)

"He's got, like, so many issues." (Two teenage girls on the London Underground.)

"So, can you see it when you wear a bikini?" (Woman on a train.) "No." (Woman's friend.)

Humans have never been short of things worth mentioning. You might have found a patch of edible mushrooms that's bigger than you can eat yourself, and you want to feed your friends and family. You might be hunting deer and want to suggest that one of your party sneaks up on the animals from behind a nearby hillock. You might have noticed that the sap from a particular tree is good for plugging leaks in a canoe, and you want to share your innovation. You might have bought a really good pair of running shoes or seen a terrific movie. If that were all that we talked about, though, life would be like a Western — long stretches of silence punctuated by the clipped exchange of a few useful words. Finding food, withstanding the elements, and keeping fit and amused are important problems, to be sure, and language is an excellent tool to help solve them. But my grotesquely unrigorous sample more or less confirmed the work of researchers who have eavesdropped in a more scientific fashion to discover what people talk about in the wild. They mostly talk about other people.

One review published in 2004 estimated that "at least 60% of adult conversations are about people who are not present."[2] For anyone who is averagely conversationally active, that amounts to several hours of chat about absent others each day.

We've seen that people and other animals invest their trust in those around them who are most successful, by watching and learning from them. We've seen that the successful also try to advertise their success, and so buy that trust, with generosity. And we've seen that people keep a record of who does what to whom, and that this information allows them to decide whether someone can be trusted. The knowledge that other people are doing the same for them gives them an incentive to be trustworthy. On a large scale, reputation might be capable of turning a bunch of self-interested individuals into a cooperative, selfless group. In the end, though, your reputation isn't what you do, or what you say about yourself. Your reputation is whatever other people say it is.

For many species, including ourselves, observation is a powerful influence on behavior. We aren't the only species that can use reputation to maintain cooperative behavior and curb cheating, and we aren't the only species that acts differently when it's being watched. (More on this later.) But enforcing cooperation by surveillance puts a severe cramp on what animals can achieve and on the size of group they can achieve it in. If you're watching your neighbors, it's difficult to do anything else at the same time, such as feed yourself or watch for predators. It's hard to keep track of more than one individual at a time. It's impossible to tell anyone else what you've seen or to learn what they've seen, and your technology is defeated by trees, rocks, and anything else opaque.

Language allows people to preserve a record of others' deeds through time and spread it through space. As a tool for finding out what other people did while you weren't there and then passing that information on to someone else, language is hard to beat. Besides being a labor-saving device, reputation is also an amplifier, a form of social leverage that makes the consequences of our actions, for good or ill, reverberate beyond their immediate time, place, and target. Language amplifies the amplifier. Nourished in the broth of talk, reputation grows from something incidental to something omnipresent and scarily powerful.

Some researchers, such as the British evolutionary biologist Robin Dunbar, have argued that the value of social information drove the evolution of language—that our ancestors began talking to one another so that they could gossip.[3] Dunbar, like Richard Alexander, believes that a big brain is a social tool. Primates, Dunbar argues, evolved bigger and more expensive brains than other mammals, relative to their body size, not because they need all of that processing power to cope with physical challenges, such as swinging through the trees, or the color vision needed to spot ripe fruit or the intelligence for tool use, but because their social world is especially demanding. In support of what he calls the social brain hypothesis, Dunbar has found a strong link across various primate species between social complexity and the size of the neocortex—the bit of the brain involved in clever stuff such as language and consciousness. Species that live in larger groups, such as macaques, form more coalitions as adults, play more as youngsters, and have relatively bigger neocortexes than do less social species such as marmosets. Among primates, humans have the biggest brains, the most complex social lives, and the most sophisticated cognitive tools for managing them, of which language is the most highly developed. To quote the evolutionary biologist David Haig, "For direct reciprocity you need a face, for indirect reciprocity you need a name."[4]

Not surprisingly, it was obvious to the first researchers on indirect reciprocity that gossip could be a means to create and communicate reputations. Martin Nowak and Karl Sigmund suggested this in their original paper on image scoring. Not surprisingly, it was Manfred Milinski's group that put the idea to the test.

The experiment was led by Ralf Sommerfeld, a graduate student in Milinski's group.[5] It was designed to test whether gossip could substitute for direct observation when people used indirect reciprocity and to compare the strength of gossip versus observation to affect people's behavior. When your ears and eyes are telling you different things, do you trust the hearsay or the data?

Sommerfeld and his colleagues gave 126 first-year biology students at the universities of Kiel, Münster, and Vienna 10 euros each. The students then played many rounds of a two-player game in which each party decided whether to pay 1.25 euros so that her partner would get 2 euros. They changed partners every few rounds. In a fair world, each player would end each round three-quarters of a euro better off. The temptation is to hold on to your own cash in the hope of making a profit of 2 euros.

In some rounds, players were shown their partners' previous decisions with other players. Not surprisingly, stingy players found that donations dried up, leaving both players zero euros better off. In other rounds, the researchers asked the players to write a brief comment about their partners and pass this on instead. Again, no shock—players who heard that their current partners had been generous in the past but did not see those decisions were more likely to hand over their 1.25 euros, and those who heard bad things held on to their cash. People assume that others are telling the truth, and gossip can drive indirect reciprocity just as well as a visible image score does.

The surprise came when players were given both gossip and raw data. Here, the researchers said, is what your current partner has done in the past, and here is what that person's previous partners said about it. In fact, these gossip statements—such as *"spendabler spieler!"* (generous player) or *"übler geizkragen"* (nasty miser)—were left over from a previous study and paired with the real data at random.

If you've got the same information that the gossiper had, shouldn't you be able to make up your own mind, unswayed? Apparently not. If people saw what their partners had done in the past, they cooperated about 60 percent of the time. Yet if this data was accompanied by a snippet of positive gossip, cooperation went up to 75 percent. A bad word, however, even if it contradicted what the player could see with his or her own eyes, destroyed trust, with cooperation dropping to 50 percent. Even when people knew that the person talking knew no more than they did, a piece of gossip was like an extra weight thrown on the scales of decision-making, influencing whether they tipped one way or another.

Sommerfeld suggests two forces that might cause this effect. First, gossip is easy to understand, but numbers need a bit more work. Faced with two streams of information on which to base a decision, our brains might grab at the source that requires the least effort and we'd make up our minds without bothering to crunch all of the data. Our brains certainly seem to have a bias for gossip: experiments have found that people transmit social information, whether it's scandalous gossip about affairs and pregnancy or mundane news about a meeting at a bus stop, more accurately than they transmit news lacking a social context, such as a story about someone oversleeping or dry facts about Colorado.[6] We are also better at working out whether a rule of the "If P, then Q" variety has been broken when it is expressed in terms of social rules and obligations (e.g., "If you borrow the tent, then you must clean it before you give it back") than when such rules are expressed in more abstract terms.[7]

Second, people like to agree with one another and are wary of making a decision that puts them at odds with the pack. So if someone else gives you an opinion, you're tempted to go along with it and act accordingly, even if it seems not to square with your own experience.

Gossip, then, is such a good medium for transmitting reputation—and is such a powerful influence on behavior—that it can warp the evidence of our own eyes. On the one hand, experiments such as Sommerfeld's reveal the fragility of our decision-making and its susceptibility to social and emotional influences. One strength of such studies is that they help reveal the sometimes hidden forces shaping our behavior and the difference between what people do and what they say they do or imagine they would do. On the other hand, it's hardly a surprise that words sway people and that they make us treat others too harshly or too leniently or act against our own best interests. We just like to think that such manipulation requires a bit more in the way of oratory than a few words picked at random and pitched into the information mix.

Language takes your reputation out of your hands. It makes your reputation not what you do, but what other people say about you, usually behind your back. Sommerfeld's experiment shows that this is true even when people know what you did. A heart of gold is no match for a silver tongue.

Faced with the power of language to warp reputation, many wise people have stressed the difference between how the world perceives us and how we truly are. "Character is like a tree and reputation is like a shadow," said Abraham Lincoln. "The shadow is what we think of it, the tree is the real thing."[8] This real thing, unfortunately, is inaccessible. Your character is like a cross between an imaginary friend (it might give you some comfort, but it won't stand up for you) and Schrödinger's cat (as soon as you look at it, it becomes something else, namely, reputation). Your reputation may indeed bear only a passing resemblance to what you have actually done, but that's because you do not own your reputation, and so it does not always serve your own interests. The mismatch reflects other people's priorities, and it comes about through how they use gossip.

When we gossip, we don't stand on a box in the street with a megaphone. We take someone or a few people whom we already know into our confidence. They might repay us with something they heard from a mutual friend about a friend of a friend and then go and tell someone we don't know what they just heard from us. Information pinballs around, and where it goes and what sort of reputation emerges depends on who tells what to whom and how they connect to one another. Social information is like water: where it ends up depends on the shape of the landscape it flows over. For gossip, social networks form the topography of this landscape.

Much of what we do, how we feel, and how our lives pan out depends on the structure of our social network. Suicide, obesity, divorce, and happiness are all contagious. Your emotions and achievements depend not only on what happens to you. They also depend on the fates of your family, friends, and colleagues and even on what happens to the people connected to them. Another important factor is how the people who connect to you connect to one another. Teenage girls are more prone to suicidal thoughts if their friends don't get along with one another than if they do.[9] Theoretical studies, meanwhile, show that stable social networks breed altruism, because cooperative individuals can form clusters where they are more likely to interact with one another, an idea called network reciprocity.[10] Social stability enhances the force of reputation. The diamond trade, for example, is one business still regulated largely by reputation: contracts are sealed with a handshake, and members of the New York Diamond Dealer's Club are fined or expelled if they try to take professional disputes to court rather than allow them to be dealt with internally. Instead, the club's trading room is lined with pictures of dealers with bad debts. This form of enforcement is possible partly because businesses are passed down within families, and most of those in the trade are Orthodox Jews, a small and tightly knit community in which the threat of ostracism carries additional force.[11] In large groups of highly mobile individuals, in contrast, it's hard to build up long-term relationships and difficult to find out a person's past, so cooperation is more fragile, something we'll return to later. It's not too surprising, then, that your reputation is also a feature—a product, even—of your social network.

Ronald Burt, a sociologist at the University of Chicago, analyzed the reputations of employees who were working on investments for what he describes as a "large American financial organization during the late 1990s, just before the dot.com bubble burst."[12] The company had a very fluid working environment—a team of employees would come together for a specific project and then disband to team up with mostly new people on a new job. To measure employees' perform-ance in this shifting social landscape, the company used 360-degree evaluation, constructing each employee's reputation from the opin-ions of those above, alongside, and beneath him or her in the busi-ness hierarchy. These ratings were used to decide promotions and bonuses.

Despite this chaotic working structure, many people showed consistent evaluations from year to year, both good and bad. Why, of course, a business president told Burt, good people do good work and get good ratings, and the reverse.

But Burt suspected that a stable reputation had more to do with a person's social environment than with his intrinsic qualities. Often people attracted very different appraisals from various colleagues, suggesting that personal chemistry mattered more than any objective measure of success. Burt looked at how the structure of a person's social network affected the stability of his reputation. If a person's reputation reflected only his intrinsic qualities, then there would have been no effect. Someone who found himself in a work team where everyone had adjacent desks and members chatted all day before going to a bar together after work would be in the same position, reputation-wise, as someone working in the Chicago office with teammates who were in London, Geneva, and Tokyo and knew one another only via conference calls.

This wasn't the case, however. The stability of a person's reputation—the extent to which his ranking, be it good or bad, remained the same from one year to the next—depended on the strength of the connections between his colleagues. Specifically, reputation was a product of networks with a cliquey structure. If a person had colleagues who gossiped with one another, then they created a picture of him within the company that was vivid enough to survive into the next year and influence how his new colleagues saw him.

Cameron Anderson and Aiwa Shirako of the University of California, Berkeley, found something similar while studying MBA students on a negotiation course.[13] The researchers measured the students' behavior in a series of role-playing exercises, looking at whether, for example, a student sought a good outcome for both parties, or whether she just tried to drive the best possible deal for herself. At the end of the course, the researchers measured the students' reputations by asking each class member to nominate the most trustworthy and kind members of the group and the most aggressive, ruthless, and slippery. They also measured social connectedness by asking each student how well she knew every other member of the group.

A person's reputation with her classmates, they found, matched her behavior only if she was widely known and well-connected. This was true for both cooperative and selfish behavior, suggesting that although there are obvious advantages to being talked about, it also limits what you can get away with. The more anonymous, less connected members of the class, in contrast, barely had reputations at all—they were seldom nominated as being either cooperative or selfish. And what reputations they did have bore little resemblance to whether they had been kind or cutthroat in negotiations.

Both Anderson and Shirako's study and Burt's work show that closed networks make for strong groups, because bad behavior is more likely to be detected. Yet for us reluctant networkers who hope that our deeds can make their own way in the world and maybe even tow us along in their wake—who hope that, to pick an example at random, writing one good piece for a magazine will lead to other pieces being commissioned—this is sobering news. You have a reputation only if you are well-connected and if your connections are interconnected. It's as if reputation is an energy that's generated by gossip, constantly dissipating and needing constant renewal. If the people who know you don't know one another, you can't expect them to gossip about you— what would they say to one another, and why would they bother? And if people don't talk about you, you remain a cipher, an unknown quantity. The issue isn't so much that your reputation will not reflect your behavior, as that you won't have a reputation at all. Your tree, to adapt Lincoln's metaphor, will cast no shadow. Or, to quote a remark I heard Burt make in a talk: "Do good work that people don't talk about, and you've got the life expectancy of morning dew."[14]

What other people say about you, then, and to whom, decides whether you're trusted, and talking about other people lets you work out whether they can be trusted. When we gossip, however, we're not pipes through which information travels to emerge unadulterated. We are more like refineries; what comes out is very different from what goes in. We shape other people's reputations by what we choose to report of them, what we leave out, and the slant we put on the information. We filter and spin in the way that we think will best serve our own interests.

Sometimes we manipulate gossip to bolster or attack the reputation of whomever we're talking about, because he is a friend or a rival or because we are angry at his antisocial behavior and want him brought into line or ostracized. This use of gossip is the subject of chapter 9. But we also warp reputations less consciously, because in the conversational moment making a friend of whomever we're talking to is usually more important than accurately portraying the person we're talking about.

Passing on some useful or entertaining tidbit about another person to your friend is a sign of commitment. If you jeopardize your relationship with the subject of the gossip by gossiping about him or her, you show that you value whom you're talking with more than whom you're talking about. Yet even more simply than that, we show people we value them by agreeing with them. The innocent urge to make friends and avoid giving offense has a profound influence on how we use gossip and the reputations that result from it. Experiments have found that if people are given an equal selection of positive and negative facts about a person and are asked to discuss him with a stranger, they accentuate the positive if they think the stranger likes the other person and the negative if they don't.[15] Just as we build bonds in conversation by unconsciously mirroring one another's posture and gestures, so we do the same with opinions.

If you work with Jeff, and you meet someone in another office who, it transpires, likes Jeff, you share an anecdote about the time that Jeff pulled an all-nighter to get his team's report ready in time for a deadline. But if, when you mention Jeff, the colleague seems to stiffen, you mention how Jeff always seems to slink off early on a Friday. Either way, both of you come away with your opinions more settled than they were before. (One reason, I think, that scientists can seem socially inept is that the combative conversational environment in which they work knocks this habit out of them. Science, like every academic discipline, is about criticizing others and yourself, and this approach becomes ingrained and generalized in its practitioners. So in a department coffee break room or at a conference dinner, every statement, be it about science, taste in music, political beliefs, or religious faith, is liable to be destruction-tested. Among scientists, this is the norm and part of the fun. It's accepted that just because you disagree with someone and will use your full rhetorical arsenal against him, it doesn't mean you think he's an idiot or a bad person. Yet I have seen that civilians who encounter this style can be left feeling as if the person ripping their views to shreds thinks precisely that.)

Again, how this bonding feature of gossip shapes the reputation of those gossiped about depends on the structure of social networks. In Ronald Burt's words, closed networks are an echo chamber within which people tell one another what they want to hear. This creates a feedback loop, amplifying the strength of opinions and turning social information into value judgments, creating both heroes and villains. In his study of social networks and reputation formation in business, Burt found that difficult interactions in an open social network tended to be blamed on the situation—perhaps neither of you was having a good day. In a closed network, they were more likely to be blamed on personality flaws—the guy must be a jerk. The issue isn't whether your reputation is based on accurate information. It's that you can't control how people interpret that information. In general, when people tell stories about one another they emphasize the characters and their deeds, and downplay the details of the situation that might have shaped or excused those deeds. This means that opinions based on hearsay tend to be more extreme than those based on direct experience.[16] By doing this, we serve our own ends by creating a simpler and sharper story that makes us a more compelling conversation partner. And we make the social information we're passing on seem more valuable, because knowing what someone is like deep down is more generally useful than knowing what they did in a particular situation.

So once a clique has formed an opinion about Jeff, it becomes extremely resistant to change, regardless of what Jeff does, because stories about Jeff are not just for working out whether he can be trusted. They are, in Burt's words, "grist for the gossip mill through which colleagues strengthen their relationships with each other."[17] To change the story would be to threaten the relationship between the gossipers. You can see this phenomenon at work in the images of public figures, particularly in the media. Once a view settles on the incompetence of a politician or a sports coach, or about the kookiness of a film star, the facts of that person's behavior get fitted into that view. If someone labeled a failure has some success, or someone labeled an oddball does something shrewd, it gets marked as a one-off or an accident or just ignored.

The study of social networks and gossip, then, shows that if reputation does not reflect character, that's hardly surprising. That's not what reputation is for. Your character belongs to you; your reputation belongs to other people, who have their own interests at heart, and they use it to control you, not to depict you. To mangle Abraham Lincoln's metaphor, if character is the tree, reputation is the tree surgeon, and gossip is her pruning saw. Of course, all of us have a degree of control over the information we feed into our social networks, through how we behave, and we all have a degree of control over how those networks refine our reputations. One of the best things you could do, in terms of nurturing your own reputation, is to introduce your friends to one another and encourage them to hit it off. In addition, if you've got something difficult and potentially damaging to discuss, it's best to do it with someone outside your immediate social network, because she is likely to be less judgmental, and what you tell her will have less gossip value.

We've already seen some of the things people do to publicize their own virtues, how they use information about others, and the consequences of that public knowledge for individuals and their groups. Yet no one gets it right all of the time. We forget birthdays, avoid washing the dishes, talk to ourselves louder than we mean to, and mistakenly use the women's toilet at Turin airport. Damage control is another vital piece of everyone's reputation tool kit. The weird thing is, we publicize our failures almost as much as our successes.

CHAPTER 5

Saving Face

In the mid-1990s, Mark Leary, who now works at Duke University in North Carolina, began to wonder what self-esteem is for. Many psychologists treat it as an end in itself, thinking that we simply prefer feeling good to feeling bad. But this is like saying that we prefer chocolate cake to cabbage because the cake tastes nicer—it's all right as far as it goes, but it raises further questions about the function of taste and the nutritional properties of cake. Leary wanted to know what might be the ultimate benefit of feeling good about yourself.

Leary was particularly struck by research on social rejection showing that when people are devalued by others, they devalue themselves. He began to think that maybe self-esteem was an internal reflection of external events, tracking the value of our social stock, monitoring our good and bad deeds, converting this data into a net sense of self-worth, and guiding us toward acts that would improve our standing. He called this tracker the "sociometer."[1] You could imagine it as a news feed showing your image score—after all, there's no point if everyone knows your reputation except you.

During the next decade, Leary tested this idea in more than a dozen experiments that looked at how rejection and acceptance by others affected self-worth. He held team-formation exercises, in which subjects were either chosen or ignored or chosen first or last; he asked people to talk about themselves and then gave positive or negative feedback about their desirability as a friend or a colleague; he asked people to imagine how a thumbs-up or thumbs-down from a professor or a date would make them feel; and he staged conversations in which subjects were either heeded or ignored. All of these studies found that the positive attention and good opinions of others led to higher self-esteem, and rejection led to lower. Likewise, when Leary asked people to rank a list of behaviors—ranging from "I cheated on a final exam," "I sneezed on the person in front of me at a checkout line," and "I took care of a friend's house plants," to "I donated a kidney to a dying person"—on two lists, one showing how socially prized or condemned these would be and the other showing how much they would boost or lower self-esteem, the two scales were almost identical. It's an old idea that how we see ourselves depends on how others see us. In 1902, the psychologist Charles Horton Cooley coined the phrase "looking-glass self" to describe the effect of other's opinions on our self-image. Leary's work shows that our internal state and our social selves are inseparable and demonstrates that personal morality steers us toward actions that will make others think well of us.

When Leary began to give talks on this work, someone always came up to him afterward and said something like, "Yeah, well, I guess that might be true for most people, but I don't care what anybody else thinks of me." We like to feel that we make our own ideas of right and wrong, and the thought that we might simply be chasing acceptance is a bit disturbing. So Leary asked a large group of people how much they cared about what other people thought of them, and he experimented on the most dismissive 10 percent and the neediest 10 percent. He divided his subjects into groups of four and had them exchange personal information. After this, each subject chose which two of the other three they would most like to be friends with. Leary then gave his guinea pigs bogus feedback on what other people had said about them. Being told that no one liked them was just as wounding to self-declared loners as it was to those who had said they craved acceptance. People do differ in their sensitivity to social judgment, but anyone who tells you he doesn't care what anyone else thinks of him is lying. (Or he's a psychopath, as we'll discuss in chapter 10, but in that case he's likely to lie and pretend that he cares.)

• • •

As well as keeping track of past behavior and its consequences, a sense of self-worth also lets us see into and test possible futures. When we imagine how we would feel if we got a promotion or if we got caught stealing a colleague's idea, we focus on the internal sensations as much as on others' responses. Those imagined feelings push us toward doing things that keep our reputations healthy. The English writer William Hazlitt put it well in his 1805 *Essay on the Principles of Human Action*: "[Imagination] must carry me out of myself into the feeling of others by one and the same process by which I am thrown forward, as it were, into my future being and interested in it. I could not love myself, if I were not capable of loving others. Self-love, used in this sense, is in its fundamental principle the same with disinterested benevolence."[2]

A recent study of people with autism, the symptoms of which include a lack of social awareness and an inability to see another's point of view, illustrates the link between self-image and the social self.[3] Neuroscientist Pearl Chiu and her colleagues had people with autism play an economic trust game, where one player must decide whether to give money to the other. The money is multiplied en route, and the other player must decide whether to reward the first player's trust by giving money back or exploit it by keeping the cash. Chiu's team found that at the moment when people with autism decide whether to trust, they show much less activity in a brain region that fires when picturing the *self* in a social situation. This suggests that when people without autism make a similar decision, they're not only thinking "Can I trust you?" and trying to put themselves in the other person's mind; they're also thinking, "How do I get you to trust me?" and trying to see themselves through the other person's eyes. Giving in the trust game, then, is a signal, as well as an investment, and the opportunity to build a reputation is as important as the opportunity to make some cash. The worry is not only that the person won't return our trust if we do give, but that he or she will be hurt if we don't— something that people with autism seem not to consider.

In a social environment in which animals both cooperate and compete, being able to put oneself in another's head and see oneself through another's eyes is such a valuable skill that many researchers believe its benefits drove the evolution of self-awareness—consciousness—itself. In the 1970s, the British psychologist and philosopher Nicholas Humphrey suggested, after spending some time watching gorillas with Dian Fossey, that self-awareness was a tool for understanding, anticipating, and manipulating others.[4] This idea, sometimes called Machiavellian intelligence, also lies behind the social brain hypothesis— the idea that a big brain is a tool for group living—that we encountered in chapter 4.[5]

It's easy to see how a cognitive arms race could develop as brains and social complexity evolve together. If you can build a bigger group, you get a competitive advantage over other groups, but this gives you more people in your own group to keep track of. You have to read other people's minds and recognize their intentions. You have to work out whether they are being nice or nasty and how well they are succeeding. You have to judge how you would feel to be on the receiving end of such behavior, and then you have to use that feeling to work out how to treat the person you're observing. Learning from other people's experience and using reputation require a huge amount of cognitive infrastructure.

If you can solve those problems, your group is more likely to stick together. You also get an advantage within your group, because you will be better at winning the trust of and, if necessary, deceiving its other members. This imposes a pressure on other groups and other members of your own group to get wise to your tricks and develop their own, which creates a more complex social environment, which creates new social pressures, and so on. Because, it seems, introspection is a good method for solving these social problems, a few million years of this arms race results in an ape that asks itself not only "What does he think of me?" but "Who am I?" and "Why am I here?"—yet which still tends to answer those questions in terms of its relationships with other members of its group.

Reputation is a game in which we must play every position on the field, monitoring others while we guard and burnish our own images. In evolutionary terms, we can understand how a stream of social information, simulated outcomes, and sociometer readings gets translated into decisions by looking at the costs and benefits of particular courses of action. Yet no one makes these decisions after a reckoning of his or her reputational credits and debits, any more than people who see a shark swimming toward them pause to weigh up the pros and cons of getting out of the water. Fear is a quick way of letting you know that your skin is in danger and a powerful prompt to do something about it. Pain and pleasure are also excellent teachers of what to avoid and seek out.

Likewise, our emotions steer us away from social injury and toward social comfort, teach us to avoid repeating our mistakes, and encourage us to repeat our successes. Only the greatest writers and stories can do justice to the force of these feelings in human life. In Shakespeare's *Othello*, Cassio feels his shame as a kind of death. When, in the 2,500-year-old Hindu epic the *Ramayana*, Rama wrongly accuses his wife, Sita, of infidelity, she calls on the earth to open up and swallow her, which it does. The body treats shame in the same way it does a physical wound, releasing a surge of the chemicals that trigger inflammation in damaged cells and of the stress hormone cortisol. Gay men infected with HIV show higher viral loads and faster declines in immune cells if they are particularly prone to shame and sensitive to social rejection; this is not seen for other negative emotions, such as anger and anxiety. A 1997 study found that patients highly sensitive to rejection died of AIDS on average two years before those who cared less about society's judgment.[6]

Yet emotions don't merely send our bodies messages about the outside world. They use our bodies to send messages the other way, so that others can read our minds and learn from our experience. We learn through empathy and through emotional contagion. If we see fear on someone's face, we feel uneasy. Seeing someone make a grimace of disgust and sniffing something rotten both trigger similar brain responses. It's easy to see the benefit of taking note of these emotions: if someone nearby is afraid or disgusted, we too may be in danger. If the person looks rapturous, there's probably something good going on.

Emotional contagion puts us in another person's shoes. But the feelings that guard our social selves have a different purpose: to show us ourselves through other eyes. The question these emotions answer isn't "What would I feel if I were experiencing the same thing as that person, and how can I achieve or avoid that?" It's "If I were that person, what would I feel about me, and what should I do about that?" That's why psychologists call shame, pride, guilt, and embarrassment the self-conscious emotions. I think of them as the emotions of reputation.

If you want people to think well of you, it seems foolish to make a display of your errors. That we do suggests that humans evolved in an environment where it was difficult to keep secrets, because people were seldom alone and because we are keen observers of one another. Yet even if people know what we have done, they may not know what to make of it. Did that woman spill her coffee over her husband out of clumsiness or rage? Did my friend not send me a birthday card because he forgot or because we're no longer friends? When we have a social accident, attaching an emotional signal to the incident is a way of revealing our motives and intentions. This helps minimize and repair the damage by letting other people know that despite our current difficulties, we know how to behave.

The negative self-conscious emotions—shame, guilt, and embarrassment—hunt as a pack and shade into one another. Some cultures lump them together—many languages use the same word to describe shame and embarrassment, and many psychologists once thought that the three were different names for the same thing. Most now believe that this is not the case, however, and that each feeling has its own triggers and consequences.[7]

Guilt is the sense of having done a bad thing. When asked to name acts they would feel guilty about, people suggest things such as lying, stealing, and infidelity. Guilt is an outward-facing emotion. People who feel guilty become more empathetic and kinder and seek to make amends by confessing, apologizing, and compensating. We have a sense that repairing the damage is at least partly within our power.

Shame, in contrast, is the sense of being a bad person. People are ashamed when they fail to meet the standards of decency, morality, or achievement that they set for themselves or that the people they care about hold, such as when they hurt someone's feelings or lose a job. Shame is more fatalistic than guilt: the guilty boy thinks he failed an exam because he didn't study; the ashamed boy thinks he failed because he's stupid. Shame also brings a feeling of unwelcome exposure and a wish to be out of sight—even if it means, like Sita, the ground opening up beneath you. This shrinking from society is the reverse of guilt's effects: instead of reaching out to the offended party, shame prevents you from doing any more damage. And rather than driving one's own hand to repair the damage, shame drives us to seek relief in others' acceptance and forgiveness.

Embarrassment's sting is not so harsh, but it is uniquely social.[8] We can feel guilt and shame when no one else is around, but embarrassment needs an audience. Rather than being specifically linked to moral failings, we feel embarrassment when we break social conventions of any sort or when we feel conspicuous. This covers physical pratfalls, breaches of etiquette, losses of control and privacy, general displays of eccentricity and ineptitude, and just about anything that involves being the center of attention; one method that is used to induce embarrassment in the lab is to ask subjects to sing to a video camera ("The Star-Spangled Banner" and "Feelings" are popular choices) and then watch the recording together with the experimenter. As a generalized response to attention, embarrassment is more promiscuous and also more contagious than shame. It strikes even when we have nothing to feel bad about, such as when we receive extravagant praise; when other people are in the wrong, as, for example, when we have to ask them if they've got the twenty dollars they said they'd pay back last week; or even on another's behalf, such as when we see our parents attempt to speak a foreign language. Embarrassment says something like "I am showing you that I know this is a social situation, that rules apply, and that people are being watched and judged," but judgment can't help bleeding into empathy, thank goodness.

These emotions, as well as stemming from different causes, take different physical forms. The signs of shame match its vocabulary: we feel small and make ourselves small, cast our eyes down, hang our heads, hunch our shoulders, and shrink into ourselves. Such movements are very similar to, and were almost certainly derived from, the displays that animals use to show that they know they're beaten and to appease an aggressor. By looking at the ground, hanging its head, and hunching its shoulders, a dog or a monkey acknowledges its subordinate status and pleads for mercy. Some primates' skin also turns red. The defeated sportsman slinking off the field or the red-faced employee dressed down by his boss show that humans have kept this aspect of shame as a response to defeat and inferiority. Many languages also reflect this property of the emotion: the Maori word *whakama*, for example, can mean shame, embarrassment, respect, deference, and unfavorable comparisons with others.[9] Humans have taken the feeling and the show of inferiority and adapted it to our more complex social lives. We have many more opportunities for social failure and need to appease a wider group than those who are bigger and stronger than ourselves.

Embarrassment also brings forth a distinctive response. Like shame, it gives us a sudden interest in studying the floor. Unlike shame, embarrassment also comes with a smile—a small, sheepish smile that turns the corner of our mouths up but, unlike a smile of amusement, doesn't engage the eye muscles. Embarrassed people also often touch their faces, which is not seen in those who are ashamed. Blushing, which is so closely associated with social discomfort, is seen in both emotions, but it's not the clear-cut signal it might seem—it doesn't always appear, and it can sometimes signal something else, such as anger.

Showing shame and embarrassment, then, involves executing a complex set of moves. Unlike what psychologists call the basic emotions of fear, disgust, happiness, anger, sadness, and surprise, which we share with many other species, facial expression alone is not enough. A smiling person might be proud or happy, a frowning one might be sad or ashamed. Self-conscious emotions become unmistakable only when bodily postures are included. Shame and embarrassment are also less consistent across cultures than basic emotions are—not every society distinguishes between them, and there are local variations in how they are expressed: in India, embarrassed people often bite their tongues, for example. Yet there are also consistencies: people from the African nation of Burkina Faso can recognize a look of shame on a white American's face.[10] Guilt, however, has no outward signs that are recognized across different cultures. It's about doing, not showing, and it protects our reputations by driving us to repair relationships, not by triggering public shows of contrition.

Unlike the expressions of the basic emotions, these emotional displays do not to make others feel what we're feeling. Instead, they make people feel better about us. Showing that we care about what other people think softens their judgment, and often what we do is less important than how we appear to feel about it. If people are asked to watch a video of a man who knocks over a stack of toilet paper in a shop, they find him more likeable if he shows embarrassment, even if he doesn't tidy up, than if he calmly puts the rolls back and saunters off.[11] It's important, however, that the transgression is accidental—if people suspect they've been tricked, they take blushing as a sign of culpability.[12]

It's easy to see why people would take notice of these signals. Seeing someone lose his balance or yield to temptation once isn't necessarily a good guide to his competence and trustworthiness, but emotions reveal the personality underlying the behavior, a more stable and better guide to the future. Not showing emotion is also revealing. One of the things that has made many people angry with investment bankers and their ilk during the last few years is not only that they made mistakes, but that they seem so unabashed. (I'll come to why this might be so in chapter 10, where I discuss psychopaths.) A person who doesn't show shame or embarrassment doesn't care about social acceptance, doesn't value the group to which he belongs, and so is a dangerous and untrustworthy person to have around. People will forgive most things, but shamelessness is hard to swallow.

Showing embarrassment doesn't change only how people feel about us. It also changes how people behave toward us. In a study carried out at Northeastern University in Boston, a woman went into classes seeking volunteers for a research study.[13] In some, the request passed without incident. In others, she dropped a sheaf of papers, embarrassedly picked them up, and soldiered on. In the third treatment she dropped her papers and fled the room in panic. She got the most volunteers when she experienced a mishap and showed mild embarrassment—the emotional display seems to have made her more likeable. A complete breakdown, on the other hand, might be a sign of incompetence. Who'd want to be experimented on by someone who gets freaked out by a sheet of paper?

Embarrassment also makes us more helpful. Working at Boston University in the 1970s, Robert Apsler asked undergraduates to make fools of themselves—imitating a toddler throwing a tantrum, for example—while an observer looked on.[14] The observer then asked subjects whether they'd mind helping out with a research project that involved spending thirty minutes each day filling out questionnaires. Embarrassed students signed up for fifteen days; unembarrassed, nine. Aspler suggested that "embarrassed individuals seek the positive experience of helping someone in order to relieve the discomfort of their embarrassment." The actions that help embarrassed people feel better about themselves also make other people feel better about them.

Science and medicine have given much more attention to what makes people feel bad than to what makes them feel good. So pride has been studied less than guilt and shame. People tend not to go to psychiatrists and say, "Doctor, I'm so proud of myself, I just go around all day thinking how good I am. Is there a pill that'll make it go away?" Yet the studies that have been conducted show that pride is the opposite of the negative self-conscious emotions in many ways.

For example, pride's physical expression reverses the signs of shame. Proud people stand tall, they put their shoulders back and puff out their chests, they look you in the eye. The psychologist who has probably given the most thought to pride, Jessica Tracy, has found that, like the signs of shame, this display is recognized around the world. Looking at Olympic judo bouts, she has seen that the winner stands tall, smiles, and so on, regardless of his or her nationality.[15] To show that athletes don't learn this from watching sports movies, she has seen that blind athletes competing in the Paralympics mark a victory in exactly the same way. Showing pride is part of our biology.

Pride gives us an internal reward—"Congratulations! You've done something that others will admire and reward. Keep it up." Pride advertises our achievement to others—"Hey! This person is a success.

You want him in your group." Beyond this immediate and short-lived effect, pride's effects on behavior also invert shame; proud people are more sociable and outgoing, and people who take a genuine, wholesome pride in their achievements also score highly on personality traits such as agreeableness and conscientiousness.

But pride has two faces. Recently, Tracy has been observing chimpanzees to try to work out the animal antecedents of human pride. She thinks that the chest-out, shoulders-back posture is related to the swaggering displays of dominance that chimpanzees give, not after they've won a fight, but before the confrontation happens.[16] These shows of strength, like shows of submission, help animals size up one another without coming to blows.

Humans seem to have a version of this preemptive pride. You might call it the opposite of shame—the sense that one is a good person, rather than the sense that one did a good thing. Hubris is a better description, and the advantage of showing it, particularly in competitive situations, is obvious. As self-help books will tell you, if you want to be a winner, act like a winner, and other people will treat you like a winner, even if you haven't won anything yet. Weakling chimps don't strut about, because you can get a good idea of how strong a chimp is by looking at him, and if in doubt, it's easy to discover whether there's any muscle behind the show by picking a fight.

Humans face a more complicated task. Unlike in chimpanzees, a display of pride is meant to be attractive, not threatening. At root, the message of all of the emotions of reputation is "trust me." They are signals that seek to bind us to other people and encourage them to cooperate with us. The problem with hubris is that it's a cheap signal—it costs little to send and a lot to believe. It might take a while to find out whether a person's pride is justified, and you could lose quite a bit in the process.

Pride is a bid to boost reputation, but reputation can also expose false pride. By consulting other people, we find out whether someone wearing a proud expression has anything to be proud of. This makes hubris more expensive, because it means that a person taken in by false pride in the present can damage the hubristic individual in the long run. We are very sensitive to any mismatch between a person's self-image and his or her social worth and have lots of words to condemn groundless pride—*arrogant, pompous, cocky, conceited, big-headed*. The labels for people lacking self-esteem, such as shy and timid, don't carry the same condemnation, perhaps because an excess of embarrassment is more self-defeating than it is damaging to others—shame and embarrassment are cheap signals, but unlike pride, there's no incentive to be deceitful in falsely displaying them, because there's little point going around saying, "I goofed," if you haven't.

Religion and culture are full of warnings about pride. Around 600 CE, Pope Gregory the Great made pride one of the seven deadly sins, and Buddhism, besides taking a generally dim view of self-consciousness, lists conceit as one of the ten fetters of existence, hindering the journey to enlightenment. Such lists tell us how to spot people whom it's dangerous to trust, as well as how to maintain our own social value. In stories, comic characters made so by the gap between their egos and the reality are harder to avoid than they are to accumulate, particularly in British humor. In the last novel I finished before writing this, Charles Dickens's *Our Mutual Friend*, the rascally but stupid Silas Wegg pines after an imaginary bond with the genteel former occupants of the house he pitches his stall outside and thinks himself worth "five hundred times" the house's current tenant and his employer, the generous and humble dust-man Noddy Boffin. We cheer when Wegg gets his comeuppance, ejected from the novel on a dustcart, but at least, in being puffed up and brought down by hubris, he joins the company of tragic heroes from Achilles to Darth Vader.

There's more to interpreting emotional signals than simply detecting and punishing false displays. Even when someone has something to be genuinely proud or ashamed of, the audience will have its own opinions about how that emotion should be displayed and how much. The effect of the display on the actor's reputation will depend on how well she meets those expectations. The result is that cultures differ in how they value the self-conscious emotions, so people in various cultures express themselves differently.

In the early 1990s, Daniel Fessler, an anthropologist at the University of California, Los Angeles, spent nearly three years doing research in a fishing village on the Indonesian island of Sumatra, among the Bengkulu people.[17] One of his aims was to investigate the presence and strength of shame in that culture and compare it with his own. He gave the villagers a deck of cards bearing fifty-two words commonly used to describe emotions and asked them to rank the words according to how often they arose in everyday conversation. When he tallied the results, *shame* came second, behind *anger* and before *sympathy*. He then repeated the experiment with Southern Californians and found that *shame* trailed in forty-ninth place, just behind *grief—love* and *stressed out* ranked one and two.

Californians and the Bengkulu, Fessler found, agreed about what shame is, but the emotion is a far less important part of social life in California than among the Bengkulu. Californians instead placed more emphasis on guilt—number thirty-two on the emotional charts. The Bengkulu, in contrast, struggled with the concept of guilt. Their language has no equivalent word for private social pain, and they tended to use broader terms, such as *regret, error,* or *sinning*. Social damage was always a public experience and always involved feeling devalued in the eyes of others, rather than against an internal standard.

Fessler also asked people what kind of experiences made them feel bad about themselves and how. There were many similarities— Californians and Bengkulu both feel ashamed when bested in competition, or when they fail to live up to society's expectations. He did find, however, that unlike Californians, the Bengkulu retained a sense of shame caused by inferior status, even when they had done nothing wrong. A young man, for example, might become tongue-tied and bashful simply when speaking to the head man in the village and would describe himself as ashamed to be doing so.

Fessler's study slots into a long line of anthropological research comparing the strength and value of shame and guilt in different cultures, going back to the anthropologist Ruth Benedict's 1946 book about Japanese society, *The Chrysanthemum and the Sword*. Benedict argued that Japan is a "shame culture," where the force of others' opinions is a stronger influence on how people feel and behave than in guilt cultures such as the United States, where people rely more on conscience and self-control.

Different cultures bring forth varying emotions through differences in the structure of their social networks. In the previous chapter, we saw from Ronald Burt's work on gossip and reputation that how an act affects the actor's reputation depends on the social connections within the audience. This will feed back to influence how people behave in the first place, particularly with regard to their emotional displays.

In tightly knit social networks abuzz with gossip, such as you'd find in a small fishing village, people become judgmental and tend to attribute social failure and success to character flaws and virtues, rather than to the situation. If you live in a dense social network, in other words, your audience will take your missteps to show that you are a bad person—that you have something to be ashamed of. When you see yourself reflected in this social mirror, you, too, are likely to feel ashamed. And if your audience thinks you have something to be ashamed of, the best way to appease it is to give it what it wants.

We should expect shame to be strong, then, in places where the links between people are tight and long-lasting, privacy and anonymity are hard to come by, and group cohesion and identity are important, because individual and group welfare are tightly linked. Nowadays, anthropologists describe such cultures with the less loaded term *collectivistic*. Bengkulu is one such culture.

In individualistic cultures such as Southern California, people are more anonymous and private, less densely connected, and less reliant on a single social group—rather, they belong to many groups that overlap to varying degrees. The patterns of gossip in such an environment may produce less judgmental attitudes and so demand less shame. People in these cultures still need to manage their reputations and avoid ostracism, but perhaps the internal promptings of guilt are more useful and noticeable than the public sting of shame. Benedict's work has been controversial—some believed it painted Japanese society as less morally advanced than its Western counterpart, and contemporary anthropologists tend to view the dichotomy as too simplistic. Yet shame and guilt may be different routes to the same end of avoiding and repairing social damage, each suited to its own social circumstances.

Collectivistic cultures value shame more highly than do individualistic ones—people don't enjoy feeling ashamed, of course, but they can see it as an appropriate and useful sensation, like the pain you feel after exercising, rather than the pain you feel when you stub your toe. In her study of judoists, Tracy found that fighters from collectivistic cultures were more likely to show shame after a defeat than were those from Western Europe and North America, who hid any shame they felt.

Pride, on the other hand, has a worse name in collectivistic cultures; it shows more cultural variation in whether it is thought of as good or bad than any other emotion. If Jessica Tracy's hunch about strutting chimpanzees is right, a hubristic display of pride is the equivalent to a display of dominance—it is saying, "I'm better than you, and you will do my bidding, whether you like it or not."[18] As we saw, people often try to discourage and undermine such displays of dominance. In a densely knit collectivistic society, where an individual's fate is closely tied to that of his group, dominance threatens widespread social damage and so will be particularly unwelcome and frowned on. In such cultures, high achievers use self-deprecation and modesty to show that although they might be excellent, they still value their neighbors' approval.

Culture and biology, then, work together to create our emotional makeup. We all have the capacity to feel these emotions, but our individual emotional palette depends on our social environment. Just as we evolved in the African forest and moved to tundra, desert, seashore, and city, so we can also adapt to many social environments and quickly: when Fessler went to live with the Bengkulu, he says, he found himself changing from a laidback West Coast type to someone more moralistic and self-righteous, taking on the code of the people he was studying.

Those of us living in large Western cities at the beginning of the twenty-first century probably feel as if we have less to be ashamed of than any other people in history. Yet we pay the price in loneliness and insecurity. I wonder whether people in the Anglo-Saxon West have become keener on revealing their emotions in the last few decades not only because repression is internally damaging, but because their society has become less interconnected. We use emotional displays to reveal ourselves to those around us, to share information and so build trust; as individuals become more isolated, emotional displays might become more pronounced as people strive to transmit enough information to make themselves trusted across greater social distances. Could emotional incontinence—gushing, chest-thumping pride, and theatrical, weeping shame—be an effort to shout across a social chasm and make yourself heard on the other side?

What's certainly true is that many of our personal and societal dilemmas originate in how, individually and en masse, we respond to and use social scrutiny and judgment. We want to be connected, and we want to be independent. We want to be ourselves, and we want to fit in. We want to be known, and we want to be private. We want tolerance, and we want agreement. We want to be in the group, and we want to be individuals. Where shame is strong, people treat one another with courtesy and consideration—Japan has a notably low crime rate—but such societies also create a pressure to conform, causing people to prefer to avoid failure, rather than take the risks entailed in creativity, innovation, and making new connections.[19] Every culture trades different social virtues off against one another, and the relative value that each, pushed by history, culture, economics, politics, and technology, comes to place on these goals will determine where it ends up on the line between collectivism and individualism, cohesion and diversity, stability and fluidity.

When a society holds its members tightly, it can be comforting and stifling. When it holds them loosely, it can be liberating and lonely. And when people have more to fear from their neighbors than to gain from them, the force of reputation can help explain not only why people help one another, but why they harm one another.

CHAPTER 6

Just to Get a Rep

In the late 1950s, Richard Nisbett, age seventeen, left his hometown in Texas for college at Tufts University in Massachusetts. Not everything about New England agreed with him. People seemed stiff and uptight, ruder, and less fun. Yet there was one thing he preferred about the Northern states: your acquaintances tended not to kill one another so much.

In 1960, Texas had 9.5 million people and saw 824 murders. In Massachusetts in the same year, there were 74 murders in a population of a little more than 5 million.[1] By moving north, Nisbett reduced the chances of a violent death to one-sixth of what they would have been had he stayed in Texas. This was not only a Texan thing: the Southern states in general have had a higher murder rate for as long as anyone has been collecting data. Nineteenth-century records show an epidemic of duels, feuds, and lynchings, with the murder rate in some areas equaling that seen in Ciudad Juarez, the drug-riven Mexican city unfortunate enough to currently hold the world record. Nor was this only poor and desperate people killing one another: one of Nisbett's relatives caught her husband in flagrante and shot him dead. She was the society editor of the *El Paso Herald Post* at the time.

Thirty-some years later, Nisbett was still in the North, working as a psychology professor at the University of Michigan in Ann Arbor.

He wanted to study cultural differences between groups, but on campus, the culture of political correctness was at its peak. Trying to tell one group of people why it was different from another group was likely to give more offense and invite more hostility than it was worth. Under the circumstances, Nisbett decided that the most diplomatic thing to do would be to study the culture he came from. Why, he decided to find out, was the South more violent?

The first clue lay in the FBI's files. The bureau records not only who kills whom but why. Where property is at stake, there was no regional difference—Americans from every part of the nation, when they rob, are equally likely to kill one another. In social disputes, however, it's very different. Southerners are far more likely to kill their friends and acquaintances in quarrels sparked by insults. This greater willingness to defend honor with deadly force accounted for all of the South's extra murders.

Nisbett recognized these attitudes in himself. He was, he realized, quicker to take offense than his Northern friends were. He was also more likely to take matters into his own hands and once pursued a burglar out of his house and down the street, a course of action that seemed idiotic once he'd calmed down. To see whether this was typical and distinctive Southern behavior, he and his colleagues recruited a hundred male students at the University of Michigan, half each from Northern and Southern states, and insulted them. Or, rather, the men were told they would be participating in a study measuring the effect of "limited response time conditions on certain facets of human judgment."[2] They were asked to complete a short questionnaire and to deliver it to a table down the corridor. The questionnaire was a decoy; the corridor was the arena for the real experiment. As the men walked down the corridor, they had to pass another man working at a filing cabinet, who closed a drawer to let them pass. As they returned, he did the same but less graciously, slamming the drawer in a show of irritation. He also bumped the subject in the shoulder and called him an asshole.

Northerners laughed the insult off—two-thirds were more amused than angered. Nearly 90 percent of Southerners, in contrast, felt a flash of anger. They also showed a spike in cortisol, a stress hormone, and in testosterone, linked to aggression. If they then met a stranger who had witnessed this minor humiliation, Southerners acted in a more domineering manner, and their handshakes became firmer, but they also reported feeling less manly in the stranger's eyes.

In their piece de resistance, Nisbett's team used tables to narrow the corridor and then, just after insulting their subjects, confronted them with someone else walking in the other direction, forcing them to step aside. Southerners who hadn't been insulted showed the good manners associated with the region, pausing when the other person was about nine feet away. Northerners who hadn't been insulted stepped aside when the other person was about six feet away, while those who had been insulted waited another foot before yielding. In the aftermath of being called an asshole, however, Southerners didn't back down until they were about three feet from bumping into the oncoming person—who was a 250-pound, 6′ 3″ college football linebacker.[3]

Social injury tends to leave someone from the southern United States more assertive and primed for violence than it does someone from the north, but why?

A person who has been insulted faces the same choices as someone who has been helped. He can either ignore the act, or he can reciprocate. If he chooses to retaliate, he must decide how much he is willing to invest in doing so. Harming people is costly, and letting the insult slide saves time and energy. Yet nearly all of us believe that harming people is justified in some circumstances. We call it punishment, and we will dish it out even if it costs us to do so.

One of the best demonstrations that people have an expensive taste for righteous punishment is an economic experiment called the ultimatum game. In this game, one player, the proposer, is given some money and then told to share it with another player, the responder. The proposer can offer as much or as little as he likes. If the other player accepts the offer, the money is divided along those lines. If he doesn't, he can reject it, and then neither player gets anything. The second player can punish the first for being mean but must pay to do so.

Experiments with the ultimatum game have been done across many cultures, and, although there is a lot of variation in what people will accept, punishment is present in all of them.[4] Even when relatively large sums of money, equivalent to about three months' wages, are on the table, offers of less than a quarter of the total pot are often rejected.[5] The ultimatum game shows that people value fairness above immediate gain, and that they would rather hurt someone who treats them unfairly than settle for a derisory offer.

If you're going to be playing the same person often, it's easy to see that the short-term cost of rejecting a small offer can be more than recouped if a chastened proposer makes larger offers in the future. This is a punisher's version of reciprocity: just as cooperation can persist if people swap favors, so meanness can be stamped out if it is returned in kind, even though by refusing the offer the responder forgoes an immediate gain.

It's a short hop from here to indirect reciprocity—it can pay to treat someone in a certain way, not because of the effect it will have on his or her future behavior, but because it will influence others who know your reputation. That could go for punishment, as well as assistance.

Two Swiss economists, Ernst Fehr and Urs Fischbacher, tested this idea by looking at reputation's influence on the ultimatum game.[6] Participants in their experiment played a series of twenty games, changing partners every time. In half of the games, the players came to one another cold, without any information about how they had behaved in the past. In the other half, responders could build a reputation, because the proposer was told what previous offers their current responder had accepted or rejected in the past.

In the blind condition, when there was no information on past behavior, any offer of more than about 30 percent of the pot was accepted. Yet when responders could bring their past to the table, this jumped to 40 percent, and anything smaller was turned down. Almost everyone in the experiment became more demanding when his or her decisions were made public. After one round, a player who turns down a 30 percent offer will be much worse off than one who accepts it. But if refusing low offers results in higher offers in the future, then toughness can pay in the long run. This is what seemed to happen: proposers made more generous offers in the open condition. This can't have been an attempt by proposers to build reputations of their own, because the researchers did not let proposers know how their partners had behaved when they had been the ones making the offer, only on which offers had been accepted and rejected in the past. Fehr and Fischbacher's experiment suggests that people drive a harder bargain in front of an audience because the benefits of gaining a reputation as a strong negotiator more than outweigh the short-term cost of rejecting small offers. If you settle for peanuts now, you're inviting paltry offers in the future. Having a reputation to consider doesn't merely amplify our helpful, generous urges. It makes us tougher, too.

Punishment is like indirect reciprocity in another regard. We don't simply harm those who have harmed us. We are willing to punish wrongdoers in general. We abhor cruelty and rapaciousness even when it doesn't affect us, and we are willing to do something about it. There are few things more satisfying than seeing someone get what's coming to him, and it's even better being the person who delivers it, even if we have to pay the postage ourselves.

Like the urge to reward kindness, the urge to punish badness emerges early in life. Kiley Hamlin, whose work on how babies use reputation was described in chapter 3, found that after watching a dog puppet either help or hinder a tiger puppet, most two-year-olds will punish the unhelpful dog by depriving it of a sponge "treat." One child in her experiment punched the bad puppet in the face.[7]

Harming someone for what he or she did to someone else is called third-party punishment. Hamlin's experiment shows that toddlers are willing to use it, but it didn't cost the children anything to punish the bad dog. A second experiment by Ernst Fehr and Urs Fischbacher shows that adult humans have a taste for third-party punishment even when it is expensive.[8] In this experiment, two people played the dictator game. This is like the ultimatum game, except the responder can't respond. He has to take what he's given, so there is much less incentive for the proposer to be generous.

The researchers gave the dictator 100 "points" and the option of transferring between 0 and 50 percent of them to the second player. They then gave a third player 50 points and told her that by spending one of her points she could deprive the dictator of three of his (the punisher did not get these points; they were removed from the game). At the end of the game, the experimenters gave the subjects 0.3 Swiss francs (about thirty cents) for every point they had left.

If the third player's aim was to leave the lab with as much cash as possible, she would never punish. Yet about six in ten subjects were willing to punish any dictator who gave less than half of his points to the second player. Confronted with a player who gave nothing, the average punisher was willing to part with 14 of her own points to knock 42 off the selfish dictator's pile. This declined as the amount the dictator gave increased, but anyone who handed over less than half of his endowment was still likely to get punished. Most people are willing to enforce fairness on behalf of others.

There's strong evidence that niceness couldn't survive without protection from this brand of righteous nastiness. In games where the choice is to help or not, the most powerful sanction against antisocial behavior available is to withdraw cooperation. This has the advantage that unlike punishment, it costs nothing to administer—it opts out of social interaction and leaves everyone where he or she started. Yet in group situations where the fate of a common resource is at stake, the results of the public goods game, where cooperation starts strong and leaches away, suggest that the threat of having cooperation withdrawn is not enough to prevent cheating and free riding.

If you add "altruistic punishment," however, as Fehr and his colleagues have dubbed it, to the range of options, this can protect public goods.[9] Generous players will pay to punish, and selfish players learn that it's cheaper to be generous. If you give people the choice of playing their economic games in experimental groups with and without punishment, most initially choose the option without punishment, but everyone eventually ends up opting for groups where punishment is possible and cooperation is protected.[10]

People punish one another with an extravagance that mirrors their drive to help one another. They go out of their way to do it, they do it to a degree that seems to defy rational calculation, they enjoy doing so—imaging studies show that punishing a cheat makes the brain's pleasure centers light up—and they believe it is the right thing to do. Yet it's a lot less certain what benefits punishment brings for individuals or society. One problem is that punishment itself is a public good. Everyone benefits from having cheats brought into line, but only those who do the punishing pay the cost in time and energy—punishing might bring a neural reward, but it comes at a material cost. If someone else is willing to do the punishing, you're better off not bothering. This creates the temptation to be what's called a second-order free rider, someone who is willing to pay the cost of cooperation but dodges the costs of punishing cheats. One solution to this is second-order punishment, so that people who don't punish are themselves punished, but this creates the incentive for third-order free riding, and so on, ad infinitum.

When we looked at cooperation, we saw that one possible reason for contributing to public goods was to earn a reputation that turns a profit in other social situations, such as one-on-one encounters. Could this be a reason to contribute to the public good of punishment? There have been only a few studies on this idea, but what little evidence there is gives it some support. An audience, for example, makes people more willing to invest in third-party punishment. One study found that when punishers had to announce what they'd done in front of one another, they spent three times as much on punishing a selfish player as when they punished anonymously.[11] Another study, which alternated the public goods game with a two-player game, found that players who invested in punishment for the public good were rated as more trustworthy and rewarded in private interactions.[12]

One route to a good reputation, in other words, is to do bad things to bad people—to be an avenger. If the rewards of having a reputation for punishing are large enough, this alone might justify individuals investing in punishment.[13] In fact, if you're going to provide a public good, punishing wrongdoers (as long as everyone understands your motives, recognizes the people as wrongdoers, and doesn't just image-score you as a bully) might be the best investment in reputation you can make, because it both deters cheats and challengers and makes you appear generous and trustworthy. Think of the politicians, such as Rudy Giuliani, elected on the basis of a crime-busting past. Giuliani did everything he could to publicize his arrests, even inventing the "perp walk," where white-collar criminals were seized in their workplaces, cuffed, and hauled off in front of TV cameras.

It would be wrong, though, to give the impression that reputation is the only game in town when it comes to punishment and cooperation. I've described lots of studies where giving people the opportunity to form a reputation makes them more likely to do something costly in the short term, be it cooperating with others or punishing them. Yet I've blithely skipped over, and you may have raised an eyebrow at, the evidence from those same studies that shows that even in anonymity and in one-shot interactions, many people are still willing pay to cooperate and pay to punish. For example, more than a third of people cooperate in one-shot, anonymous prisoner's dilemmas, and Fehr and Fischbacher found that offers in the ultimatum game of less than 30 percent of the pot were still likely to be rejected, even when players will never meet again and no one else will ever know what they did. People spend money on third-party punishment even when no one will know they were the punishers. This is something that's hard to account for by seeing people's instincts as an evolutionary response to self-interested calculations of present and future pay-offs. If reputation were the only thing that made people cooperate, wouldn't cooperation vanish in its absence?

One possibility is that experiments that sought to examine behavior in anonymous situations unwittingly included subtle, unconscious cues that trigger a concern for reputation. We'll see in chapter 8 how sensitive people are to scrutiny and how little it takes for them to sense that their reputations are at stake. A second possibility is that people mix up their strategies and don't feel comfortable doing the same thing all of the time: in experiments where always cooperating yields the highest returns, and so selfishness becomes irrational, people still cheat occasionally, just to see what happens.[14] A third is that as a species with its roots in small groups where anonymity, privacy, and secrecy were hard to come by and strangers almost nonexistent, we can never quite bring ourselves to act as if our reputations are perfectly insulated, and we err on the side of assuming that our deeds and identities will be revealed. This also avoids the risk that we'll betray ourselves, blurting out some shaming truth in an unguarded moment.

But some researchers take a different view and argue that the high levels of cooperation and punishment that are seen even in anonymous, one-shot social interactions are not caused by an experimental error or a hangover from our past. Instead, they believe that human social behavior is driven by a predisposition to help others, reward cooperative behavior, and punish cheats even when such behavior can't be justified by kin selection, reciprocity, or reputation.

This combination of helping and punishment is called strong reciprocity.[15] Its advocates argue that cooperation and punishment are driven into societies not because they benefit individuals, but by competition between groups. Models show that a group in which individuals cooperate with one another and punish free riders without any regard for personal gain is a superior force to a group of self-regarding reciprocators who never act without asking, "What's in it for me?" In models of strong reciprocity, these practices spread not through genes, but as a set of cultural norms that are transmitted when, for example, an immigrant to a group adopts its mores or a group copies a neighboring group that seems to be doing well. Strong reciprocity thus provides another potential answer to the problem of collective action and another pillar to support human cooperation.

This view of the forces driving our behavior echoes Charles Darwin. Puzzling over the evolutionary advantages of morality in his 1871 book *The Descent of Man*, he wrote that "although a high standard of morality gives but a slight or no advantage to each individual man and his children over the other men of the same tribe . . . an advancement in the standard of morality will certainly give an immense advantage to one tribe over another." Yet the tribe's-eye view is what makes strong reciprocity controversial today. One thing that made Bill Hamilton and Robert Trivers's work on altruism so important was that it showed how cooperation can arise from individual self-interest. This overcame the problem that cooperative groups are vulnerable to selfish invaders and the difficulty of working out a way in which groups can reproduce themselves and pass on their traits in a way similar to replicating genes or reproducing individuals. The critics of strong reciprocity, who include Manfred Milinski and Richard Alexander, tend to be evolutionary biologists, among whom a group-level view of natural selection is still unpopular. Many of the idea's leading advocates, such as Ernst Fehr, come from economics, where the study of companies and other institutions has made group-level thinking less problematic.

I mention strong reciprocity because it is an important focus of research and debate on human social behavior and evolution. It is, however, a detour away from our story of reputation, which is a far less controversial influence on human behavior. There's uncertainty on why people help and punish one another in the ways that they do, but there's a consensus that reputation makes those behaviors more pronounced.

In some cultures, the urge to punish becomes more prominent than in others. This takes us back to the differences between the northern and southern United States. Southerners are more likely to believe that a man has the right to kill in defense of his home or family, more likely to spank their children, and more likely to endorse the police in shooting to kill. Southern states have fewer laws on gun control, domestic violence, and corporal punishment and use capital punishment more. Relative to people from the northern United States, Southerners are more likely to believe that insults and bullying should be met with violence. In Texas, the law viewed killings provoked by adultery as justifiable homicide until 1977. (Nisbett is almost sure that his husband-shooting relative did no jail time.) When Nisbett gives talks on his research to Southern audiences, they wonder why Yankees are such wimps.

So why do Texans, on average, endorse harsher punishments—representing a willingness to invest more in punishment—than Bostonians? Southerners' quickness to anger, taste for physical confrontation, and belief in punishment, Nisbett and his colleagues believe, have their roots in the benefits of a reputation for responding to cheats with swift and extreme violence. This, in turn, reflects the origins and livelihoods of the region's European settlers. In the South, most white people trace their roots back to Scotland and Ireland. In the old country, they had lived on moors and mountains, making a living herding sheep and cattle. Many continued as herders in the New World.

Livestock is mobile, and herders face the constant risk of losing their livelihood to rustling, which is a feature of herding cultures around the world. Herders also live in sparse populations in rugged environments, where institutions such as the police are slow and distant. People themselves must defend their property. In such a situation, a reputation for vigilante justice is one of the most useful things a man can have. Those who are thought to be willing to kill and, if necessary, die in their own defense are much less likely to be preyed on. By blowing up at the smallest slight, with what might seem like excessive vehemence and aggression, people show society what they are capable of and earn a reputation that deters any more serious challenge to their wealth and well-being.

The northern United States, on the other hand, was settled mainly by Germans and the Dutch. These people were crop-growing farmers and remained so. Stealing a field of wheat is more difficult and less profitable than stealing a flock of sheep, and in an arable village people are in closer and more regular contact and so easier to control, whether by the state or, as would have been the case for most of human history, by informal forces in the community itself. In such an environment, property is less at risk and people have less call to defend it in person, so a reputation for being reasonable and mild-mannered is more useful than one for aggression. Likewise, in the crop-growing regions of the South, where the economy was based on plantations and slavery, the murder rate is historically lower than in drier and more mountainous regions where herding predominates.

Another feature of herding is that the opportunities for coopera-tion are relatively small. If the land is not enclosed and overgrazing isn't a problem, there's little that two herders have to gain from each other—in contrast, say, to two farmers who might benefit from collaborating on building an irrigation system. The biggest favor one herder can do for another is to stay out of his way, and the imperative is to protect and monopolize the wealth, just as it is for minerals such as gold, diamonds, and oil, which are taken from the land, rather than built on it. The scramble for natural resources rarely brings out the best in people, because those who seek to exploit such resources do not get rich by following their better natures. In such circumstances, a reputation for cooperation isn't much use, because reputation protects cooperation only when cooperation pays. If it doesn't, people pursue whatever kind of reputation is most useful.

The South, says Nisbett, has a culture of honor. It's also a culture of self-defense, rather than collective-defense, against cheats. "Death before dishonor," for example, is a motto adopted by groups and individuals that expect to be doing a lot of fighting and don't expect anyone else to do it for them; the message, of course, isn't "Please kill me," it's "You'd better not mess with me."

Cultures of honor arise in places where peoples' resources are vulnerable and government is weak—places where individuals must be their own police force and where dominance, the power to repel, is more valuable than prestige, the power to attract. Herders around the world are known for their toughness, and once attitudes are in place, they seem to persist even when the circumstances that bred them disappear. Studies of students in Mexico and Costa Rica have found that people from herding areas, such as Sonora in Mexico and Gunacaste in Costa Rica, endorse vengeful responses to insults more strongly than do those from farming areas, such as the capitals of Mexico City and San Jose.[16]

Rustlers are unlikely to be a worry for contemporary under-graduates in Mexico, Costa Rica, or the United States. One big factor in the persistence of cultures of honor is probably cultural inertia. Generations don't invent their attitudes anew; they learn how to behave from their parents. If your mother and father (and having a Southern mother is a particularly strong predictor of having a strong sense of honor) tell you not to take any crap and to stand up and fight for yourself, that's what you'll do, and that's how you'll raise your children, regardless of how much livestock you own.

• • •

Another group of people vulnerable to theft and with little recourse to the law are drug dealers. The anthropologist Philippe Bourgois spent the latter half of the 1980s living among and studying workers in the crack economy of New York's Spanish Harlem. The gripping book he wrote about the experience, *In Search of Respect*, shows that running a crack house in an urban ghetto poses similar challenges to herding animals in the hills.[17] Customers steal from dealers, dealers steal from one another, and a specialized class of armed robber has evolved to prey on the drug economy (Omar Little, in the TV series *The Wire*, is a fictional example). The police are unlikely to be sympathetic—indeed, they scarcely protect the law-abiding—and once drugs take hold in a community, other authority figures lose their power. Describing his teenage years selling crack in Brooklyn, the rapper Jay-Z told an interviewer how the people who once kept him in line became his customers: "Before, when our elders told us something, you had to listen. But now we were in power because the people who were supposed to be our support system were on crack, and they was telling us, 'I'll do anything to get it.' So we were like elders in the village, with a whole community on drugs. There was no one to police us. And we were out of control."[18]

In such an environment, the best protection is a reputation for violence. "Behaviour that appears irrationally violent, 'barbaric,' and ultimately self-destructive to the outsider," Bourgois wrote, "can be reinterpreted according to the logic of the underground economy as judicious public relations and long-term investment in one's 'human capital development.'" Or, as one crack-house employee puts it, "You can't let people push you around, because when the other guys see that, they want to do the same thing." This man was notorious for his violent rages; one of his favorite anecdotes concerned the time he fractured a threatening customer's skull with a baseball bat. (Many of the drug dealers Bourgois knew were ashamed of how they made a living, but the alternative was an insecure and demeaning job—or, given the pay, jobs—in the service sector. Nevertheless, many strove to enter the regular economy, and some succeeded or moved back and forth between a drug job and regular employment.)

Once a culture of honor—a street culture—governed by violence and intimidation takes hold, it spreads beyond those directly involved in criminal transactions. The economist Dan Silverman has used game theory to show that when notoriety is a way to deter attack, otherwise law-abiding people, with no stake in the underground economy, have an incentive to do violence as a means of armoring themselves with a tough-guy reputation.[19] If there are predators in the streets, the best way to move among them is to appear to be one of them. You can do that through the way that you dress, walk, and talk, but these are cheap signals and thus unreliable. Only violence truly reveals dominance.

Notions of honor and the behaviors they trigger are not hard-wired into one group and missing from another. Most of us are probably capable of becoming proud firebrands, depending on our culture and upbringing. What gave humans this potential? The psychologist Todd Shackelford doubts that it was the need to protect flocks. Although the economics of herding and rustling seem to trigger a strong sense of honor, herding, he argues, is too specialized and too recent a way of life to have been the thing that caused honor to originate. Instead, he suggests that the psychology of honor has its roots in men's attempts to monopolize their women. Female abduction, adultery, and rape, he wrote, were common enough in the environment in which humans evolved to drive the evolution of male honor as a means of guarding against it.[20]

Protecting female honor certainly figures large in the South's culture, as the legal stance on killing adulterers shows. So does preventing female behavior from damaging male honor. How women behave is a major feature of other cultures of honor, such as in Kurdistan, the region that overlaps the borders of Iraq, Turkey, Syria, and Iran. Kurdistan well fits the template for a culture of honor. It is mountainous, and society has been centered on tribes, each of which is bonded by a mixture of family and social ties. There is no governing body overseeing tribal life and little central authority in general; many Kurds reject the rule of the nations in which they live and seek an independent Kurdish state.

The concern for honor means that what seems like a trivial slight can trigger a feud between tribes that lasts for generations and claims many lives. The Norwegian sociologist Haci Akman, who has studied honor violence in Kurdistan, described a feud between two Kurdish tribes that began in the late nineteenth century when one tribe's sheep crossed onto another's land.[21] This tribe slaughtered the sheep. Yet things couldn't rest there. To leave the encroachment unavenged would have destroyed the tribe's reputation, revealing its members as weak and cowardly, lowering its status, and raising the offender's stock among all of the other groups who came to know of the incident. So they retaliated by burning the first tribe's hay. The first tribe in turn retaliated by killing all of the kid goats belonging to the other tribe, who then killed their enemy's dogs with poisoned meat. After losing their dogs, one young man of this tribe started putting it about that a young woman of his enemy's tribe was in love with him. He had a photo of her to prove it. As a result, wrote Akman, the woman would "remain unclean forever" and, with no prospects of marriage, would be a burden to her family—in effect, she was "socially dead." This young woman's tribe learned where in town the young man spent his time and, after lying in wait, shot him dead. The cycle of killing continued for decades.

Akman, unlike Shackelford, believes that honor and feuding are more about power than sex. "Violations like abduction or rape," he wrote, "are primarily committed in order to strike the enemy tribe; the abused woman is just an unfortunate victim in the power struggle that is primarily a man's game." (In *Othello*, Iago uses Desdemona's honor as a weapon against Othello.) Some accounts of feuding make it sound as if the different groups involved are looking for any excuse to fight, so that they can display their strength as a collective and gain glory as individuals. Another sociologist, the Norwegian Tor Aase, has called honor violence a "tournament of power."

Shackelford's evolutionary argument and Akman's political one are not mutually exclusive. If female reproductive behavior didn't affect male evolutionary interests, men wouldn't be so worried about it. Men have an evolutionary incentive to control women's sexual behavior because, while a woman is sure of being the mother of any child she bears, a man is less certain about the paternity of the children he is raising. Men deal with this imbalance in information by placing a high value on women's sexual reputation and by adopting a harsh and unforgiving attitude toward promiscuity. Again, reputation becomes a way of dealing with social risks and uncertainty; again, it's about how other people judge us as much as it is about what we do; and again, it's all about control. Women tend to be judged more harshly than men for the same sexual behavior, something known as the sexual double standard, and sexual behavior is a more important aspect of their reputation than it is for men. To quote the literary scholar Patricia Meyer Spacks: "A man's good name concerns behaviour in many situations; a woman's sexual conduct is definitive."[22]

A young man interviewed by a British lawyer investigating honor violence against women compared male reputation to gold and female reputation to silk: "If gold gets dirty you can just wipe it clean, but if a piece of silk gets dirty you can never get it clean again—and you might as well just throw it away."[23] This makes a woman's sexual reputation an obvious target for her or her group's enemies. Gossip alone can be enough to destroy a woman's good name and marriage prospects, and once a woman in a culture of honor becomes socially dead, her family may think it better that she were dead. The United Nations estimates that there are about five thousand such honor killings each year, although this is probably an underestimate. Honor violence is a crime that seems as baffling as it is obscene to those from outside the culture, yet it can be endorsed and even celebrated within it. Understanding cultures of honor helps reveal the social and evolutionary forces that lead to such violence. Like the Southern culture of honor, such cultures persist when transplanted from their native soil.

Reputation helps explain many features of violence. Given that fighting invites social disapproval and legal penalties, you might think that it would be a private business and that an audience would be a calming influence, but it's the reverse. The psychologist Richard Felson questioned a mixture of former prisoners, former mental patients, and people who'd never been incarcerated about past confrontations in their lives.[24] The presence of bystanders, he found, doubled the chances of a confrontation escalating from the verbal to the physical. In the United States, two-thirds of violent confrontations occur in public, with the proportion rising to three-quarters among young people. It's not hard to find cases, tragically inexplicable to those on the outside, of young men in inner cities killing one another over petty, even imaginary, acts of disrespect. Even when the motive seems to be money, the return is often terrible—one-third of robberies in the United States yield less than $50. Nearly half of them occur in daylight, suggesting that concealment isn't uppermost in the perpetrators' minds. Even when others aren't there to see the attacks, men boast about the beatings they've dished out, as Philippe Bourgois found. If you view such crimes in the light of reputation, they make a lot more sense. This is not mindless violence; it's strategic violence, and the perpetrators are doing what they do not to gain money, but to buy reputation.

Like generosity and cooperation, then, violence can be used as a signal. Because doing violence is so costly, it is an ideal show of strength. The bigger the audience, the more valuable the signal becomes, so the more it pays to invest in it. In fact, when violence is less risky, men are less likely to do it in public. Felson found that an audience only increases the chances of a fight between two men. In an altercation between the sexes, an audience made physical violence less likely. If a man is fighting to send a message to those watching, beating up someone who is less able to fight back is a less reliable sign of strength. A man beating up women in public is more likely to earn himself a reputation as a sleazebag than a tough guy.

Violence can also yield benefits through a form of indirect reciprocity. Instead of Adam helping Bob so that the watching Charlie aids him in the future, Adam fights Bob so as to make Charlie think twice about attacking him. The name for this sort of behavior, in which both parties come off worse—because fighting is costly, no matter how much you damage the other guy—is spite. Theoretical studies of the effect of indirect reciprocity on spite suggest that an audience will make spiteful behavior more common.[25] Experiments show the benefits of intimidating someone in front of an audience — men perceive an angry face as more dominant if it is paired with a picture of a fearful reaction than if it is matched with a similarly angry, aggressive response.[26] It even might pay to start fights you know you're going to lose, if the benefits of deterrence are large enough. Economists have applied very similar logic to explain why companies use predatory tactics such as price-cutting, even though they lose more in revenue than they gain in sales. If you show that you are willing to crush your rivals at almost any price, it will pay off in the long term by making any future competitors wary of entering the market.[27]

This isn't to say that people consciously choose violence as a way to cultivate a certain type of reputation. Rather, people are spurred into violence by an emotional reaction to being cheated or insulted — they feel as if they are defending their honor, not managing their images. Psychiatrist James Gilligan, director of the Center for the Study of Violence at Harvard Medical School has written that he has "yet to see a serious act of violence that was not provoked by the experience of feeling shamed and humiliated."[28] As the work of Richard Nisbett and others has shown, how deeply people care about their honor and the lengths they will go to protect it depend on culture, environment, and economics.

At this point, we can do no better than quote Niccolò Machiavelli: "From this arises the following question: whether it is better to be loved than feared, or the reverse." Machiavelli's reply to his own question, which he posed in his book *The Prince*, is discouraging: "The answer is that one would like to be both the one and the other; but because it is difficult to combine them, it is far better to be feared than loved if you cannot be both. . . . Men worry less about doing an injury to one who makes himself loved than to one who makes himself feared."[29]

The Prince, written in 1513, is an attempt to solve the same problem that Richard Alexander grappled with more than 450 years later when he began to think about human evolution, morality, and indirect reciprocity. How does a group remain strong enough to survive and prosper in competition with other groups? For Machiavelli, this was an applied problem. Italy was a patchwork of city-states, competing with one another and threatened by other European powers. During Machiavelli's lifetime, Italy was invaded by France, Spain, and the Holy Roman Empire. In his beloved Florence, he saw the ruling Medici family replaced by a republic in 1494, saw the Medicis regain power in 1512, and saw them re-ousted in 1527, the year of his death. Florence's glory declined all the while.

In his book, Machiavelli addresses a leader who finds himself in the kind of environment that produces a culture of honor. He has a lot to lose, faces attack from within and outside his group, and has no one else to protect him. It's easy to see how such a man could benefit from a fearsome reputation. Yet Machiavelli did not worship dictators and power for their own sake. He fought to defend the Florentine republic, and the Medicis tortured him on regaining the city. *The Prince* is amoral, but it advises a ruler to use his dominance in the service of his people and to use brutality as a public good:

> [A] prince must not worry if he incurs reproach for his cruelty so long as he keeps his subjects united and loyal. By making an example or two he will prove more compassionate than those who, being too compassionate, allow disorders which lead to murder and rapine. These nearly always harm the whole community, whereas executions ordered by a prince only affect individuals.[30]

Machiavelli also knew that dominance alone was not enough, and that if he was to last, a ruler must also pursue prestige: no one conspires against a prince if he thinks that doing so will outrage the people. Likewise, Bourgois found that top crack dealers strengthened their positions by using a skillful blend of friendship, largesse, and violence. Intimidation's great disadvantage is that fear on its own is simply a repellent. It reduces the risks of being cheated, but it closes off the benefits of cooperation. Although the threat of punishment gives people an incentive to acquiesce, it also gives them an incentive to remove the threat and take back their autonomy. As we've seen from numerous examples, people fight against being dominated by members of their own group. This applies to cultures of honor in every place and era: the title of this chapter is taken from a 1990 song by the hip hop group Gang Starr, which charts the life of a young criminal whose career is advanced by the use of extreme violence and ended by a victim's revenge.

Societies governed by intimidation eat themselves from within, exhausting their energies in vengeance and deterrence, leaving themselves prey to more cohesive groups. In his study of feuding in Kurdistan, Haci Akman noted that ever since the late sixteenth century, outside observers have pointed out that the tribal obsession with honor is a barrier to social cohesion and thus prevents Kurdish unity and hinders the formation of a Kurdish state. Tribes' attempts to band together, Akman wrote, are undermined by quarrels over honor, allowing other powers in the region to divide and rule Kurdistan.

To undermine cultures of honor and violence, communities and governments must change the economics of reputation. The Dutch economist Robert Dur has argued that zero-tolerance policing, where the police try to curb small crimes such as shoplifting and fare-dodging, makes committing a minor crime a more daring thing to do and so a better investment in one's reputation. This, he said, is why a zero-tolerance approach has been seen to reduce crime across the board: by making minor crimes more risky, it makes them stronger signals.[31] If you can prove your toughness by breaking a window, you don't need to stab anyone (although Dan Silverman also cautions that if conspicuous policing spreads news of a crime, it might counter this effect by enhancing the signaling benefits of crime in general). If you're not tough enough, you'll be dissuaded from committing any crime at all.

By increasing the probability and scope of third-party punishment, policing can reduce the benefits of participating in the underground economy and provide an external authority that lessens people's need to take matters into their own hands. Punishment works best when it is an extension of a community's will, when as many people as possible are signed up to a policy for punishment and are willing to contribute to its cost, so that this cost does not fall too heavily on any one individual. We are ashamed to be punished by people like ourselves and will change our behavior as a result, but when control and punishment appear to come from outside, it seems more like an attack than a sanction and so is less effective at changing behavior (a subject we'll return to in our final chapter on the workings of reputation between groups). Societies must work both to embed the forces of law and order in the communities they are policing and to enhance the standing of informal police such as elders.

Cultural change follows shifts in social networks and power. In his book *The Honor Code*, the philosopher Kwame Anthony Appiah discusses how practices that were once sustained by notions of honor, such as dueling in Britain and foot binding in China, disappeared not because of some moral insight or legal reform, but because economic and social changes made them disreputable.[32] In Britain, the rise of the middle and working classes and the waning of the hereditary aristocracy's social isolation and political dominance made dueling seem ridiculous. Nineteenth-century China was opened up to economic, intellectual, and philosophical exchange with the West and suffered a number of humiliating military defeats at the hands of Western nations. This caused Chinese intellectuals to question their traditions, and what had once seemed sophisticated and erotic quickly came to appear backward and cruel. Appiah argues that, similarly, the best way to fight honor violence against women is to make it shameful. The way to do that is to build social bonds between the people and societies that practice such violence and those that abhor it, along which social norms, reputation, prestige, shame, and punishment can flow.

In this chapter and its predecessors, we've looked at how reputations are made. Humans strive to show others both what we have and who we are. Conspicuous displays of generosity can be status symbols that advertise our physical and material wealth. Helping one person encourages a bystander to help you. Harming another person deters a bystander from attacking you. Our emotions reveal the motives behind both our successes and our mishaps to anyone watching. Gossip sucks up all of this information and spreads it far and wide, creating and shaping reputation as it goes.

A reputation can be a tool for getting people to do things for you, as well as a tool for getting people not to do things to you. Trust isn't about how nice you are, it's about how predictable you are and how confident people can be about your response to a given situation. The benefits of using how we treat one person to shape how other people treat us make us more altruistic, but these benefits can also make us more brutal.

Yet reputations aren't only built. They are protected, avoided, and attacked, and sometimes your reputation is best served by restraint, not action. To see what threatens reputation and how it is defended, we can return to the rest of the animal kingdom. Things are about to get sneaky.

CHAPTER 7

Nosy Neighbors

Peter McGregor's first thought was to call what he was hearing the "Margaret Thatcher effect." During the previous couple of years, McGregor had become an expert at antagonizing great tits, small but pugnacious songbirds that in Britain are often seen taking peanuts from garden bird feeders but that have also been known to kill and eat small bats. Like other small woodland birds, male great tits sing to mark the borders of their territory, repel other males, and attract a mate. For us, a springtime walk through a woodland trilling with birdsong is a wholesome delight. For the animals involved, it's more like a rowdy bar on a Saturday night—a fight breaking out over in one corner, a seduction attempt launching in another. For animal-behavior researchers, the great thing is that for the price of some weatherproof audio equipment, they can join in, picking fights and pitching woo as the mood takes them.

The way to annoy a male great tit, McGregor found, is to interrupt him. When a male sings over his neighbor, he challenges that male's status and the boundaries of his territory. Using a playback of recorded songs, McGregor was able to do the same to the great tits living in the woodlands around the English city of Nottingham. The birds hated this intrusion and would respond with acoustic gymnastics, switching rapidly between short and long songs to avoid being overlapped and to barge in on their challenger's song. This aggression-through-interruption reminded McGregor of the former prime minister's habit in interviews of beginning her answer quite a long time before the interviewer had finished the question. But you have to get up brain-scramblingly early to study birdsong; what struck McGregor as clever during the dawn chorus seemed like the product of sleep deprivation by lunchtime, so he never committed the term "Margaret Thatcher effect" to print.

The disappointment was soon forgotten, though, as McGregor noticed an unforeseen factor in his woodland confrontations. As soon as McGregor started a song duel in one territory, that bird's neighbor would show up and hang around the experiment. At first, this was frustrating, because McGregor could no longer be sure that the male he was interested in was responding to the playback and not to its neighbor. Yet as this kept happening, McGregor began to get more interested in the neighbor than in the male he was picking on. Perhaps, he thought, neighbors were not just passing by. Perhaps they had arrived to check out the scuffle next door and learn something from it, such as, Can the male next door defend what's his? And should I be worried about this new guy?

McGregor thus became a pioneer in the study of what's now known as behavioral eavesdropping. He and his colleagues embarked on a series of studies designed to test whether male great tits really eavesdrop on others' song duels, and if so, what they do with the information. Using playback, the researchers either "won" a bout with a male, in the sense of aggressively overlapping his song, or they showed deference in the same way that another great tit would, by waiting for the male to stop his song before beginning their own. They also staged artificial encounters using two sets of speakers playing different songs—every male great tit sings differently, so a song is a badge of identity, as well as of status—and then confronted a nearby male with either the winner or the loser.

The results showed that male great tits do indeed eavesdrop on their neighbors' encounters and use that information to plot their own tactics. When a winning speaker intruded into a male's territory, the resident sang less and instead approached the winning speaker in silence, a more hostile move than singing from a distance. It seems that an intruder with a record of successful aggression is seen as more of a threat and so gets a more vigorous response.[1]

Territorial songbirds show what's called the "dear enemy" effect. Once boundaries are established, neighbors exercise mutual restraint in respecting them. This saves them the effort of constant fighting, but it leaves the birds open to intrusion across their undefended borders. In other words, it's a situation a lot like the prisoner's dilemma, where the benefits of defection make cooperation difficult to achieve. One use of eavesdropping is that it can solve this problem by letting you work out which of your neighbors can be trusted to respect your boundaries and which can't. By recording the songs of another bird species (those of song sparrows living in Discovery Park, Seattle) and then playing them back to simulate trespassing, Çağlar Akçay and his colleagues showed that the birds monitor their neighbors in just this fashion.[2] If a male hears one neighbor intrude on another's territory, he becomes more wary toward the aggressor, approaching his song more quickly and closely and singing more vociferously in response. That this indirect reciprocity helps maintain the peace and does not trigger a cascade of aggression as other eavesdroppers become hostile to the retaliating bird suggests that song sparrows may have sophisticated rules about how to judge the motives behind an aggressive act and know that a male fighting off an intruder can still be trusted to respect others' territories. As we saw in the discussion of human cooperation and indirect reciprocity in chapter 3, it's not clear how much our species uses these rules.

Animal communication, then, isn't only a two-player game. Many signals travel far and reach many more animals than just their obvious target. The leakiness of animal communication channels allows eavesdroppers to listen, look, or sniff in and use the information gleaned to plan their own advances or retreats.

When animals started to eavesdrop on one another, they invented reputation. In chapter 1, we saw how widespread copying is in the animal kingdom and its benefits. Yet we also saw that this is more like brand building than reputation in its strict sense—there's no social interaction in social learning. Eavesdroppers, though, are not imitating another animal. They are studying its behavior to work out how they should treat it, saving time and effort by using someone else's experiences to aid their decision-making.

Some animals are so good at this that they can predict the results of fights that haven't happened. For example, if you see animal A defeat animal B and then see animal B defeat animal C, you might conclude that animal A is likely to be dominant to animal C. One species that can reason in this way is Burton's mouthbrooder, an African freshwater fish. If you let the fish watch the A-beats-B-beats-C fights described previously and then give it a choice between approaching fish A or C, it chooses C, as the weaker of the two, even though it has never seen A defeat C.[3]

Another similarity between behavioral eavesdropping and humans' use of reputation is that the audience shapes the performance. Animals can adapt their behavior to influence not only how their immediate opponent sees them, but also how bystanders treat them. They can manage their reputations by changing what they do, depending on who's watching. For example, when McGregor was listening in on song duels, he could usually tell which bird was going to win after a few seconds. Great tits, which are born to make this sort of judgment, are presumably better at spotting a winner than biologists are, so it's odd that the males usually sing for several minutes before they break off the encounter. If you know the outcome—particularly if you know you're going to lose—why use up all of that time and energy putting up a fight?

McGregor thinks that males prolong losing bouts because they're not merely performing to their opponent. By singing on, a male shows eavesdroppers that he's no pushover. He won't win this encounter, but he may show his ability to any other birds that are listening and perhaps make them wary of challenging him.

McGregor never tested this idea in great tits, but other researchers have shown that it applies to other animals. The green swordtail, a small freshwater fish from Central America, is a popular aquarium species, but some hobbyists recommend keeping only one male in a tank, because males tend to attack one another. They also eavesdrop: male bystanders are less aggressive toward fish they have seen win a contest and less aggressive to losers that put up a fight than toward those that back down quickly.[4] The swordtail shows how, during the course of evolution, eavesdroppers may have shaped the animal signals they observe—even if, as in the case of songbirds, dense woodland means that the singer can't be sure there are any eavesdroppers about.

As well as performing to the eavesdroppers, male birds can try to hide from them. Besides their loud and melodious songs, many songbirds also have a quiet song that is used in particularly tense encounters, when two evenly matched birds find themselves in the same territory, with neither confident that he will win. This song is more variable than the male's loud song, which consists of a limited repertoire that makes him easy to identify. Instead of broadcasting from a few well-used song perches within the territory, quietly singing males flit about from spot to spot. It's not clear what function the quiet song has, but one possibility is that it is used when both birds want to fight in private, concealing their identities from eavesdroppers.[5]

A male bird defeated in a public confrontation has a lot to lose, because it's not only other males that are eavesdropping. Territory-holding and song-dueling are just a means to the end of attracting and keeping a mate, and one way that females choose their mates is by eavesdropping on male contests. McGregor, besides observing great tits, has studied eavesdropping in Siamese fighting fish, where the males wave their samurai-like fins and tails at one another in ritualized duels that sometimes escalate into deadly violence. Females that have seen a confrontation prefer to spend time with the winner. This is not because they can judge a male on his inherent qualities—if they don't watch the fight, they show no preference.[6] Male fish, knowing this, do the best they can to protect their image. By staging fights in an aquarium with a mixture of public and secluded spots, McGregor has found that males are keener to fight in front of a female if their opponent is obviously weaker. If forced to confront a superior, they will try to do so in private. Yet females of some species do not always reward machismo: in the Japanese quail, females actually prefer losing males, perhaps because dominant birds take the same robust approach to courting that they do to fighting, and females are often injured in the process.[7]

Pairing up with a mate does not make a male safe from eaves-dropping. If a female overhears her mate having his song trounced by another male, or if she hears a better performance coming from next door, she is liable to act on that information. McGregor's team created just such a scenario, using speakers to escalate a fight with a male great tit and then going to the adjacent territory and treating the resident male more politely. Females that heard their neighbor defeat a bird that had beaten their own mate were much more likely to visit the more successful male's territories than were those paired with winners.[8]

The defeated males did not seem to pay a price for their mates' wandering interest, as DNA tests showed that chicks in a losing male's nest were no less likely to be his own offspring than were those raised by the winners. Male black-capped chickadees, however, are not so lucky. Daniel Mennill and his colleagues carried out a similar experiment in the woods of Ontario on these birds, which are closely related to great tits (they are the American and British names for the same group of species). Female chickadees paired to low-ranking males often explore other options: paternity tests show that about half of these females have chicks by a male other than the one they are mated to. High-ranking males normally have no such worries; only about one nest in ten contains the fruit of what's technically known as an extra-pair copulation. Yet one defeat for a high-ranking male at the hands of Mennill's playback experiment—the entire test took only six minutes—raised this to 50 percent, the same proportion as seen in low-ranked males.[9] Tough crowd.

For animals whose social encounters revolve around fighting and mating, there are few uses for reputation besides as an indirect measure of dominance. Many animals, however, have social lives that go beyond the two basics. The advantages of group living apply to other animals just as much as they do to humans. For hunters, teaming up with others brings bigger prey within reach. For the hunted, a herd's many eyes make spotting predators more likely and allow each individual to spend more time feeding. Groups provide economies of scale, allow for division of labor, and can ensure against fluctuating individual fortunes, through food sharing, for example. Yet just as social life has costs with humans, it has costs and risks for animals. A group needs more land and more food. Competition within a group never goes away—there will be fights over status, resources, and mates—and any collective effort creates an opportunity for freeloaders to take the benefits without paying the costs.

The life of lions shows both sides of group living's balance sheet. Lions hunt, care for cubs, and defend their territory as a pride. Prides need to be strong, because the struggle with other prides is a major part of life. Neighbors face off once or twice a week, large groups take territory from smaller ones, and solitary lions are often attacked and sometimes killed. Group cohesion is a matter of life and death. Yet while studying the lions of the Serengeti in the 1990s, Robert Heinsohn and Craig Packer found that the pride's solidarity is fragile and imperfect.[10]

The question of how to antagonize a lion has two answers: carefully, and in the same way as you would a great tit. The researchers approached the pride with a stuffed lion and a roaring loudspeaker. Some lions were quick to rise to the challenge, approaching and attacking the model, before realizing their mistake and, according to Packer, "look[ing] embarrassed about it."[11] Yet others only showed up several minutes later, by which time, had the intruder been a real lion, any confrontation might well have been over. Some of the laggards stepped up more quickly when Heinsohn and Packer used the recorded roars of several lions to pose a more serious threat, but others hung farther back still.

It seems that laggardly lions get a reputation as such. When the researchers separated a leader and a laggard from the rest of the pride, forcing them to confront the threat in tandem, the leader would become cautious and untrusting. It would hesitate and look back at the lion bringing up the rear before eventually soldiering on regardless. Apparently unable to force the laggard into the fray, the leader seemed to realize that it was stuck with a companion that wasn't pulling its weight. In contrast, when the lion was paired with another leader, they both confronted the threat as equals.

The study shows that lions experience one key problem of group living—free riders—and it shows that lions can recognize when a member of their group isn't contributing. It also raises a thicket of questions. Are leaders rewarded or laggards punished? Do laggards make up for their slacking in other areas, such as caring for cubs or hunting? How many laggards can a group support before it collapses? Unfortunately, another disadvantage of group living is that disease spreads more easily between animals that live close together. In 1994, just after Heinsohn and Packer had identified the leaders and the laggards in the pride they were studying, most of the lions died in an outbreak of canine distemper virus, leaving these questions unanswered.

Another animal of the African plains shows a better grasp of public relations than the laggardly lion does. Sociable weavers are only about the size of sparrows, but their communal nests are some of the largest structures made by any bird. These avian apartment blocks, built in trees and, lately, on telephone poles in the Kalahari of southern Africa, contain dozens of nest chambers, stitched together from plant material. A single nest can be the size of a haystack, might house dozens of families, and may be more than a century old.

Weavers are one of about three hundred bird species that breeds cooperatively, meaning that other birds besides the breeding pair feed the chicks in a nest. A breeding pair of sociable weavers (and in this case, it really is the breeding pair, because extra-pair copulations are rare) can have between one and five helpers. The more helpers a nest has, the more chicks it fledges. Helpers, in turn, are often related to the chicks they feed, so they get some of their genes sent into the next generation.

If a helper cannot hold down a mate or territory itself, helping may be its best option. Yet even while a helper is feeding another bird's chicks, it keeps one eye on the future and tries to burnish its reputation as a provider, by making its aid as conspicuous as it can.

When a sociable weaver shows up at the colony with some food, it tends not to go straight into its nest. A parent hangs around on average for about forty seconds, but a helper waits for around double this, close to a minute and a half. The fewer birds there are in the audience, the longer the bird waits, loitering until it can be sure that its charity won't go unobserved. A bird delivering a particularly large morsel waits longer than one with a smaller meal, and the same goes during dry spells, when food is scarce and thus helping is more valuable.[12]

Helpers do not act differently in front of the parents they are helping and the other birds in the colony, and there's no evidence that slackers are ever expelled from a nest. So it looks as if helpers aren't trying to impress the resident pair and show their landlords that they are paying their way. Instead, Claire Doutrelant and her colleagues, who have studied the weaver's helping behavior, believe that the weaver gets the same benefit from displaying its competence as a food gatherer that a Meriam turtle hunter gets from sharing his catch. Helping, as a costly signal of quality, is a means to attract a mate. The weaver seems to make a display of its helping and tunes that behavior to make the signal as effective as it can.

All of these wily fish and birds show that different aspects of the ability to judge and manipulate reputation are present on many different branches of the animal family tree. As with social learning, they show that what determines whether a species evolves the ability to use reputation is not what it's got in terms of brainpower, but what it needs in its particular social environment. But sparrows and swordtails don't tell us much about the evolutionary roots of our own abilities. To get an idea of how humans got to be such skilled users of reputation and so sensitive about what others think of us, we need to look at species more closely related to ourselves.

One key aspect of the human ability to use reputation is our understanding that others have minds. Using this theory of mind, as researchers call it, we can work out what others know and want and can second-guess their reactions to our own deeds. We know when someone is trying to help or cheat us and when we've given pleasure or offense. We worry about what people think of us.

Yet a theory of mind isn't essential for a species to use reputation. No biologist thinks that a male Siamese fighting fish ponders what's going on in a rival's head, but a fish can learn to protect its reputation or deceive bystanders by seeing the outward effects of its actions on other animals and then arrive at simple rules, such as, "If I can see a bystander fish, then I should be more aggressive than if I can't."

Primatologists are still divided over whether chimpanzees, humans' closest relatives, have a theory of mind or whether they are simply gifted students of behavior, but lots of evidence suggests that the apes can work out what other animals know and what they want.[13] Much of this centers on chimps' capacity for deception, their ability to conceal what they are up to from other members of their group, particularly, the more dominant ones. To deceive people or other animals, you must have some idea of what they expect, which involves being able to grasp what they're thinking.

Dominant male chimpanzees beat up lower-ranking males that try to mate. The primatologist Frans de Waal, in his book *Chimpanzee Politics*, based on his study of a captive group living in Arnhem Zoo in the Netherlands, describes how, faced with this threat, Dandy, the youngest adult male in the group, tried to lead a furtive sex life.[14] "[E]very now and again he does succeed in mating . . . after having made a 'date'," wrote de Waal. "When this happens, the female and Dandy pretend to be walking in the same direction by chance, and if all goes well, they meet behind a few tree trunks."

Yet Dandy had to stay watchful and be ready to hide his intentions. "Dandy began to make advances to the female, while at the same time restlessly looking around to see if any other males were watching. Male chimpanzees start their advances by sitting with their legs wide apart revealing their erection. Precisely at the point where Dandy was exhibiting his sexual urge in this way, Luit, one of the older males, unexpectedly came around the corner. Dandy immediately dropped his hands over his penis concealing it from view."

De Waal also describes how one female, when mating surreptitiously with a low-ranking male, suppressed the scream that female chimps typically give at the moment of climax. Wild chimpanzees have also been seen deceiving one another, and there's experimental evidence that chimps can be deceptive about food—something else they compete for—taking a hidden route to a treat if they think another chimp or human is likely to try to beat them to it.[15] Chimpanzees also play to their audience in less deceptive ways. High-ranking animals often intervene to stop fights, seemingly responding to a particular type of scream that the apes give when attacked. Chimpanzees under attack scream extra-loud if they know that another animal that outranks their aggressor is within earshot.[16]

So chimps seem to manipulate what others know about them and use what they know about others' actions and abilities to subvert dominance and avoid getting beaten up. They cooperate in the wild, sharing food and hunting as a team. Lab experiments in which chimpanzees must collaborate to get a food reward have shown that they can learn from experience who will be the best collaborator.[17] All of this shows a keen political sense and a keen awareness of the abilities of other animals.

But whether chimpanzees use reputation to decide whom to trust and thus whom to cooperate with is less certain. A couple of experiments using captive apes suggest that they can. In one, chimpanzees and their close relatives bonobos (but not gorillas or orangutans) preferred to approach a human they had seen share grapes with another over one they had seen refuse to share.[18] In another, some of the chimpanzees tested learned, after a couple of months' training, that a stranger who shared fruit with their human trainer was more likely to give a chimpanzee a treat than someone who hadn't shared, and approached them accordingly.[19] These chimps could then apply the same rule when they saw a strange human reward or snub another chimp, which isn't surprising, as you'd expect chimpanzees to take a keener interest in what happens to other chimps than in what happens to people.

This, then, is a hint that our closest relative at least has the capacity to use information about others' experience to plan its own behavior. It's a tentative hint, though, and whether wild chimpanzees actually use reputation's power to promote cooperation is unclear. It would be a surprise if chimpanzees couldn't work out dominance hierarchies by observation, but the evidence that chimpanzees trade favors directly — practice reciprocal altruism, in other words — is inconclusive, so you might think it less likely that they use reputation to work out whom to help.[20] Broadly put, chimpanzee society is less cooperative and more competitive and hierarchical than our own, so the apes probably have fewer opportunities to exercise such a talent.

In contrast to the chimpanzee's need for special training, domestic dogs breeze through tests like these, much preferring to beg a treat from a human they have seen share food with another human than from one they have seen behave selfishly. A pet dog, of course, gets plenty of chances to watch humans. Its species has spent thousands of years in intimacy and cooperation with us, giving it the evolutionary opportunity and incentive to get good at reading our behavior.[21] Yet if you were looking to proclaim a species besides ourselves champion in the use of reputation—a species that knows what others know about it, knows how to win the trust of those it relies on, and knows when it can get away with dirty tricks without damaging its future prospects— it wouldn't be a dog or an ape. It would be another fish.

On a coral reef, the social bustle revolves around cleaner fish. Cleaning stations are found every twenty yards or so, each consisting of about a hundred cubic feet of water occupied by one or a few fish that have chosen that spot to do business. Many species of fish visit the stations to get spruced up. Queues often develop, and if a shoaling species needs a cleaning, it will visit en masse. There's quite a buzz, and scuba divers know that one of the best ways to see a lot of reef species quickly is to hang out at a cleaning station.

On reefs everywhere from the Red Sea to the Great Barrier Reef, the most important cleaner fish is the bluestreak cleaner wrasse. A single fish can do more than two thousand cleaning jobs in a single day, removing parasites, particularly small crustaceans, from clients' gills and skin. The biologist Redouan Bshary began to study the wrasse because he wanted to work on biological markets—situations where questions of supply and demand influence how animals behave when they meet. The fish turned out to be a far sharper operator than he had ever suspected.

One thing he found, for example, is that the fish treats its clients differently, depending on their ability to shop around. Some reef species roam over a wide area. Others spend their lives within small territories that contain a single cleaning station. Cleaners can recognize individual clients. They also recognize wide-ranging species, which can and do take their business elsewhere if they're not serviced immediately, and allow them to jump the queue ahead of the locals.

But there's a greater indignity than getting bumped for a more cosmopolitan client. When Bshary began to study the cleaner wrasse, it was already known that tissue from clients, in the form of scales, skin, and mucus, ended up in cleaners' stomachs, but it wasn't clear whether this was because cleaners bit their clients deliberately or it was an accidental result of overzealous cleaning.

You can tell when a cleaner wrasse bites a client, because the client gives a jolt. Bshary, watching cleaning stations in the Red Sea, could see that sometimes these jolts are quite common. When the client is a small local fish that is unlikely to go elsewhere, there's about one jolt for every fifteen seconds of cleaning time. When the client is a predatory fish, on the other hand—and sometimes cleaner fish end up becoming the meal, rather than getting one—there are no jolts. Cleaner wrasse can clearly avoid biting their clients. So why bite at all?

A choice between eating parasites and eating mucus might not sound like much of a choice, but it matters to the wrasse. When Bshary offered the two options separately, presenting the fish with one plate bearing parasites and another smeared with fish mucus, more often than not the cleaners went for the mucus.[22] The wrasse would rather feed on its clients than on their parasites, because mucus is more nutritious. So every time the cleaner wrasse goes to work it has a dilemma: keep its side of the bargain or cheat and get a better meal.

Bshary also noticed that a small proportion of the cleaners do most of the biting. These biting fish are all spawning females. Such fish are burning a lot of energy making eggs. They are also diverting resources away from growth, because the food they eat ends up in their offspring, rather than in themselves. Making more fish is obviously sound evolutionary business, but for a female cleaner wrasse, choosing reproduction over growth is not as obvious a call as it first appears. That's because a female, if she grows, can get another prize: she can turn into a male. The cleaner wrasse is what's called a sequential hermaphrodite. When they are small, fish are female and live on a territory controlled by a male. When they get big enough, they can become male, control a territory themselves, and mate with its resident females. By reproducing, females delay this moment, but by biting clients, Bshary believes, females get a rapid nutritional hit that allows them to make eggs without stunting their growth too much.

The client fish have something to say about all of this, of course. A fish that doesn't roam widely can't go elsewhere for a clean, but it can bite back, and a jolt is usually followed by the client whirling around and chasing the cleaner wrasse for a second or two. A wide-ranging client, which can afford to be choosy, simply swims off when bitten. This gives the cleaner wrasse an incentive to cooperate—but it's not the only incentive. If the wrasse decides to bite, it could lose more than just the energy that's needed to evade a disgruntled client. It also risks alienating its client base.

Remember that there are often several clients hanging around a cleaning station, waiting their turn. If they see the current client jolt, they are likely to swim away. Clients also prefer to go to cleaner fish that they know give good service. Using an aquarium in the lab, Bshary set up two cleaning stations observed by a potential client. At each station, he put a model fish and a cleaning wrasse. At one station, the model was smeared with prawn paste, which the cleaner wrasse nibbled off, giving the observing client the impression that it was doing a diligent job. The other model bore no such inducements, so the cleaner ignored it. Given a choice, the client visited the cleaner it had seen "clean," rather than the one it had never seen at work. So, as well as avoiding cleaners they suspect will cheat, clients choose those they have reason to trust.[23] Faced with this discriminating clientele, the cleaner fish does the sensible thing, and bites only when no other fish are watching.[24]

In the wild, the cleaner wrasse hardly bites at all if there is a wide-ranging, choosy fish nearby. Having a large local fish in the queue also deters biting, because the larger the client, the more food to be gained by cleaning it. Such fish are bystanders at about half of the wrasse's cleaning bouts. There are nearly always some small local fish watching, but the wrasse doesn't take any notice of them. They have little to offer in the way of food and thus no sanctions to impose. In fact, the cleaner often refuses to clean small local fish altogether.

It does, however, sometimes make an exception. In particular, when a female cleaner fish is going through a biting phase, she is more likely to clean small fish, as long as there's a big fish nearby. It's a tactic remarkably similar to a type of fraud called "pump and chump": cleaner fish exploit the client's discriminating nature by using small fish to inflate their reputation and so lure in a fish worth cheating.[25] So, the game goes like this: clients benefit from being cleaned, but this gives cleaners the chance to exploit them. So clients use reputation to choose the best cleaner and to keep cleaners honest. As a result, cleaners evolve confidence tricks. Each move closes down some options and creates others; every fix produces new vulnerabilities.

Humans face the same social choices and dilemmas as cleaning fish and their clients. We need to build and maintain our own reputations, prevent others from cheating us—and detect and punish them if they do—and stay alert for the best moment to steal a bite of mucus. You can see our species' answers to these problems in our bodies, our brains, and even, you might say, our souls.

CHAPTER 8

Panopticon

I n the coffee room at the University of Newcastle's psychology department, there's no one to collect your payment for your drink. Instead, the researchers use an honor system, putting their money into an honesty box.

Melissa Bateson, an animal behavior researcher in the department, looks after the box. In early 2006, she began tinkering with the sign that shows the prices of the drinks (30 pence for a cup of tea, 50 pence for a coffee, 10 pence for a shot of milk), which is hung on a cabinet door over the counter where the kettle, the coffee, and the tea bags sit. For ten weeks, from late January to early April, Bateson put a letterbox-shaped banner image, downloaded from the Web, along the top of the price sheet. On odd-numbered weeks, the banner was a picture of some flowers. On other weeks, the picture was a photo of some human eyes, ranging from a coy, sidelong female glance to a belligerent male stare.[1]

Different numbers of people used the coffee room each week, so when Bateson calculated the effects of various images on how much people put in the honesty box, she corrected for this by dividing the amount of money collected by the amount of milk consumed. On average, she found that during a "flower" week, the honesty box contained 15 pence for every liter of milk used. During an "eye" week, the figure was 42 pence per liter. That is, when there was a picture of some eyes on the price sheet, people nearly tripled their contributions. When the eyes were mad and staring, people paid about 70 pence a liter. Bateson, as coffee-room monitor, had been hoping to get people to pay more, but the results were staggering. Her colleagues were equally flabbergasted: a couple of people in the department had commented on the changing images while the study was running, but most seemed oblivious, and none knew they were being experimented on.

Bateson speculates that the eye pictures might have signaled either "I have seen your good deed and will reward you," "I find your honesty sexually arousing," or "I will punish you if you do not behave well." The fact that the scariest eyes extracted the most money hints that the last of these might be most potent. A doe-eyed female gaze extracted scarcely more money from the scientists than did a picture of some flowers, showing perhaps that such inducements affected only the coffee room's male users, or that scientists are less susceptible to that sort of thing, or that no one ever acted like a goody-goody to impress a woman. Bateson and her colleagues have since repeated the trick in the university canteen, where diners are asked to bus their own trays. The results were similar: in a "flower" week, twice as many people failed to clear their tables as in an "eye" week.[2] Meanwhile, a picture of Bateson's own eyes keeps watch over the psychology department coffee room.

"The more strictly we are watched, the better we behave," wrote the English philosopher Jeremy Bentham in 1791, an insight that led him to argue for transparency in public life and to design a prison he called the panopticon, in which open-fronted cells are arranged in a circle around a watchtower, allowing for constant surveillance.[3] None were built in his lifetime, but several have been since. Psychologists have long known that the less anonymous you make people—if people have to look at one another or reveal their names, for example— the fairer, more generous, and more cooperative they become. Just as with client fish watching the cleaning wrasse, an audience improves our manners. You are more likely to wash your hands after using a public toilet if someone else is present; if you are driving a convertible, you are less likely to toot your horn when the top is down; and church-goers put more into an open collection basket than into a closed bag that conceals their donations.[4]

Bateson's study shows that even when we feel ourselves unself-conscious and oblivious to judgment, our sense of reputation is manipulating us. Her findings are not a lone example: testing how artificial eyes affect how people play economic games has become a busy micro-discipline. Different groups of researchers have found that people playing such games via computer behave more generously if their screen bears an image of Kismet the robot (which looks a bit like a robot deer, with a metal skull, pointy ears, blond eyebrows, pink lips, and large, soft eyes) or the Eye of Horus, an ancient Egyptian symbol.[5] Another study, in which participants were questioned about their emotions during the experiment, found that as well as making people more generous, the gaze of the Eye seemed to make them think that their generosity would be noticed and rewarded.[6] In the most daringly austere experiment in this vein, Mary Rigdon and her colleagues found that people were more generous if they had to write their decision on whether to share on a piece of paper bearing three dots in an upside-down triangle, about the most abstracted representation of a face you can imagine.[7]

Not every experiment finds as powerful an effect as seen in Newcastle. In Rigdon's study, for example, only men responded to the three dots (other studies have likewise tended to find that women have a higher level of baseline generosity and men are more influenced by eyespot cues). In addition, if the experiment gives players a sense of interacting with a genuine person, rather than simply making a decision on whether to be honest or to share, this seems to swamp the influence of more artificial cues.[8] Yet there have been enough positive findings to show that we are so sensitive to scrutiny that we respond even when we are not consciously aware of being watched and even when the observer is an obvious fake. This sensitivity is reputation's first line of defense, and cheating's first line of attack. In a world where your actions are monitored, analyzed, and acted on, but where there might also be the opportunity to sneak an advantage, it pays to know when you're in public.

Image-makers of all stripes have long understood and exploited this sensitivity. One unintended consequence of this form of manipulation fell on my maternal grandfather, whose middle name was Kitchener.

This has never been a common boy's name in Bermondsey, a poor neighborhood in central London, but my grandfather happened to be born in the autumn of 1915, while the eyes of Lord Kitchener of Khartoum were boring into my great-grandparents from out of the most famous recruiting poster of World War I, letting them know that their country needed them (across the Atlantic, Uncle Sam did the same job). Burglars have been known to turn their victims' family photos face-down, and I'd guess that adulterers sometimes do the same. Even our own gaze matters—college students are less likely to cheat on a test if they have to look at themselves in a mirror while they do it, and in the 1970s, a team of psychologists in Seattle found that trick-or-treaters were less likely to take more than their share if there was a mirror behind the candy bowl.[9] The need to look yourself in the eye is not merely a proverbial motive for doing the right thing.

Language looms so large in humans' idea of themselves that it's easy to overlook how much we communicate with our eyes.[10] Adult humans can detect an eye movement of a degree or two from a couple of yards away, corresponding to about a two-inch shift in the point of attention, such as from the left eye to the right. To a baby, other peoples' eyes are just about the most interesting things in the world. A baby will look at a picture of a pair of eyes for almost as long as one of a whole face and much longer than at an eyeless face with all of the other features. From a few days old, babies look longer if the eyes on a picture are directed at them than if they are pointing elsewhere.[11]

What other people are looking at is one of our most important and most avidly consumed sources of social information. The quickest way to find what's important in your environment, such as sources of food or danger, is to follow others' gaze. The urge to do this is difficult to resist, which is why soccer or basketball players can fool their opponents by looking one way and sending the ball the other. Experiments asking people to locate an object on a screen show that they will follow the gaze of a photograph even if the person always looks in the wrong direction—although they rate that person as less trustworthy after the experiment.[12]

It is extra important when someone is looking at you, because it means you're the most important thing in his or her environment. Eye contact can mean lots of things: complicity, challenge, climb-down, go away, come hither. These messages are complex and nuanced: someone who looks you in the eye is good and inspires trust, but at some point a held gaze tips over into a threat—hence responses such as, "It's rude to stare," or, "What are you looking at?" A variety of brain regions detect and interpret all of this eye-sent information. Some areas simply register where people are looking and whether it's at you. Others work out what the gaze means: one region that fires when we detect someone looking at us is the amygdala, part of the brain's emotional system that is particularly involved with fear. It responds more actively when it spots a stranger than when someone familiar looks at us.

The symptoms of autism are another indicator of the importance of gaze to our social lives and how it links in with our other abilities. Besides lacking social awareness, self-consciousness, and theory of mind, people with autism are less interested in looking at eyes, not as good at detecting gaze direction, and less skilled at reading the mean-ings of eye contact. The autism researcher Simon Baron-Cohen tells of the mother of a severely autistic little boy who went into a room to find her son pointing at a toy on a high shelf. He'd worked out that pointing at the things you want was a good way to get them, but not that the trick only worked in front of an audience.

All primates pay attention to where the other members of their group are looking, but humans' skills are the more honed. If a human experimenter points her face to the ceiling with her eyes closed, a chimp will look in the same direction. Human infants are only likely to do the same if they can see that the person's eyes are open.[13] Compared to our closest relatives, we are especially well equipped to send mes-sages with our gaze. No matter how close you get, you'll never see the whites of a chimpanzee's eyes. The sclera—the bit surrounding the iris—is dark, as are the iris and the ape's face. The same goes for other primates and most other animals, and this makes it hard to tell where they're looking. Only we have large white sclera that high-light where our pupils are pointing.[14] Human eyes are also more elliptical, compared with the rounder eyes of other primates, making our shifty left-right glances more obvious.

Easy-to-read eyes have limitations. They make it much harder to conceal where you are looking and thus more difficult for you to gather social information covertly—the type of information that ought to reveal the most about another person's personality and intentions. In other words, our eyes are not good for spying. Spies aim to discover what people do when they believe they're not being watched and, in theory, prevent antisocial behavior by catching plotters red-handed. The police, in contrast, reveal themselves and, in theory, prevent antisocial behavior by letting people know they're being watched. It looks as if in the evolution of human society the benefits of policing have won out over those of spying, and the advantage of letting others know that you're watching them has proved greater than the advantage of catching them unawares. Or at least, that's how it is in a hunter-gatherer group. Large and complex modern states can combine both policing and spying for maximum control. The propaganda of totalitarian regimes lets their citizens know that Big Brother is watching, while dictators and their secret police hide their gaze behind sunglasses.

And if all that wasn't enough, our reputations have yet another line of defense. The watchers have set up home in our heads.

Jesse Bering and his colleagues at Queen's University Belfast gave a group of students a spatial intelligence test. Participants saw an image on a computer screen and then picked which of several other shapes was the same, only rotated. This, the researchers told their subjects, was a cutting-edge test—so new that there were still some bugs in the program. One glitch they should look out for was that sometimes the answer flashed up before the multiple-choice options appeared, accompanied by the word *answer*. If this happened, could they just hit the space bar to clear the screen, so that they could take the test honestly? Oh, and there's a $50 prize for whoever gets the most questions right.

Two-thirds of the participants were shown another piece of information after these instructions. The experiment, they were told, was dedicated to the memory of Paul J. Kellogg, a graduate student in the department who had worked on the test's design but had died unexpectedly before it could be carried out. To half of these people (that is, one-third of all of the participants) the researcher running the test then mentioned, in passing but sincerely, something else: They'd seen Paul's ghost, right here in this room, where you're taking the test. Several other people had seen it, too. Okay, you're all set—I'm going to leave you alone now and shut the door. I'll be waiting outside. Good luck!

The researchers, as you've guessed, weren't testing people's spatial intelligence. They were testing whether people are more honest in the presence of a supernatural observer.[15] Plus, the computer bug wasn't a bug—of the twenty-five items in the test, a random five were programmed to flash up the answer before the question. The people in the control group, who knew nothing of Paul Kellogg, waited an average of 7.2 seconds before pressing the space bar to get rid of their temptation (although they didn't get more of these questions right than either of the other two groups). Those who were told of Kellogg's passing but not of his ghost waited 6.3 seconds, a statistically insignificant difference. Those who were told that Paul's ghost might be watching (two of whom would do the test only if the researcher left the door ajar) hit the space bar after an average of 4.3 seconds, significantly quicker than either of the groups that hadn't heard the ghost story.

This group also got fewer right answers overall, so perhaps they had been puzzling over the researcher's superstitious ravings, rather than concentrating on the test. Yet if the spooked people really were simply distracted, you'd expect them to take longer to hit the space bar and get rid of their unfair advantage; instead, it looks as if a fear of provoking Kellogg's ghost kept them honest.

In a similar study, Azim Shariff and Ara Norenzayan, two psychologists working at the University of British Columbia in Vancouver, got fifty subjects to play dictator in the give-what-you-like, take-what-you're-given dictator game, in anonymous conditions, dividing $10 with another player.[16] Before the test, they gave half of the participants a short task: a list of five words, which could be rearranged into a sentence if you got rid of one word. So, for example, "dessert divine was fork the" would be "the dessert was divine." Of the ten sentences, half contained one of either *spirit*, *divine*, *God*, *sacred*, or *prophet*.

Psychologists call this priming: priming people with words related to rudeness makes them more likely to interrupt a conversation; priming them with the idea of old age makes them walk more slowly. In Shariff and Norenzayan's experiment, the unprimed players gave up an average of $1.82, and a little more than half gave a dollar or less. Those who had been primed with religious words gave up, on average, $4.22—more than twice as much—and nearly two-thirds gave $5 or more. The effect did not depend on religious belief: priming worked equally well on the students who professed a religion as it did on non-denominational believers and atheists. Religion without priming, on the other hand, made no difference: an unprimed believer was as stingy as his or her atheistic counterpart.

The duo repeated the experiment with seventy-five people, mostly nonstudents, ages seventeen to eighty-two. Again, religious priming made a big difference to donations—$4.56, compared to $2.56. Happily for secularists, priming with words related to legal scrutiny such as *civic*, *jury*, *police*, *court*, and *contract* was as good as spiritual priming, with donations averaging $4.44. Perhaps priming gives people a feel-good shot of moral uplift, although primed participants did not report feeling happier or more empathic, which suggests that it doesn't make them feel noble; nor did they deduce the purpose of the experiment. The most likely explanation, say Shariff and Norenzayan, is that putting the idea of scrutiny, be it legal or religious, in people's heads makes them feel watched and behave accordingly.

Religion does a lot of priming. Every Sunday, before Holy Communion and just after the Lord's Prayer, Anglicans using the 1662 *Book of Common Prayer* ask, "Almighty God, unto whom all hearts are open, all desires known, and from whom no secrets are hid" to "cleanse the thoughts of our hearts." In the Old Testament, verse 7 of Psalm 66 runs: "He ruleth by his power for ever; his eyes behold the nations: let not the rebellious exalt themselves." The Koran, too, mentions divine surveillance: "Dost thou not perceive that God knoweth whatever is in heaven and in Earth? There is no private discourse among three persons but that he is the fourth of them."

Nor is this unique to monotheism. Religion is a human universal, seen in every society. All religions invoke supernatural beings, such as gods or the spirits of ancestors, and a universal feature of such beings is their omniscience. In his 1955 essay "On the Attributes of God," the Italian anthropologist Raffaele Pettazoni lists dozens of examples of all-knowing and particularly all-seeing gods.[17] Many pantheons are led by sky gods who watch over their flocks, such as Zeus, or the Finno-Ugrian Torem, who has "eyes as big as lakes." The animals on Native American totem poles often have humanlike whites to their eyes, the better, perhaps, to provide a watchful gaze over their community. The Egyptian sky god, the aforementioned Horus, has the head of a falcon, the sharpest-eyed animal. East African Masai and Polynesian islanders are among the many societies that believe the stars, the sun, and the moon are the eyes of god. Hindu gods such as Brahma, Vishnu, and Shiva are often represented with many heads. "If one stands or goes, or that which has two persons seated say to each other, [the sky god] King Varuna is the third and knows it," says the Hindu *Atharva-Veda*, written about a thousand years before the birth of Christ. Look at the dollar bill: on one side, George Washington, one of America's intelligent designers, looks you in the eye; on the other is the Masonic all-seeing eye. You could spend an entire academic career trying to untangle what that says about the power of money and how that relates to religion.

Like police officers everywhere, gods are more interested in bad deeds than in good and are more likely to punish sin, with hell in the afterlife, reincarnation lower down the food chain, or plagues and curses in this life, than they are to reward virtue. The god Nyalich, of the Dinka of West Africa, takes a special interest in robbers and murderers, whereas Puluga, the supreme being of the Andaman Islanders, is, wrote Pettazoni, "angry when he sees anyone quarter a boar badly or uproot tubers at the wrong season." Such bad housekeeping is likely to provoke the standard response of offended deities: storms, deluges, and thunderbolts. One special benefit of subcontracting your vengeance to supernatural entities is that it lifts the burden of punishment from human shoulders. When gods provide a threat of punishment that curbs bad behavior, people can spend less on the public good of punishment. Even nice supernatural beings, such as Santa, have this in their job description, seeing when you're sleeping, knowing when you're awake, scoring your image, and reciprocating indirectly.

You can see the effects of supernatural policing in people's attitudes, behavior, and societies. Analyzing data from the World Values Survey for eighty-seven countries, Quentin Atkinson and Pierrick Bourrat found that believers take a sterner view of moral transgressions, ranging from littering to bribery to underage sex, than atheists do.[18] Believers' attitudes reflect how accountable to God they feel: those who believe in the rewards and punishments of heaven and hell make stronger moral judgments than those who do not, as do those who believe in a personal, watching God, rather than a diffuse spirit or life force. Religious people put their money where their minds are: churchgoers give more time and money to charity, and in economic games they are more trusting and more trustworthy. (People who are more fundamentalist in their religious beliefs, however, tend to confine their help to people who share their values.)[19]

Another piece of evidence that religion serves a policing function is that the form of religion a society adopts seems to depend partly on the type of policing it needs. In particular, deities who take an active role in human affairs and morality, known as high gods, are more common in larger societies with institutions, such as money and taxation, that require large-scale cooperation between strangers.[20] In large groups, it's harder for people to control one another, because it's more difficult to know another person's reputation and easier to escape your own. The temptation to cheat is stronger, and trust is harder to achieve, so stronger and further-reaching gods are needed. The threat posed by your particular set of ancestors or nature spirits is probably too local and personal to scare someone from another town into treating you well.

High gods need not mean one God—the Romans, the Egyptians, and the Indians, among others, have developed large, sophisticated, and polytheistic societies. Yet it's striking that the world's two most currently popular religions encourage their followers to have a personal relationship with a single, all-seeing, all-knowing, ever-present, and all-powerful God, who, in contrast to, say, the bickering, capricious, and horny inhabitants of Ancient Rome's pantheon, does little save watch and judge, reward and punish. Such a God is particularly useful in a large, relatively anonymous society where strangers must rely on one another, because he makes everyone play by the same rules and feel the same pressures. The anthropologist Joseph Henrich, whose ideas about prestige and dominance we encountered in chapter 1, and his colleagues have found that when people from Islamic or Christian societies play economic games with strangers, they tend to behave more equably than do people whose societies follow more local religions. "Religion may have coevolved with complex societies to facilitate large-scale interactions," they wrote.[21] The need to protect and enhance a reputation with God, in other words, can compensate for the weakening force of reputation among people and thus help hold large groups together.

These features of religion and its practitioners are a strong hint that one advantage of being religious is that it unlocks the benefits of cooperation, and that one way it does this is by providing the sense of an omnipotent policeman, curbing selfishness and deviance, and thus protecting a believer's social self. If you allow religious considerations to guide behavior, you miss out on some opportunities to be selfish by, for example, taking a free cup of coffee when no one is guarding the honesty box. Yet you are less likely, for example, to try to sneak a free cup of coffee when there's an emeritus professor lurking quietly in the corner armchair. You also avoid the risk of betraying yourself at a later date. If mistakenly believing that no one is watching does more damage than passing up the chance to be selfish—which, given the consequences of losing your reputation, is likely—then it pays to believe in God.[22]

This is an evolutionary psychologist's version of Pascal's wager, the idea famously mooted by the seventeenth-century French philosopher Blaise Pascal that although God's existence cannot be proved, it's better to assume that he does exist and to live a virtuous life. Because if it turns out that he does, you gain salvation and avoid damnation, and if he doesn't, you haven't lost much. Likewise if, in a world of reputation, you act as if no one can see you and you're wrong, you risk losing more than you'd have gained by being right. So it pays to act as if someone powerful and thin-skinned is watching, even if this entity is not.

Society is a panopticon, and we are all inmates and warders—although the result is cooperation, rather than paranoia. Yet if reputation were spread only through our eyes and shaped by our deeds, we'd be on a par with a cleaner fish. Humans aren't so lucky: one selfish, rash, weird, or indiscreet deed can damage your reputation with everybody, forever. That's because our eyes are only the second most powerful agents of reputation and the second most effective means we have of controlling one another. The first is that noisy hole a few inches lower down the face.

CHAPTER 9

A Tool and a Weapon

U niversity rowing demands commitment. Boats are on the water before dawn and sometimes back there later in the day. When rowers are not in the boat, they're often in the gym. Besides reaching peak condition as individuals, rowers in a pair or in a group of four or eight practice so as to become parts of a whole, meshing their strength into a collective poise and rhythm. Boat speed is a product of group effort—a public good—and if a rower isn't pulling his or her weight, the whole boat suffers.

Richard Dawkins, in his book *The Selfish Gene*, compares the genes in a genome to rowers in a boat. The competition between genomes, he notes, is decided partly by how well genes work with one another—teamwork, as well as individual attributes, is important. It's no good being big and strong if you can't pull in time with your colleagues.

This passage set the anthropologist Kevin Kniffin thinking. In *The Selfish Gene*, Dawkins makes a powerful case for the idea that evolution is best understood as a process that makes individual genes better at competing with one another, even if this harms the species, populations, or individuals that carry those genes. Kniffin, however, had just begun graduate school at Binghamton University in New York, where his adviser was the evolutionary biologist David Sloan Wilson. Wilson is one of the leading advocates of what's become known as multilevel

141

selection. This theory argues that as well as genes and individuals, natural selection can work at the level of groups, and that some features of biology are adaptations that evolved to help the group, rather than the individual. Strong reciprocity, the combination of helping and punishment discussed in chapter 6, is held up as an example of just such a set of adaptations.

In this view, if we see an animal doing something costly, it might not be getting some ultimate selfish payoff. Instead, the benefit might be shared around its group as a whole. Kniffin decided to take Dawkins's metaphor literally; rowers, he thought, where individuals merge their skills and fates into a group, would be an excellent system to probe how selection worked on groups and individuals. So he signed up for the university rowing team.[1]

Most people with no appetite for early starts and fatigue don't last long in a rowing club, but Kniffin, in his first semester, was lucky enough to be presented with a natural experiment in the club's social dynamics. Also present was a man whom he came to know as "the slacker." The slacker had joined the boat club the semester before Kniffin, but he had attended hardly any of the off-season gym practices. When the racing season began and the practice schedule stepped up a notch, he was just as flaky.

While Kniffin trained, he monitored, with the team's permission, what the other rowers talked about when, for example, they were driving to and from practice. Soon, the rowing club was aflame with harsh judgments and unkind jokes about the slacker, both behind his back and, less often, to his face. "I don't understand how he accomplishes anything in life," said one rower, exhibiting the human tendency to generalize from how people behave in one sphere of activity to their competence in others. "He just doesn't have the crew mentality," volunteered another.

By gossiping in this way, the rowers were ignoring millennia of moral instruction. The Ninth Commandment prohibits bearing false witness. Besides that, the holy books of the Abrahamic faiths express a lot of disapproval about bearing any kind of witness. "You shall not go about as a talebearer among your people," says Leviticus. "Do not spy nor let some of you backbite others," says the

Quran. And St. Paul, in his first letter to the Romans, lists whispering and backbiting among the vices of the unrighteous, along with murder, deceit, and fornication, adding that "they that commit such things are worthy of death." Patricia Meyer Spacks's book *Gossip* catalogues centuries of opprobrium, from medieval warnings that gossip killed souls and was "more cruel than hell" to Renaissance associations with noxious beasts such as scorpions, wasps, and leeches to a modern view of gossiping as a crime against good manners, rather than against God. The French philosopher Roland Barthes called it "murder by language," and a 1976 column from the pseudonymous American agony aunt Ann Landers is headlined "Gossip's a Vicious Killer." "I've said it before but I'll say it again," she wrote. "Superior people talk about ideas. Mediocre people talk about things. Little people talk about other people."[2] For something that we all do, a lot, gossip has gotten a terrible press.

Yet it's hard to argue that the most antisocial behavior revealed by Kniffin's study was coming from the gossipers. The rowers had a serious problem, in the shape of a social parasite who threatened their collective endeavor. The negative gossip was like an immune reaction— it identified the threat, spread the news around the social body, and activated defense systems that attacked the slacker by damaging his reputation, with the aim of either reforming or expelling him.

Talk was the rowing club's first line of defense against the ever-present threat of selfishness. That's true of any society, and it makes gossip a crucial component of our ability to trust one another and cooperate without any external authority or impartial arbiter to enforce the rules. Put like that, badmouthing slackers becomes a moral duty.

That's how many people see it. In another study of how groups use gossip to regulate their members, Kniffin's adviser, David Sloan Wilson, presented undergraduates with scenarios taken from a study of cattle ranchers in northern California. In his 1991 book *Order without Law*, the legal scholar Robert Ellickson described how the ranchers of Shasta County hardly ever needed police or lawyers to resolve their disputes.[3] When someone broke a rule, by letting his animals roam on another's land, for example, or failing to maintain his fences, the wronged party's first response was to tell his neighbors. This created a social pressure that usually brought the offender into line.

Was it okay, Wilson asked his subjects, for Tom Stark to complain to his fellow ranchers that Jim Turner's cattle had broken through a fence and were eating Stark's grass? It was not only okay, they replied, it was his duty—in another scenario in the study, they disapproved of Stark when they were told he kept quiet about the breach.[4] Sometimes, not gossiping is antisocial, because stepping up to deal with the selfish individual is part of being a good member of society. By keeping quiet, Stark was dodging the cost of punishment (being a second-order free rider, in the jargon) and relying on someone else to police his community.

Granted, gossip is only talk. If negative gossip is to make its target change or leave, there needs to be something concrete behind it. Among the ranchers of Shasta County, more drastic measures, such as shooting a trespassing animal, were sometimes used if gossip didn't do the trick. When the rowing-team slacker continued to skip practices as the racing season loomed, there were threats of physical violence. Once, when he failed to show for early morning practice, more than forty club members went to his home to wake him as rudely as they could.

The rowing crew also punished the slacker in another, more subtle way. When Kniffin asked strangers to rate his physical appearance, they found him reasonably good looking. Boat-club insiders, who knew of his antisocial behavior, rated him significantly less attractive.[5] Those who knew him had translated his moral failings into physical shortcomings, and if he'd had to find a mate within the rowing club—if it were, say, an isolated hunter-gatherer group and not a university sport club—his genes would probably have suffered.

After a semester of this, the slacker got the message and left the club. The rowing club had protected itself through social pressure alone. It didn't need to resort to violence, and perhaps surprisingly, gossip didn't find a new target when he left. Post-slacker, Kniffin found, negative gossip almost disappeared: he recorded more than a hundred incidents of trash-talking in his first semester of study and only eleven in his second and third combined. Kniffin also noticed that positive gossip vanished entirely. When the slacker had been in the club, the rowers were sure to praise their hard-working and committed fellows, reaffirming and repairing their collective values. When the slacker disappeared, people went back to talking about movies they'd seen or music they'd heard. In a group under threat, gossip is used to both attack the bad and boost the good.

People seem to devote rather little of their conversational time to criticizing people behind their backs—one eavesdropping study put the figure at less than 5 percent.[6] (Although such numbers should not be seen as written in stone, as definitions of what constitutes gossip and methods of measuring it vary from study to study.) That gossip's corrosive effect on reputation looms so large in our idea of it suggests both that like all good deterrents, gossip rarely needs to be used and that the threat alone is enough to prevent a lot of antisocial behavior. It also suggests that a little such talk goes a long way.

One source of bad gossip's power is a deep-seated bias in how humans respond to what happens to them. In nearly every aspect of our mental life, bad things make more of an impression than good. The brain responds more strongly to pictures of nasty things than to nice ones. Bad events are remembered far longer than good ones. The pain of losing $10 is greater than the pleasure of finding $10—so if you lose some money and find it again, you'll think yourself worse off. A single piece of rude or inconsiderate behavior can spoil your day, but small acts of politeness leave no trace. A single terrible event can result in a lifetime of post-traumatic stress disorder, but there's no equivalent post-triumphant euphoric glow.

One illustration of this is in the way that gossip fine-tunes our visual surveillance systems. If each eye is presented with a different image—say, a face and a house—the brain toggles between them, so that we see the house, then the face, then the house, and so on. Normally, each image gets equal time, but when the psychologist Eric Anderson and his colleagues showed their subjects a house in one eye and the face of a stranger about whom they had heard a piece of bad gossip, such as "threw a chair at a classmate," in the other, that face dominated their vision, as the brain focused on the purported villain. Gossip shapes what we see, in other words, but only if it's bad; faces associated with good gossip got no extra attention.[7]

This negativity bias, as it's called, starts early. A couple of years after Kiley Hamlin did her experiments showing that six- and ten-month-olds are acute judges of social worth, she repeated the study using three-month-old babies.[8] Three-month-olds can't reach for an object, but they do show what they like by the amount of time they spend looking at a thing. Given a choice between a helping block and a hinderer, they looked longest at the helper, showing the same preference as their elders did. Yet when Hamlin tried them out on the more complex scenario, seeing how the babies rated a neutral block relative to a helper and a hinderer, she saw something new. Helpers and neutral blocks drew about the same amount of attention, showing, it seems, that babies didn't strongly prefer either. Neutral blocks, however, were far more popular than hinderers. When Hamlin compared babies' reaction to a neutral character to a nasty one that blocked the hill-climber, she found that the neutral block got twelve seconds of attention and the nasty block three. The difference between a bad deed and no deed was much larger than that between no deed and a good deed.

Negativity bias lies behind Warren Buffett's remark that it takes twenty years to build a reputation and five minutes to ruin it. Ranchers might ignore years of Jim Turner's following the rules, but a break in the fence makes an immediate and powerful impression. In the 1970s, the psychologist Michael Birnbaum conducted a number of studies that looked at how bad and good acts combine into an overall character assessment, in which he asked undergraduates to rate the cumulative moral weight of good (helping an old lady across the road, rescuing a family from a burning house) and bad (bribing your way out of a speeding ticket, torturing prisoners of war) deeds. Not only do bad acts have a greater impact on a person's standing than do good ones, he found, no amount of good deeds was enough to redeem someone who had done something really bad.[9] "The overall goodness of a person is determined by his worst bad deed," he wrote, noting that this is the attitude reflected in the Old Testament Book of Ezekiel 3:20: "When a righteous man doth turn from his righteousness, and commit iniquity . . . he shall die in his sin, and his righteousness which he hath done shall not be remembered." It also brings to mind the joke that starts with a man walking around his village and pointing out his many achievements—"I built that bridge, but do they call me Angus the bridge builder? No, they don't"—and ends with the punch line "but you fuck one sheep . . ."

The reason we have a negativity bias is probably the same reason it's safest to assume that someone, be it a ghost, a friend, or a god, might see you acting inappropriately. Some kinds of mistake are more expensive than others. If you show a negativity bias and react strongly to mild threats—running away at the first hint of danger, for example—you'll expend some unnecessary energy and miss some opportunities, but you're less likely to wind up dead. Avoiding bad choices, people, and situations is more important, and mistakes are harder to correct, than missing out on good things. If someone cries wolf in error and you run away, you'll lose nothing worse than your breath. If you ignore the person and he's right, you might lose your life.

When I first discussed gossip in chapter 4, we saw how essential it is for your reputation that people talk about you. Yet we also saw that what people say about you serves their own ends more than it does yours. Sometimes, as in a rowing crew, the needs of the individual are aligned with those of the group. In that context, backbiting becomes almost noble—nobody stood to gain more than anybody else from criticizing the slacker behind his back. If this were all that people gossiped about, though, we would have been spared the finger-wagging of moralists from Leviticus to Ann Landers. In many groups—political parties, magazines, universities, you name it—people's desire to get to the top of the pile is often more important to them than their ambition to work toward a common goal. There's one thing about social status that makes it particularly vulnerable to gossip: it's relative. You don't have to raise yourself; lowering someone else works just as well.

People are experts at using gossip to manipulate social status in their own interests. The psychologist Frank McAndrew and his colleagues found that in hypothetical scenarios, people are most likely to pass on good news about their friends and family and most likely to spread dirt on their rivals, enemies, and superiors.[10] If a friend tells you that your professor has won a Nobel Prize, you smile politely. If you hear that your professor has been pilfering computers from campus or that the noisy guy in the apartment above yours was spotted falling down drunk in the street, you reach for your cell phone. If someone lets slip that a mutual friend has just gotten a great job, you put the word out. If you hear that this same friend has a drug problem, you keep it to yourself. In all, McAndrew's findings support the idea that gossip is a tool we use to boost our friends and harm our rivals—and in the process, improve our own standing in the social order.

New media reproduce these old patterns. A team led by Lars Kai Hansen, a Danish researcher working at the boundary of neuroscience and technology, has analyzed what kind of messages were most likely to be passed on via Twitter.[11] They found that negative news stories had a higher "virality," matching the conclusion reached by studies of old news media, but that, similar to McAndrew's finding, positive social messages were more likely to be re-tweeted among networks of friends. As with real-world gossip, communication with social media is as much about building bonds as it is about imparting information. The secret of creating those bonds and making a message that spreads is to arouse the receiver's emotions. If you want to grab someone's attention, exploit his negativity bias and tell him something bad; if you want to build a relationship with him, tell him something good and make him associate you with feeling good.

The urge to spread bad news about anyone powerful, even if the person is not an adversary, also shows gossip's power as a weapon against dominance. As many scholars have pointed out, gossip is one of the few means for the weak to attack the strong. By damaging the reputations of high-status men and women, we limit their power. This is not to say that gossip works disproportionately against the powerful. Countless people have suffered or died because they were unable to defend themselves against whispers in corners. That might be why religious philosophies speak against gossip. A less charitable interpretation would be that scripture tends to be written, interpreted, and enforced by high-status men, who have the most to lose from damaging words.

You can see gossip being used to attack reputation on every newsstand and all over the Web. I just Googled "celebrity friends worried," to discover that Christina Aguilera, Lindsay Lohan, and Charlie Sheen are some of the people whose friends have been moved to reveal their excesses and mishaps. By attacking the reputations of the alpha males and females in their group, these Iagos-lite take themselves a little nearer to the top.

The challenge to listeners is to work out the motives of someone passing on a juicy piece of gossip. It's very similar to the problem of judging motive in indirect reciprocity: is what we're witnessing a justifiable punishment or a selfish attack? Experiments asking people how they judge gossip have found that people have several ways to do this.

One is to analyze the content of what's being said. In David Sloan Wilson's study using repurposed gossip about cattle ranchers, he found that although students approved of gossip about social transgressions, they disapproved of scenarios in which the gossip was gratuitous (with Stark ascribing Turner's slip-up to drunkenness) or only part of the story (with Stark failing to mention that Turner hadn't retrieved his cattle because he was out of town).

Listeners also go beyond the content of what people are saying and become informal opinion pollsters, seeking a range of opinions and discounting information if it is rare. Experiments have found that despite our negativity bias, one bad opinion about a person is not enough to override a positive majority.[12] We also discount the extremes: a bit like the scoring in diving, where the highest and the lowest marks are discarded, making it harder for a single biased judge to sway the result, people seem to be proportionately less influenced by extremely good or bad gossip than they are by more moderate opinions.[13] Gossip also becomes more credible if it flows from more than one independent source and less credible if we know the gossiper is passing on something she heard from someone else or in competition with the person she's telling tales about.[14]

When we hear gossip, then, we apply the same criteria that responsible journalists use to judge a story. Is damaging this person's reputation in the public interest? Do we have multiple sources? Are they independent? Does our source have ulterior motives or a conflict of interest? (If, for example, this book gets a good review in *Nature*, you might wonder whether it's because I'm married to that journal's chief opinion editor.)

Most celebrity gossip fails all of these tests, so why do people have such an appetite for bad news about famous people? One possible answer is that celebrity gossip is the social equivalent of junk food. Until recently, each of us had only a few people to be curious about—those we lived around and dealt with from day to day. The benefits of knowing a lot about such people's tastes and tendencies are obvious, and so is the benefit of making some effort to gather such information. If strangers are rare, it makes little sense being choosy whom you are curious about, because everyone it's possible to know well is also likely to be influential in your life. In this view, the mass media hijack our general, indiscriminating appetite for social information in the same way that the food industry taps into an ancient hunger for fat and sugar. We don't know a lot about Charlie Sheen because we think he's important to us; we think he's important because we know a lot about him. The less flattering our knowledge becomes, the higher we feel in comparison.

Another study by Frank McAndrew and his colleagues lends support to the idea that we see celebrities as members of our group, and that we use gossip to compete with them. They found that people are most interested in gossip about celebrities of the same age and sex as themselves. As of the late 1990s, women under thirty ranked a story about figure skater Oksana Baiul as most interesting; young men went for a story about Robert Downey Jr., then thirty-one. Among the over-thirties, the most eye-catching celebrities for women and men were model Christie Brinkley (b. 1954) and Kelsey Grammer (b. 1955), respectively. Stories about the oldest members of the sample, such as Frank Sinatra, consistently aroused the least interest.[15]

In everyday life, McAndrew reasons, people's closest allies and also their stiffest competitors for mates, riches, and status are those most similar to themselves. These are the people you need to watch; these are the people you want to know about. And this, McAndrew believes, is the interest that magazines and tabloids exploit when they use the latest changes in Britney Spears's or Angelina Jolie's weight, hair, behavior, and relationships to sell copies to young women. Which is mostly whom they sell copies to: the readership of *OK!* (one of the top British celebrity magazines) is 84 percent female.[16] This brings us to the question of whether gossip really is a female specialty, and if so, why.

When we think of what makes a group an effective fighting force, cohesion is one of the first things that springs to mind, in the discipline and the courage that are needed if a collection of individuals is to attack and stand its ground as a unit, and in the camaraderie that makes people want to fight for their friends. This was as true 250,000 years ago as it is now, and many evolutionary psychologists believe that one reason that men form close and enduring friendships is that, in the environment in which our species evolved, it made their group better at fighting other groups. In battle, soldiers don't give their lives for their country or their ideals. They do it for one another.

Women are less violent than men, and female friendship has received much less academic attention. One idea is that female alliances help defend against male aggression; another, sometimes called "tend and befriend," is that women form close relationships so as to help rear one another's children. To the anthropologist Nicole Hess, this didn't chime with experience. As she went through adolescence and into adulthood, she formed a group of close female friends, but they spent far more time chatting about what their old schoolmates were up to than they did babysitting one another's kids. It doesn't fit with what our relatives do, either. For female baboons, for example, alliances with other females are crucial to compete with the rest of the group for food. Are human females unique in forming alliances that are solely peaceable?

It seems unlikely. Humans—at least in their original environment—are like other primates, in that the stuff of evolutionary success is in short supply. Food (and, for males, mates) are worth fighting for, even if you have to fight your neighbor, but almost every human society frowns on settling internal conflicts with violence, perhaps because if you're not part of the quarrel, you don't want to see your group weakened by infighting.

Gossip, on the other hand, is everywhere. Compared with a physical assault, it's harder to detect, easier to deny, pleasurable to engage in, and valuable to its consumers. This opens up a much more promising line of attack. Harming reputation may well be as effective as an outright assault: in other primates, animals of low social status are less fertile than their higher-ranking counterparts. The effect passes down the generations, with the daughters of low-ranking females also suffering. The lowest-ranking, most put-upon individuals are effectively sterile. Yet they are no less capable of working for their group than are the most fertile and superior individuals.

Hess began to wonder whether one benefit of female friendship revealed itself in wars of words. On the battlefield of rumor and propaganda, allies are as important as they are in any other conflict. Friends can play on both offense, collecting and analyzing information on your rivals and spreading gossip, and defense, to deter others from spreading malicious gossip about you and to detect and counter with explanations and alibis any that does get going. Nipping gossip in the bud is especially valuable, because malicious rumors gain power from being about things—fidelity, promiscuity, and, depending on what century and continent you live in, witchcraft and substance abuse—that, true or not, are difficult for their targets to disprove. The private nature of sex and the greater part that sexual behavior plays in female reputation make women particularly vulnerable to malicious gossip.

To test the idea that cliques are gossip patrols, Hess went into a sorority at an unnamed university in Southern California armed with the following scenario. Imagine, she told the sisters, that you're at a party with another member of your sorority. Let's call her Nina. Late in the evening, looking for the bathroom, you wander into a room without knocking and stumble on Nina snorting cocaine with Hank, one of the university's most notorious rakes. You make your excuses and leave, then eventually walk home from the party with Ryan, Nina's boyfriend, although nothing happens, and thankfully he doesn't ask you anything about Nina. Yet the next day, Nina starts spreading a rumor that you hit on Ryan.[17]

Hess told this story to seventy-five young women of the sorority and then asked them how much they agreed with a set of statements such as, "It would get around that Nina was using cocaine" and "It would get around that Nina was a liar." She also asked the students to tell her about their real-world social networks. As we saw earlier, a person's reputation, good or bad, depends both on what she does and on the structure of her social network. Gossip makes reputation as it flows along social connections, and tight networks, where everyone speaks with everyone else, are especially good at creating and stabilizing reputation. Hess thought that as well as applying to the reputations within a clique, this might also affect a clique's ability to attack an outsider's reputation—the tighter the group, the tougher it is. So she also asked the young women how close they were to their four closest friends and how close the members of this quartet were to one another.

The closer a person's friends, Hess found, the more they expected Nina's reputation to suffer. Those with solid cliques felt more confident in their ability to mount a gossip counterattack than did those whose social networks were less tightly interconnected. In another study, using an online questionnaire, Hess found that both men and women were less likely to pass on damaging gossip about a competitor for a promotion if that rival had a close friend in the same office. (A friend in the same neighborhood was rated as posing a greater physical threat than another coworker, but such a friend was a weaker deterrent to malicious gossip, suggesting that allies' power to curb gossip is social, not physical.) In other words, when people compete with someone close to them for something, such as a job, that's difficult or impossible to share, gossip is part of their armory, and one of the many things that friends are for is mounting and resisting such attacks.

Psychologists call it indirect aggression. If you study what goes on in school playgrounds, indirect aggression seems pretty clearly a girl's game. Children and adolescents divide clearly in their aggressive tactics. Boys punch and yell, whereas girls live in a web of alliance and enmity, where who's in and out is always changing. For adults, the picture is less clear-cut. Men remain, on average, more physically aggressive than women throughout their lives, and the sexes do seem to have different strategies in how they spread gossip. Frank McAndrew found that men were most likely to pass on juicy tidbits to their romantic partners, whereas women were more likely to tell female friends. Beyond adolescence, however, the sexes haven't been found to differ much in the amount they use indirect aggression. This is a serious challenge to the idea that female friendship has a competitive function.

To try to meet this challenge, Hess investigated whether the two sexes think about gossip and reputation differently. To do so, she took another painful scenario to a group of undergraduates at the University of California, Santa Barbara.[18] It went like this: On a class project, you are paired with a partner of your own sex who leaves you to do the work while he or she nips off to Mexico for an impromptu vacation. One Friday night, you're at a party, where you hear this person (the woman in the story was called Melissa) complaining to the class's teaching assistant that she's doing all of the work, and you keep showing up at meetings with a hangover. She thinks you have a drinking problem. None of this is true, and in fact you have kept an incriminating voice-mail message from Melissa about the Mexican trip. The overheard conversation breaks up, and right away you bump into Melissa. "How are things going?" she says brightly. "Hasn't the weather been great lately?"

Hess then gave her subjects a range of options, which included punching the person, revealing the holiday to the teaching assistant, badmouthing Melissa to other people at the party, or simply saying, without irony, "Yeah, the weather has been nice." How badly, Hess asked the students, did they want to pursue each course? She also forced them to choose whether they were more inclined to attack Melissa's person or her reputation.

Forced to choose between indirect or physical aggression, 90 percent of women chose an attack on reputation, compared with 55 percent of men. Women also reported a stronger desire to gossip about their tormentor, whereas men were more inclined to either punch or threaten to punch him. Men also rated punching as more socially acceptable. Neither sex showed much of an urge to turn the other cheek and talk about the weather.

If you force people to choose, then, women are more inclined than men to attack their tormentors with gossip. So why doesn't this translate into their behavior? It might be a reflection of our culture, a sign that men have become bigger users of indirect aggression because settling disputes with fists or dueling pistols has become less acceptable. (Studying aggression among hunter-gatherers in central Africa, Hess and her colleagues found a bias for indirect aggression among adult females.)[19] It might also be that by the time women reach adulthood, they are past their aggressive peak. The biggest difference between the sexes in the amount of indirect aggression they use is seen for eleven- to seventeen-year-olds, whereas for physical aggression eighteen- to thirty-year-olds show the biggest sex difference. This may also reflect women's tendency to get married at a younger age than men: each sex's most aggressive phase seems to match the age at which it is most likely to be seeking, attracting, and competing for a mate and thus is in stiffest competition with other members of its own sex. This is also the age at which women have the greatest appetite for gossip—more than a third of OK!'s readers are ages fifteen to twenty-four.

None of this is saying that men never bitch about one another or that women can't be the soul of kindness and discretion. Rather, Hess's idea is that indirect aggression is particularly useful in fights within groups, and that in our evolutionary history women have found themselves in this type of competition more often than men have. This, she suggests, is because of the differing patterns of migration seen in men and women. In many human societies, males tend to remain in the group they were born in—creating blood ties and thus another reason for male group members to stand by one another—whereas females move to their husbands' groups when they marry.

(In most other primates, the reverse is true, and males are the migratory sex.)

In such a situation, a woman must find allies among a group of strangers. Women are certainly good at building social bonds. Eavesdropping studies have found that although the amount of time spent gossiping by men and women doesn't differ much, the content of their conversations does. Men talk more about themselves—showing off, in other words—and try to dominate one another in conversation, through interruption and one-upmanship. Women talk more about other people, inquiring and empathizing.[20] Their conversations are devoted more to building and strengthening social ties than men's are. As the anthropologist Lars Rodseth and his colleagues wrote, in "striking contrast" with other primates, "even unrelated women in the most extreme patriarchal societies . . . regularly engage in peaceful cooperation toward common goals with close and enduring friendships."[21]

But if you can't join 'em, you'd better beat 'em. And if you find yourself a newcomer among a group of women, some of whom see you as rivals for resources, status, and male attention, you'd do better to fight with the weapons you're most skilled at using. In a woman's case, that's conversation: according to some studies, women are quicker, more fluent, and less likely to flub in speech than men, and they are less prone to speech disorders such as stammering.

This is neither a seamless nor uncontested picture (Hess's sorority study is as yet unpublished and so hasn't received the endorsement of peer review). There's been some debate about whether human society really was originally based on males staying put and females moving, or whether we were more like other primates, with females using gossip more to cement alliances within their home group than to attack strangers in their new group. Some researchers have argued that women are less physically aggressive than men because injury would damage their ability to care for their children (they are the less disposable sex, in other words), although this does not explain why females of other species fight.[22] And gossip has other uses besides controlling and harming: it underpins social learning, for example. The Belgian psychologist Charlotte De Backer argues that the primary function of celebrity gossip is to provide useful lessons for our own lives. This, she notes, would explain why young women, who have the least personal experience and the greatest need for social information, are gossip's most avid consumers.[23]

The size of the psychological differences between the sexes is also disputed. Some researchers point to the vast amount of overlap seen in male and female behavior and abilities and feel that emphasizing the relatively few areas in which we differ risks enforcing sexism at school and work.[24] There's certainly a lot of overlap between the sexes: in Hess's "Melissa" scenario, for example, more men than women wanted to punch their antagonist, but more than half of the men still chose to attack reputation. There's also a risk that one will pick and choose one's evidence—taking one suggestive fact from apes, another from hunter-gatherers, a third from sorority girls, a fourth from supermarket tabloids, and so on—and stitch them together into a quilt that obscures the fact that these are all rather different situations. Sometimes it's tempting to argue that people behave as they do because of the legacies of their evolutionary past, other times that they're cannily adapting to their present circumstances. Even if you accept the results so far, there's still a lot left uncertain. We don't know why sorority girls with tight social networks feel better able to damage a rival's reputation—the link doesn't tell us the cause. Likewise, we don't know whether the slacker left the SUNY rowing club because of all of the gossip against him, or because he took up racquetball or got a new girlfriend who liked to sleep in.

Nevertheless, it's incontrovertible that people do attack one another with gossip. One also needs to explain the strong evidence for sex differences in aggressive behavior, the almost equally strong evidence for a similar difference in verbal abilities, and the differing leitmotifs in masculine and feminine conversation. Hypotheses such as Hess's don't have all of the answers, but they seem to be on the right track. It would certainly help explain why most of the celebrities who popped out of my Google search were young women and why young, famous, and successful women are the targets of the most intense and ugly gossip.

People don't gossip for or about any one thing. How we use it depends on our goals and the incentives and threats in our environment. Most particularly, it depends on whether the strength of our group is more important than our status within it. In a rowing team, there's little point in moving up the pecking order by dragging down the guy sitting in front of you. To do so would harm the whole boat and thus hurt your chances as an individual. Your most serious rivals are in the other boats, so the best thing to do is whatever makes your group a more effective competitor. In a sorority, on the other hand, your most serious competitors for social status are in your own house. Hess entered the sorority she studied expecting to find a society in solidarity but instead found a warren of competing cliques.

Unfortunately, the only thing worse than a society of gossips is a society where nobody gossips.

CHAPTER 10

Future Discounting

Transcranial magnetic stimulation (TMS), says the neuroscientist Daria Knoch, creates a "very subtle tickle" inside your head. TMS is so subtle that unless you know it's happening, it's difficult to detect, so as an experimental control, researchers can use a sham treatment, holding an electromagnet to a subject's head without actually sending any magnetic pulses into his brain. When the magnet is switched on, it alters electrical activity in the brain, and by positioning the magnet the activity of specific brain areas can be temporarily and noninvasively dimmed or enhanced.

Knoch and her colleagues gave transcranial magnetic stimulation to subjects as they played a trust game with multiple partners. Players had to decide how much of the endowment to return, multiplied by the experimenters, that the first player had given them. Without TMS or with sham TMS, people returned about a quarter of what they received if they were anonymous and nearly half if their decisions were made public. They understood, of course, that if they betrayed one partner's trust, the next partner would not trust them.

When Knoch used TMS to suppress the activity of the right prefrontal cortex (PFC), though, people behaved as if no one was watching, even in public.[1] The amount of money returned was almost identical to the anonymous condition. Disrupting this region at the front of the brain, which is involved in social behavior and complex planning, made people oblivious of their reputations. When questioned after the experiment, they knew what the fair thing to do would have been and knew that they hadn't done it, but they hadn't been able to stop themselves from taking the quick win. They shrugged, rather than blushed, about their decision.

Knoch's work shows that concern for reputation is a species of self-control. It's the ability to resist the chance of a small win now in the hope of a bigger one later. Within the brain, the right PFC, which is one of the most recent brain areas to evolve and one of the last to form during development, asserts this control. In other experiments, Knoch's team has found that disrupting the same region also makes people accept lower offers in the ultimatum game and choose riskier options in gambling games—reputation, fairness, and reciprocity are all related, and all rely on allowing the future to influence the present. Without the right PFC to act as the angel on our shoulder, we are swayed by a more primitive voice that wants the reward now. Heeding this voice is often a bad move—in Knoch's experiment for example, players made untrustworthy by TMS ended up with less money than those who guarded their reputations. Yet in some people, a lack of self-control, no sense of fairness, and a disregard for reputation seem to be features, not a bug.

About one in every hundred people doesn't value a good reputation and doesn't care if others think well of him or her. These people are hard to spot. Physically, they are usually healthy and normal. They have stable and sometimes privileged upbringings. Their intelligence is often above average. And in the words of the psychiatrist David Lykken, who spent his life studying these people, they lie without compunction, cheat, steal, and casually violate any and all norms of social conduct whenever it suits their whim. They have little or no empathy for others' suffering, little or no remorse when caught, and punishment does little or nothing to change their behavior.[2] They are called psychopaths.

Mental-health professionals have usually treated psychopathic behavior as evidence of something gone wrong, but viewed from an evolutionary angle, being a psychopath can make sense. Despite the short-term benefits of cheating and free riding, people's first moves toward one another tend to be trusting and generous. This pays off over time, because it releases the benefits of cooperation. Yet it also creates an opening for anyone who would rather prey on society than join it, just as cellular life created a niche for viruses to fill.

A psychopath's deceitful, manipulative, and callous nature equips him (it's three times more likely to be a "him") to fill this niche. Psychopaths' deficit is in empathy, not reason. Like the subjects in Knoch's study, they understand moral principles and rules perfectly well, but they are immune to other people's emotions and therefore don't care about the effect of their actions. Society doesn't have many openings for psychopaths, because if there were lots of them, they would always be bumping into one another, leading to mutual cheating or mutual destruction. Evolutionary biologists call this frequency dependence: it means that the rarer a trait becomes, the more it pays off. This advantage when rare prevents the trait from becoming extinct, but the disadvantage of being common prevents it from taking over. The net effect is to keep multiple traits in balance. Sex is one example of frequency dependence: if males were more common than females, they would be less likely to find a mate, so it would pay to have female offspring, pushing the sex ratio back toward equality. Similarly, mathematical models suggest that if antisocial behavior is rare enough, it can prosper.[3]

Like every strategy, psychopathy involves trade-offs. The benefit of psychopathy is that you take the rewards of other people's altruism without paying the cost of being altruistic yourself. The downside is that people's cooperation is conditional. You can cheat a person only so many times before he refuses to have anything more to do with you. Your victims are also likely to warn their friends not to trust you. And they or outraged third parties may seek revenge. So a psychopath must stay one step ahead of his reputation.

Psychopaths' psychology reflects this. They tend to be drifters and often change their names as they change places. They have nonexistent boredom thresholds and a dread of long-term commitment in work, friendship, or romance. Rather than play the long game of reciprocity, they go for the quick buck and the one-night stand.[4] They are impulsive and uninhibited, with little self-control, little regard for the future consequences of their actions, and short attention spans. A psychopath is someone who lives fast, doing everything he can to escape the future's shadow. The right prefrontal cortex of a psychopath is asleep on the job, and this does seem to be one of the brain areas that shows differences between psychopathic and social people.

One obvious criticism of the idea that psychopathy is a strategy, rather than a malfunction, is that it often leads to a disastrous life. It's only in comics where injury turns ordinary folk into master criminals. In reality, when disease, dementia, or injury affects the brain areas involved in social judgment and self-control, sufferers fall into ruinous violence, crime, substance abuse, and recklessness, losing their livelihoods and relationships.[5] (Phineas Gage, the railroad worker whose personality was transformed when an iron bar went through his skull in 1848, is a famous example.) It's been estimated that more than half of the U.S. federal prison population has some form of antisocial personality disorder, the blanket diagnosis replacing psychopathy and sociopathy in the current edition of the American Psychiatric Association's *Diagnostic and Statistical Manual of Mental Disorders (DSM)*.

On the other hand, these are the ones who get caught. Just because many prisoners are psychopaths doesn't mean that most psychopaths are in prison. In fact, psychopaths function in society far more successfully than do people with conditions such as severe autism, schizophrenia, or bipolar disorder—one psychiatrist called psychopathy "the mask of sanity." The *DSM*'s list focuses on personality flaws, whereas some of the symptoms of psychopathy have an obvious upside. Psychopaths are aggressive, quick to anger, violent, fearless, and cool under pressure. As Lykken put it, "the hero and psychopath may be twigs on the same genetic branch."[6] It's easy to see how a lack of empathy might give rise to both the conman who seeks to deceive and the warrior who must strike without pity. This has led some psychologists to suggest that such people may be specialized warriors, instead of, or as well as, cheats—they may not value others' prestige, but they are more than capable of understanding and using dominance, as the management techniques of gangsters and despots illustrate.[7]

The psychopathy checklist used by clinicians also lists "glibness/superficial charm," "cunning/manipulative," and "promiscuous sexual behavior" as defining features of the condition. All have their advantages: even if you end up jailed or dead, natural selection won't penalize you if you have several children beforehand. In addition, psychopathy may not be an all-or-nothing lifestyle. I've emphasized how sensitive our social behavior is to the environment, but that's not the whole story. Different people place different values on fairness, reciprocity, or punishment and are willing to invest different amounts in them, regardless of the immediate rewards or who's watching. Some of us, in other words, are more self-interested than others. These personality differences are called social preferences, although how fixed or sensitive to the environment they are is still unknown and debated. Out-and-out psychopaths exist out at the far end of social preferences, where all that matters is immediate self-interest, but it's easy to imagine that ruthless and manipulative behavior, combined with a degree of self-control, could be a winning combination in business, politics, or just about any other human endeavor. As with autism and schizophrenia, psychopathy may reflect traits that are valuable in moderation taken to damaging extremes.

It's difficult to detect successful psychopaths, but in a survey of professional and academic psychologists and criminal law attorneys, Stephanie Mullins-Sweatt and her colleagues found that nearly three-quarters of respondents believed they had known a successful psychopath. These people, as respondents described them, bore all of the classic traits of the type, but they also rated high on conscientiousness, an ability to get the job done that is seemingly lacking in the less successful members of their kind.[8] Mullins-Sweatt and her colleagues argue that we should update our definitions of psychopathy to include its advantages.

The psychologist Linda Mealey argued that there were two routes to antisocial behavior.[9] Some psychopaths are born that way, because natural selection has preserved genes that equip people to exploit the psychopathic niche (and the trait does seem to have a genetic component). Others are made antisocial by their environments. Given a poor, disadvantaged, unhealthy, and chaotic upbringing, she suggested, you might have no faith in the future and so settle on an exploitative lifestyle as a way to make the best of a bad lot.

She also noted that some societies are better than others at excluding psychopaths. Cultures where people live in small groups with strong connections, such as the Inuit and Israeli kibbutzes, have particularly low levels of antisocial behavior. This, she argued, is because children become antisocial more rarely in such conditions, and those who are born antisocial emigrate—or are pushed off the ice, as one anthropologist working with the Inuit was told. This also hints at why small communities tend to distrust newcomers. The very fact that someone has moved from somewhere else raises the question of why he moved. Having no reputation is the equivalent of having a bad reputation.

A few of us are psychopaths and a few of us are saints, who would never do a bad thing regardless of who's watching. Most of us are somewhere in the middle. We are not predisposed to antisocial behavior by genes or environment, but we do, unconsciously or not, weigh up the benefits of cheating against the likelihood and consequences of getting caught. For a psychopath, no one matters—you don't control yourself, you move on. For the rest of us, concern for our reputations prods us toward the saintly end of the spectrum.

Yet not every environment provokes the same concerns. In a small village or a hunter-gatherer group numbering a few dozen people, everyone knows everyone else's business. There's little secrecy or anonymity and slim chance of getting away with anything. It's easy to resist temptation in such an environment. Modern urban life, on the other hand, is much more conducive to cheating.

The more people there are in a group, the harder it becomes to sustain cooperation. Emilia Yamamoto and her colleagues got Brazilian schoolchildren, with an average age slightly below nine, to play the public goods game, except instead of putting money in the common pot, they gave each child three candy bars and the option of investing none, some, or all of them into a common urn. For every bar the children put in, the experimenters added another two and then divided the spoils equally. Donations were anonymous—the urn was behind a partition, allowing the kids to put their "public" bars in an envelope and pocket the rest without anyone else seeing.[10]

At least, that was the plan. In fact, the researchers found that the children had a keen eye for spotting who was holding onto his or her candy. The kids tried to add up how much everyone had at the end of the experiment and probably carried on the surveillance as they left the classroom and went for their lunch break—where it would also be possible to punish free riders. Yet there are limits to the number of people you can keep your eye on at once, and this seemed to influence the children's public contributions. In large groups of twelve or more children, where boys and girls seemed able to keep track only of what their close friends had done, children put less than a third of their candy in the common pot. In small groups of between five and seven, it was possible to keep tabs on everybody, and children in these groups were more cooperative, putting a little more than half of their candy into the pot.

The size of a community has a big effect on how its members behave. Pathologically antisocial behavior is about twice as common in large cities as in small towns and rural communities. There's a similar difference in crime rates. In his book *Bowling Alone*, the sociologist Robert Putnam lists how people in small towns are more helpful, charitable, and honest than their big-city counterparts.[11] Small-town folk are more likely to give directions on the street and to return overpayment in a shop, less likely to cheat in their doings with officials, and less likely to repair a car when it doesn't need it. It might be that the antisocial types move to the city, leaving the honest folk behind (that's what a psychopath would do). But it seems probable that a small-town environment encourages good behavior partly because people are better able to keep tabs on one another, making it harder to escape one's reputation.

The number of people in a group isn't the only thing that affects how its members behave. Reputation flows through social networks, and the size and shape of a person's network have a massive influence on how that individual treats his or her reputation. It's no mystery what conditions make reputation powerful and encourage good behavior: transparency, accountability, and interdependence. Secrecy, impunity, and isolation do the reverse.

• • •

Two recent scandals illustrate this. In 2009, the expense claims of UK members of Parliament (MPs) were made public for the first time, after dogged campaigning by freedom-of-information advocates and dogged resistance by the MPs. (The claims were eventually leaked to a newspaper before they were officially released.) These revealed some of the things that the British public had been buying for its politicians. The then home secretary Jacqui Smith had claimed more than £150,000 for furnishing her second home with everything from two wide-screen TVs to a bath plug and, most notoriously, two pay-per-view porn movies watched by her husband. At the more aristocratic end of the political spectrum, the Conservative MP Douglas Hogg submitted a list of expenses for his country estate that included £2,200 for cleaning the moat and £40 for tuning the piano. He also claimed £20 for a toaster and £2.99 for garbage bags.

Why did they do it? Whatever their public image, it's hard to imagine that politicians are, on average, any greedier than other Britons. The problem was the MPs' environment, not their social preferences. They thought their claims were anonymous, so the voice of short-term self-interest drowned out the voice of reputation. Because most of their peers were doing the same thing—more than half of all MPs put in excessive claims, according to one official investigation into the affair—and no one outside knew about it, there seemed to be no reputational jeopardy.

If their actions become public, however, the population that politicians have to care about expands to practically every citizen. Every elected official relies on thousands of connections that reach beyond the political bubble, in the form of the voters who put her or him in office. When the claims for expenses were revealed—the stream of disclosures filled British newspapers and bulletins for more than a month—these connections became conduits of punishment, ranging from the legitimate rough-and-tumble of democratic life to death threats and hate mail against family members. Many MPs laid low, and one spoke of her fears that one of their number would commit suicide. Peter Viggers, who claimed £1,600 for a floating duck house for his garden pond, described himself as "ashamed and humiliated."[12] He was one of more than 120 who decided not to run for another term in the 2010 general election, which had the most retirements at any election since World War II. Jacqui Smith ran for reelection but lost her seat anyway. Attempts at reforming the expenses system have been criticized as feeble, piecemeal, and grudging, yet there has been a shift toward openness and accountability, and the emotional impact on MPs is undeniable.

In contrast, look at how investment bankers responded to the near-collapse and stratospherically expensive rescue of their industry in 2008. At the bottom rung, lenders granted mortgages with no regard for the borrowers' financial reputations. They then shed much of this risk by packaging the loans into financial instruments such as mortgage-backed securities, which vanished into an unfathomably complex and opaque network of deals and derivatives. When the loans went bad, these links became sources of contagion, rather than control. The banks took pains to keep their business in general private and created "special purpose vehicles" to conceal much of their risk. The financial ratings agencies, whose job it is to measure and broadcast the reputations of financial products and instruments, gave an unrealistically rosy view of the risks of trading in bonds related to subprime mortgages. Even ignoring fraudsters such as Bernie Madoff, who were able to operate in the information gap, this reputational vacuum made it impossible to know whom to trust; as the financial journalist Michael Lewis wrote in his book *The Big Short*, blind faith took trust's place.

When the scale of the problem and its consequences became clear, the drop in bankers' reputations among the wider public was every bit as precipitous as it was for British MPs. And yet judging from the bonuses they continue to reward themselves and their efforts to resist tighter regulation, they feel no need to repair the damage. The journalist Andrew Ross Sorkin has said that when he asked leading figures in the industry whether they felt any remorse, "The answer, almost unequivocally, was no."[13] Bankers, he says, see themselves more as "survivors" of the crisis than its cause.

British MPs could just as easily say the same—they were undone as much by their environments as by their characters. The reason, I think, for MPs' and bankers' differing emotional reactions to failure and opprobrium lies in the structure of their social networks. People in the financial sector, I suspect, have few ties to nonbankers and fewer still to people less well-off than themselves. They work long hours and socialize mainly with their colleagues. While politicians have to worry about their reputations with the public at large, bankers worry only about their fellow bankers and possibly about their equally wealthy neighbors. This gives people on the outside who have picked up the bill few ways of making their displeasure felt. Bankers undoubtedly care very much about what other bankers think of them, but they live in a transnational money-world, too remote from the rest of society for anyone else's opinion to matter very much—and within banking, the behavior that led to the meltdown was somewhere between normal and virtuous, so no need to feel bad. If bankers look like money-hungry psychopaths to many of us, that's because they don't need to care what we think.

Another thing that weakens the power that society can wield over the financial sector is that bankers tend to be rich. In a study of Greek herding villagers, Sally Engle Merry found that only the people in the middle worried about gossip, scandal, and what other people thought of them.[14] Those at the bottom had nowhere further to fall. If life looks as if it will be hard and short, there's no reason to worry about your reputation, and immediate gratification and the chance of a big score become rational choices. If you've got no future, it doesn't cast any shadow. Those at the top, on the other hand, did pretty much what they liked, oblivious to common notions of propriety, because their wealth provided an armor against any social or economic punishment the rest of the community might try to inflict. Reputation is strongest within a group of people who need one another and are on about the same level (and as we've seen, people have ways of keeping one another on the same level). In the village Merry studied, this made it primarily a bourgeois concern.

The chance to make a lot of money quickly is an obvious incentive to behave selfishly. The economist and writer Will Hutton blamed the 2008 banking crisis on huge bonuses that "trashed the need for individuals to worry about integrity."[15] Such people, he wrote, "don't need to be concerned about their reputations; they just need one deal or one year at the top and they need never work again." If you have deep enough pockets, you can spend your way out of a bad reputation, as the individuals, companies, and countries that buy their way to approval and support show. "I am ugly," wrote Karl Marx, hypothetically, in 1844, "but I can buy for myself the most beautiful of women. Therefore I am not ugly, for the effect of ugliness—its deterrent power—is nullified by money. I am bad, dishonest, unscrupulous, stupid, but money is honoured, and therefore so is its possessor." Money, he concluded, was the "universal agent of divorce," dissolving all human ties.[16]

Money is surely a temptation, a shield, and an alternative to reputation, but you can overestimate this aspect of its power. Experiments with the ultimatum game show that relatively large sums do not dissolve people's concerns for fairness, although it is obviously impractical for behavioral economists to work with the kind of sums handed out as bonuses on Wall Street. British MPs were willing to sell their reputations for a piffling return—one MP submitted a claim for a hot drink he had bought in the House of Commons tearoom. Mark Leary's experiments on self-esteem and the human sociometer showed that most people can't help but care about what other people think of them. In addition, status is relative: if everyone you know makes $20 million, walking away from the table with your $5 million will feel like failure in comparison.

Money's most potent effect on behavior probably comes not through its power to corrupt, but from its power to isolate, to cut people off from anyone in different economic circumstances. The effect of economic equality on social networks may be one of the causes of the corrosive (if controversial) effects of economic inequality on a society, regardless of its wealth.[17] As well as imposing the costs and anxieties of low status on those at the bottom of the heap, inequality severs social connections and splits a society into groups whose norms evolve separately and whose members cannot influence one another.

The problem in the financial sector was not that its members were willing to sacrifice their reputations if the rewards were great enough. It was that rewards and reputation had little to do with one another. We care about a person's reputation when what he does might affect us. In banking, the ways that fees and bonuses were decided, for both companies and individuals, made the incentives to take risks so much greater than the incentives to avoid failure that, coupled with the feebleness of government regulation and fines, it became quite difficult for anyone, regardless of how greedy, dishonest, or incompetent he might be, to do anyone else much damage. So bankers had little reason to regulate one another. In contrast, the British expenses scandal caused an electoral backlash against all mainstream politicians, so those who behaved badly took the innocent down with them, giving everyone a reason to reform.

In a prescient article written in 2005, Stanislas Yassukovich, a London banker with more than forty years' experience, wrote that investment banks caught using sharp practices saw any scandal as an advertisement, rather than an indictment, and noted that a Wall Street trader who was fired for losing a then-world-record amount of money was snapped up by a different firm days later. "Reputational risk is no longer a meaningful element of corporate policy, regardless of the lip service paid to it," he wrote. "For the practitioner, it is no longer a question of knowing right from wrong; it is a matter of knowing what you can get away with and what might be the cost of getting caught."[18] When the answers to these questions are, respectively, "plenty" and "not much," it's hard to behave well.

When we don't cheat, it is often because the environment, particularly our dependence on those around us, makes cheating the losing option. The challenge for governments is to reshape the environment in the financial sector so that bankers' self-interest and the public good are more closely aligned. If bankers could harm themselves when their decisions harmed society—or even better, if they could harm one another—they would police one another's behavior more keenly. Several banks have moved to paying a higher percentage of bonuses in shares that can be cashed in only after a number of years, to make their employees more concerned for the long-term health of their institutions. It might be even more effective if they were given shares in one another's companies, so that a fund manager was tending the bonus of the guy up the street. The social rewards for success and penalties for failure delivered by such a policy might make money's mad scientists think carefully before blowing up the lab. We could also put Kismet the robot on every trading floor and a pair of staring eyes on every computer desktop, just to be on the safe side.

It's not only bankers whose social networks aren't what they used to be. Robert Putnam's *Bowling Alone* describes the fraying of America's social connections in the last third of the twentieth century. This is reflected in declining membership of organized groups, such as labor unions, professional associations, PTAs, and bowling leagues, and informal connections, such as having dinner or playing cards with friends, neighbors, and family. At the same time, people became less trusting of strangers and developed a more jaundiced view of human nature (we tend to project our own traits onto others, so those who are least trusting are also least trustworthy, and vice versa). Low-level cheating, such as running stop signs, became more common. Most of this change is generational: since World War II, each succeeding cohort of Americans has been less sociable, less altruistic, and less trusting than the last.

Many of the factors that Putnam blames for this change are linked to increasing privacy and anonymity. For example, rather than causing a reversion to small-town ways, the move from the urban anthill into suburban seclusion seems to have had the opposite effect of making people even less connected. Putnam quotes the historian and philosopher Lewis Mumford's 1938 remark that "suburbia is a collective effort to lead a private life." Americans have left public transport for automotive privacy, spending an increasing amount of time traveling to work or anywhere else alone in the car. They have abandoned public and social leisure, such as movies and clubs, in favor of staying at home and watching TV. Even in public, we are more private. When the Sony Walkman launched, it had two headphone sockets, and advertisements showed people plugged in together, sharing an experience. Instead, personal stereos and their successors became a way to shut out the rest of the world.

No one did this in the pursuit of a more miserable existence. Technology and affluence have brought convenience, comfort, and self-sufficiency, particularly in leisure and transport. Privacy and mobility release social pressure, bringing freedom and possibility, more options, and the chance for self-expression and reinvention. Small communities where everyone knows your business, the past weighs heavy, and the window of acceptable behavior is small walk a fine line between being supportive and being stultifying.

Privacy and anonymity are appealing, because if no one knows what you've been doing, they can't use that knowledge to control you. Living outside society has an obvious appeal, and individual wealth, be it material, physical, or intellectual, has a concreteness and controllability that reputation lacks. If, when you meet me, you notice that I have huge biceps, a Patek Philippe watch, and/or a string of letters after my name, you know instantly that I am strong, rich, and/ or learned, and there's little that you or anyone else can do about it. Yet if I try to win your trust and harness your efforts toward a common goal, you'd be wise to get a second, third, and fourth opinion. My social capital belongs to other people, and that's scary. Loners and mavericks, who can live their lives without anyone else's help or approval, are powerful and charismatic fantasy figures. Homer made sympathetic and heroic characters of the warrior Achilles and the conman Odysseus, each of whom would probably have scored highly on a psychopathy checklist. Fiction has a taste for psychopathic antiheroes such as Tom Ripley, Hannibal Lecter, and Dexter Morgan, and real-life criminals can become folk heroes, such as the Briton Raoul Moat, who attracted more than thirty thousand people to the "RIP Raoul Moat you legend" Facebook group set up in his honor after he killed one person, wounded two others, and then shot himself in July 2010. There's something about freedom from others' opinions and influence that appeals, even if such people scare us in the flesh.

Without some means to control other people, however, we cannot trust them, invest in them, or work with them toward a common purpose. Without social contact, you can't get to know people directly, of course, and build up the bonds that enable reciprocity. Yet because people mainly talk about those who aren't there, you're also cut off from the supply of gossip that creates reputations, indirect reciprocity, and collective action. If you live a private life, you miss out on the chance to image-score your neighbors and to exchange small kindnesses with strangers, the kind of stuff that goes to make up a faith in humanity.

In sum, America is one of those societies—the United Kingdom is another—that has become less collective and cooperative and more individualistic and competitive. Surveys find that people have become less motivated by public service and more focused on material gain and self-fulfillment. It's tempting to blame governments for this trend, with Margaret Thatcher famously saying that there is no such thing as society, only individuals and families, thereby overemphasizing kin selection as a means for promoting cooperation. The unpopularity of the inheritance tax is another sign of a shift toward a society that sees kin selection as a more reliable basis for altruism than social ties are, and the unpopularity of taxes in general is a hint that we feel less responsible for one another's well-being. Yet although politicians such as Thatcher and Ronald Reagan were partly responsible for these changes, prioritizing private wealth over public goods, they were also following social and technological shifts that had cut people off from one another. If privacy and anonymity increase, reputation and cooperation grow harder to come by, so it makes more sense to shift from a cooperative outlook to a competitive one and put your faith in things you can hold for yourself. Then, if you see what you do to cope presented as a political philosophy, you vote for it.

How might we increase transparency, accountability, and interdependence? And how might we do so without invading privacy and making society less tolerant? Here are some of the options already practiced around the world. Each autumn, Norway publishes how much everyone in the country earned the previous year and how much tax he or she paid. The United States did the same until quite recently, and several states reveal the earnings of public employees. I spent an autumn in Santa Fe, in the New Mexico desert, during which the *Santa Fe Reporter* published a list of the city's top ten water users during the preceding summer. About half of these people made shamefaced promises to do better; the other half were unavailable for comment. A German welfare-to-work scheme has paid long-term unemployed families to get out of the house and attend evening classes or simply go to the cinema. In Japan, where people must sort their garbage into dozens of categories, garbage bags are transparent, so your neighbors can see whether you're recycling.

Of course, what seems reasonable in one culture seems intrusive in another. When Stockport Council in northern England tried to introduce transparent garbage bags, locals took it as a sign of government snooping—"1984 here we come," wrote one online commenter.[19] And many people would rather reveal the details of their sex lives than their income. This is a catch-22: if you don't trust your neighbors, you don't want to reveal yourself to them, but if you don't reveal yourself, you can't create trust. It's an additional argument for all of those good things that encourage people to live more of their lives in public, such as cheap and efficient public transport; safe and pleasant parks; subsidized arts events; low-rise, high-density housing on streets free of traffic; sports and exercise facilities; community gardens and allotments; even cafes, bars, and churches. What we know about reputation suggests that a strong public realm enables a kind of benign surveillance that, by connecting people to those around them, makes them behave better. Keeping an eye on someone or something implies both protection and control, as in "Can you keep an eye on my bike?" and "I've got my eye on you." Society works best when we keep an eye on one another.

But if, in the last half-century, technology has cut us off from one another, it's also created new ways for us to connect and new ways to use reputation to control one another.

CHAPTER 11

Panopticon 2.0

L anguage probably began as a way to spread gossip and has allowed us to discuss highly technical things, such as particle physics. The Web was invented as a way for particle physicists to share data and ideas and is stampeding in the opposite direction to become where the world goes to tittle-tattle.

That's no surprise. In the wild, people spend more time gossiping than they do anything else. As we devote more of our waking hours to online societies and communication, so the amount of electronic gossip grows, and the Web becomes primarily, like language, a medium for social interaction, rather than, say, a publishing platform or a commercial marketplace. In March 2010, the social networking site Facebook passed the search engine Google as the most visited website in the United States.

Although Google and Facebook might seem very different, they both rely on reputation. Facebook, along with Twitter, MySpace, and other social media, revolves around making and measuring social connections and creating prestige. These sites are tools for people to manage their reputations and to judge others. Google's search engine is an eavesdropping machine, detecting the links between websites and measuring their reputation by who links to whom. In fact, almost every major website uses reputation. EBay feedback ratings help buyers and sellers who know nothing about one another and may never interact again trust one another based on how they have treated others in the past. Amazon lets its users review its products and also rate its reviewers. Sites that aggregate and filter content, such as Slashdot and Digg, use reputation to help readers find the grains of wheat amid the endless plains of chaff. They reward the sharpest gleaners with kudos, rather than cash, as does Wikipedia. YouTube and Flickr use rating systems to bring the best videos and pictures to viewers' attention. Reputation regulates the Web, providing a legal system, a constitution, and an economic policy rolled into one, encouraging and rewarding some behaviors and proscribing and suppressing others.

Yet reputation online is different. Imagine that you moved to a moon base. Transported to a gravity only one-sixth of what you were used to, you'd have some exciting new abilities—you could jump higher and lift heavier weights than you'd ever been able to on Earth. Until your muscles adjusted, though, you'd also be forever bumping your head on the ceiling of your habitation module. The changed physics of your new environment would require some adjustment. Moving to online society is like that, except that instead of matter, it's the behavior of social information that changes, giving us new powers but also presenting new hazards.

A few million years ago, humans' invention of gossip added a verbal element to what had been a visual system. This made reputation longer lived in time and more mobile in space, allowing greater social complexity and cooperation. The Web turbo-charges both properties. Gossip spreads faster, farther, and wider than ever before, and it is recorded for everyone to see for all time. Yet it is also weaker, because it carries none of the biological cues and social context that we use, alongside what we say, to work out whether to trust one another. The Web might be the biggest thing that's happened to reputation since people started talking to one another, but living there takes some getting used to.

We started this book with the story of how Pierre Omidyar harnessed reputation, in the form of a feedback system, to promote good behavior on eBay. Around the turn of the millennium, academics at the boundary of economics and computer science began to wonder whether it worked.

In one experiment, Paul Resnick of the University of Michigan and his colleagues enlisted John Swanson, a well-established seller of vintage postcards on the site. Swanson prepared paired lots of post-cards, such as three dozen Valentines, that he thought were of equal value. Then he sold one lot through his established eBay identity, which at the time had more than two thousand positive ratings and only one negative, and the other through one of seven new identities created for the experiment, each with its own virtual storefront and e-mail address. This experimental approach avoids the problem of simply looking at eBay in the raw and seeing how feedback score compares with selling price. In the complex ecosystem of eBay, there might be a lot of confounding factors that affect success—the design of the seller's virtual storefront, for example, or the quality of his spelling.

In the controlled environment of the experiment—Resnick's team strove to make sure that feedback rating was the only significant differ-ence between the various sellers—good feedback paid off. Postcards sold under Swanson's established identity fetched an average of 8.1 percent more than the equivalent lot sold by the newbies. Buyers on eBay, it seems, really do use feedback ratings to guide their behavior, and a good reputation translates into cash.[1]

Omidyar's original idea of letting eBayers rate one another was an inspired move, but his system had weaknesses. Turning a seller's reputation from something created and held in the minds and the gossip of his clients into a label pinned on the seller himself made it far easier for people to artificially inflate their own reputations. Turning reputation into a number had the same effect. In the real world, we piece a person's reputation together from many sources. It's a bit like following your football team: you can go to games, watch them on TV, read articles and blogs, talk to other fans, listen to radio phone-ins, and build up a picture of their performance that's full of detail and subtlety. Online reputation is like following your football team by looking at the standings in the Monday paper. You can tell who's doing well but not why or how. Turning reputation from a narrative into a number, shorn of nuance, made it easy to cheat.

The result is that eBay is in an arms race with those seeking to game its feedback system. At first, anyone could give anyone else feedback for any reason—if they'd left a helpful comment on a message board, for example. This, Omidyar believed, would mean that a person's feedback score became a broad reflection of her contribution to the eBay community. This is similar to how we perceive reputation in real life—we recognize that people have strengths and weaknesses, but we generally either trust them or we don't. If you encounter people repeatedly and have many sources of information, you see the big picture of their behavior. In a large, anonymous world, however, where a person's reputation is boiled down to a score, it's difficult to know what that number means. Allowing unrestricted feedback meant that people could collude in inflating one another's score, swapping positive ratings back and forth until they looked like old and trusted hands.

In 2000, eBay changed the rules so that you could give feedback on a person only when you bought from or sold to him or her. This was the first in a series of changes that have made feedback more detailed. These days, each user's buyer and seller feedback can be viewed separately. There are also stars-out-of-five verdicts on factors such as whether the purchase arrived promptly and whether it matched the seller's description. Feedback is broken down over periods of a month, six months, and a year, revealing whether someone has been building up his or her rating and then exploiting it.

Making eBay feedback more detailed and specific has pushed feedback farmers to work harder but has not driven them extinct. Allowing only people who do business to swap feedback created a market in worthless items—jpegs, poems, jokes—sold solely so that the buyer and the seller can boost one another's score. In a 2006 paper, Jennifer Brown and John Morgan described the tactics of an eBay trader who inflated his or her reputation this way by selling jokes for a cent before moving on to selling parcels of undeveloped land in Texas priced at several thousand dollars each.[2] EBay prohibits this sort of feedback manipulation, but a search for "feedback" on eBay.com shows that the market is still there.

Along with creating new opportunities for cheating, having your image score pinned to your name creates new ways to be cheated. In 2008, eBay prevented sellers from leaving negative comments about buyers, as a way to encourage buyers to voice their gripes without fear of retaliatory feedback from the seller (more than 99 percent of eBay ratings are positive). Sites like eBay that display negative ratings are particularly vulnerable to malicious users, because such feedback is easily weaponized.

To give an example: I asked Randall Farmer for his favorite instance of gaming reputation systems. He has been working with online societies for more than thirty years, since he added real-time chat to a multiuser text adventure game based on *Star Trek* that ran on his high school's computer network, and he wrote the book, literally, on building Web reputation systems.[3] Farmer told the story of the Sims Mafia. The Sims is a computer game where people pilot avatars through an artificial world. The online version of the game allowed players to express their approval of one another, in which case the friend's face and a green arrow appeared in the player's social hub. They could also show dislike and distrust, in which case a red mark showed up in the same place. The Sims Mafia would approach new players and instruct them to hand over all of their Simoleons, the game's currency. When the victim asked why he should do such a thing, the extorter told him to look at his hub. Mafia members had filled it with red marks, making it impossible for the new player to form relationships or get a virtual apartment.

Turning reputation into a number encourages us to think of it as being like money, something to be accumulated and something that is good in all sorts of situations. This has led some people to try to create a true online currency based on reputation, a general and precise accounting of your social worth based on your own deeds and other people's ratings. The touchstone for such efforts is Cory Doctorow's 2003 science fiction novel *Down and Out in the Magic Kingdom*. Doctorow imagines a world where scarcity and death have vanished, so instead, wealth and access to luxuries depend on the esteem awarded by others, in the form of whuffie, a system inspired by Slashdot's karma ratings and named after a word Doctorow had used in high school.[4] The idea of whuffie has been a powerful meme, and several attempts have been made to turn it into the reality of a portable and universal online reputation.

Yet the only people who truly treat reputation like money are hustlers, who build up a name for being one thing, and then cash in their reputations by revealing their true, fraudulent selves. Reputation can't be spent, only destroyed. It's not a medium of exchange; it's more like an energy or a force of nature, something that we direct and distort. A person with an eBay score of 1,000 isn't twice as trust-worthy as someone with a score of 500. He's probably just been on the site twice as long.

Efforts to create a generalized measure of online reputation are built on an assumption of prestige bias, our tendency to think that because a person is good or bad in one regard, he or she is the same in others. Yet the lesson of successful online reputation systems—or at least, their first fifteen years—is that they work best when they are most tightly focused on doing one particular job and on regulating and manipulating one particular aspect of human behavior. Online reputation is a pencil-thin beam, picking out one small aspect of behavior, not a floodlight illuminating a large space in which many things can happen. That's one important difference between online and old-style reputation and one possible limit on what can be achieved in online societies. You wouldn't recruit someone to your World of Warcraft guild based on his eBay feedback, and it's doubtful whether your credit score reveals anything besides your creditwor-thiness, even though several employers have sought to use it to make hiring decisions.[5] Numerical ratings of trustworthiness, unlike dollars and euros, do not convert easily from one form into another.

This limitation arises because online society is unbiological. We think that the Web drowns us in information, but as a conduit of gossip it's thin. Turning reputation into a number gives it an air of precision, but in fact online reputation systems capture far less social information than the stories we create in the real world. Systems such as eBay's turn the emotions of the person doing the rating into a number, combine that number with ratings from other people, and attach the resulting number to the person being rated. The system's users turn the rating back into an emotion, which they act on. In the flesh, people read and exchange emotions expertly and without thought, but turning emotions into numbers and back again is an imperfect art, with the potential for noise and distortion at every step. Even when we exchange words online, we lose all of the information we unconsciously extract from the look on a person's face and the tone of her voice, making it much harder to judge her seriousness and honesty.

Online relationships are also unbiological. We are used to, and we evolved into, a society where people lived close together for long periods and interacted with and depended on one another in all kinds of ways. We had experience of people's previous judgments, achievements, biases, and allegiances and a mutual interest in a continuing relationship to understand and trust one another. We formed friendships, in other words. If we want to, we can separate different strands of reputation—someone might be a great cook but have terrible taste in music. Yet the people I interact with on eBay can't have that sort of relationship with me, and they can't find that type of broad-spectrum information even if they want to and even if it is of some use to them. If I was a shopkeeper and treated my customers badly, life in my hometown would become difficult, but I can be a hopeless eBay trader, a brilliant Amazon reviewer, a mediocre Digger, and so on, without any one having much to do with the other. Until online communication and friendship become a lot more like real life—which, with increasing speed and bandwidth of communication, they may do—online reputation will stay limited.

One appeal of social networking sites such as Twitter and Facebook is that they import some of the benefits of real life into online society. Embedding electronic relationships in a social network makes them more biological, and so makes it easier for relationships to develop and for people to trust one another. Recommendations and opinions flowing out of a social network will probably be much more trustworthy and useful than naked information plucked from the fog of the Web. If you see a rave restaurant review online, for example, it might come from the head waiter's sister; a brickbat might originate from the restaurant next door. If you're already connected to the information's source, it's easier to judge that information's worth. Reducing anonymity and increasing social stability allows reputation building and the trading of favors. This promotes cooperation, albeit with the downside of making online identities easier targets for cyber bullies and stalkers.

EBay feedback is a public good. It takes a small amount of time and effort to create, and the benefit goes to the rest of the community, not to the person who left it—she, after all, already knows about that particular eBayer. The benefit of feedback also goes to eBay, which, like any site that exploits user-generated content, aims to turn other people's unpaid activity into private profit. A few sites pay for feedback—the review site Epinions shares its income with its best reviewers, and in 2010 Amazon started the Vine program, which allows the best reviewers to get their hands on early versions of products for free. Most of what's online, though, was created entirely for free, showing that people are motivated by plenty of things besides cash, and reminding us that lab experiments that deal only in cash reveal just a slice of human behavior. From book reviews to blog entries to Wikipedia articles to YouTube videos to open-source software projects such as the Firefox browser, the Web brims over with content and software created by people for nothing. Or at least, for something other than money. What might that be?

When we discussed conspicuous generosity and competitive altruism, we saw that young men seem to contribute to online file-sharing as a way of showing off. It's a risky form of helping that acts as a costly signal, displaying their technological capabilities and social intentions. Legitimate websites can't offer the incentive of illegality, but they can exploit costly signaling and indirect reciprocity by harnessing people's desire to appear good and helpful. In doing so, reputation systems have helped fertilize an outpouring of creativity and altruism, so that we now take it for granted that nearly anything you want to know, hear, or see can be found online for free.

If you ask people what they get out of online altruism, the answer is egoboo, as the digitally hip call the warm glow of having done good and useful things online.[6] You could also call it pride or self-esteem, an internal reward for being socially useful. Most people who write open-source software or review products say that they do so for the pleasure of being altruistic, not because they are trying to make a name for themselves. Yet this doesn't mean that they're not boosting their reputations in the process.

Some online reputation systems try to reward and encourage (and milk) a site's users by increasing the amount of egoboo they receive for their work. Just about any site whose job is to filter or recommend has some form of reputation system, used to rate both the content on the site and those doing the rating. Get enough karma points on Slashdot, and you can become a moderator, moving stories to more or less prominent positions on the site. Amazon publishes a ranking of those whose work the site's users rate as most useful. These systems are beginning to create minor celebrities, such as Andrew Sorcini, who under the username MrBabyMan developed an almost supernatural knack for knowing what stories the visitors to Digg, the social news aggregator, will like best.[7] Harriet Klausner, the most prolific book reviewer on Amazon, has been profiled in both *Time* and the *Wall Street Journal*.

This seems like a win all around. Digg and Amazon get a huge amount of added value; Sorcini gets slightly famous; Klausner gets sent publishers' latest titles; and the rest of us get steered toward the best books and news stories. Something similar happens in the open-source software community, where working on public projects for free advertises your programming skills to those handing out the paid work (it also encourages other people to help you solve your own programming problems). Yet this sort of reputation system has pitfalls and perverse incentives and is just as vulnerable to manipulation as those where hard cash is at stake. Again, developing a formula for measuring one person's online behavior that reflects what the rest of us value is a constant challenge.

Reputation systems such as Amazon's and Digg's are popularity contests, mixed with a soupçon of a video-game high-score table. Perhaps the correct sporting analogy for such contests isn't football but the Tour de France. When you look at who's in the lead, you hope that the standings reflect honest endeavor, but it's hard to escape the suspicion that some of the leaders might be cheating. Klausner, the Lance Armstrong of online book reviewing, has attracted suspicion and ridicule for her ability to read and review seven books a day. Digg removed its league table of Top Diggers in 2007, because, in an echo of the eBay experience, it was thought that groups of users were colluding to puff one another's recommendations and so climb the rankings. (In 2010, it also temporarily removed users' ability to vote down stories after it was shown that a group of activists were colluding to bury political stories they didn't agree with.)

Partly, people try to game reputation systems because anything time consuming or effortful can be a costly signal. This means that any time you rank an activity, getting to the top becomes a costly signal, and some people become obsessed with sending it. "Friend hoarding" on social network sites, for example, where people link up with anyone and everyone, would be a lot less common if these sites didn't display your number of friends so prominently. If you set up the world blinking championship and offered a paper cup to the winner, some people would enter, and some entrants would squirt Tabasco in their eyes in search of an unfair advantage.

Yet there are also more concrete benefits to be had. If a publication can get its stories high up on Digg, the extra traffic will translate into extra advertising revenue, and some people have been willing to employ middlemen to organize just such a boost using paid Diggers. There are now marketing companies in the business of targeting the "influentials" in social media—those whose opinions carry the greatest weight—and paying them to plug a particular product, a reminder that private benefits might corrupt public contributions, as well as promote them.

In contrast to the eBay approach of helping people judge one another more accurately by making more and more data available (in the same way that every season brings new sports statistics), many status-driven reputation systems are guarded by their opacity—security through obscurity, as it's called. Making it harder to work out how a system calculates its rankings means it's more difficult to manipulate, albeit at the cost of being less transparent and thus harder to trust. Slashdot no longer displays its users' karma, because the type of behavior that runs up a high karma score isn't the kind of behavior that's best for the community as a whole. Sites such as YouTube, Digg, Flickr, and Amazon keep the criteria by which they rank their users and their contributions secret, making them harder to manipulate.

None of this is a sign of failure. Just as companies face different demands and need different strategies as they grow and mature, so online reputation systems need to reflect changes in their communities. When a site is small and trying to attract users and encourage participation, rewarding and ranking activity are useful incentives—a league table of total contributions will get everyone pitching in and competing to climb the rankings. Plus, as we've seen, it's easier to keep track of everyone's reputation (scored or otherwise) in a small community. As the site grows, however, quality and freshness and keeping out malicious users who are drawn to a large audience become more important than sheer quantity. If you rank people on their lifetime activity, the top of the leader board will soon become set in stone, with the leading users running up such vast scores that new contributors are discouraged. So online reputation systems have to balance the benefits of the loyalty that comes from rewarding long service with the advantages of allowing reputation to decay—as it does in the real world, where you can hope your embarrassments will fade and where you can live on past glories for only so long. This allows new users to make a mark and discourages old ones from resting on their laurels.

In 2008, Amazon did just this, changing the way its top reviewers are calculated to give more weight to recent reviews; to reward the quality of a reviewer's work, based on the percentage of positive comments her work receives from other users, above the number of reviews she posts; and to discount "fan" voters, who repeatedly laud a particular reviewer's work. The site didn't junk the old rankings, though, because that would have made the old reviewers very unhappy.

Instead, it has split its rankings. There's the new table and a "classic" format, which displays the total number of reviews and positive ratings. Klausner, who has written more than twenty-three thousand reviews, reigns atop this in likely perpetuity.

Those who design online reputation systems must try to balance the strong and weak points of online social interaction. There's no one right answer: various reputation systems aim to manipulate behavior in different ways. One system might try to create trust and curb cheating. Another might encourage people to create public resources. A third might try to convert showing off and competition into some wider benefit. A fourth might be a labor-saving device, providing a shortcut to a good decision. Online, reputation is refracted and refined. It's a source of social energy that software engineers can harness as a mechanical engineer might use coal or flowing water—and if it's not handled carefully, it can be as destructive to social constructions as fire and flood are to buildings. The wrong reputation system can sink an online community. Reputation systems also offer new ways for fraudsters and information warriors to subvert and corrupt reputation, creating an arms race between designers and users who wish to use reputation for the good of their group and those who try to game the system for their own selfish purposes.

All online reputation systems seek to counter the property of online life that most undermines reputation and good behavior: anonymity. When you're at your computer, none of the cues exist, such as eyes, that we use to monitor who knows what about us. The shedding of inhibitions that ensues can have good consequences, allowing people to discuss and share their problems and predilections without shame. Yet anonymity does not encourage good manners, as anyone who reads online comment threads will know.

Besides hiding yourself online, it's also easy to assume fake or multiple identities. If one fraudulent eBay persona is caught and expelled or dragged down by a bad reputation—what's been called karma bankruptcy—it takes only a moment to fire up another one and begin again.

There are so many different ways to attack reputation through fake online identities that the behavior has developed its own vocabulary. "Concern trolls" are the online equivalent of worried celebrity friends: they enter online discussions posing as fans of sports teams or politicians they actually despise and try to undermine them with weasel words. "Astroturfing" creates fake grass roots, with companies paying people to pose as private citizens on blogs and discussion boards. "Sybil attacks," named after the psychiatric case of a woman with multiple personalities, create multiple accounts. These are then used to attack or boost a site—again, Digg has been a target—or a point of view, as in the mysterious case of the bogus network of stem-cell researchers set up on Facebook. Several authors have been embarrassed to be caught using fake online identities to praise their own efforts and lambast rivals, something known as "sockpuppeting."

Again, though, these attempts to manipulate reputation reveal the mismatch between online society and our social instincts. People are experts at pretending to be themselves. After millions of years of practice, managing our identities and showing the world our most flattering side comes naturally, but pretending to be someone or no one else does not come naturally at all. Working out whether you've revealed enough online to be identified is a new social problem and not one that we are good at. Yet another Web-spawned neologism entered the language in 2002, when Heather Armstrong, a Web designer in Los Angeles, found herself unemployed thanks to comments she made about her colleagues on her blog, dooce.com. The list of people dooced because their uncomplimentary blog posts were less anonymous than they imagined continues to grow.

It's hard to imagine people running this sort of risk in the real world, amid the warning signs that help us protect our reputations. Take sockpuppeting. It's impossible to know how many writers have done it successfully, but that doesn't make it a smart thing to do, any more than the fact that you might get away with stealing gum nine times out of ten makes the free gum worth the risk of a shoplifting conviction.

A successful sockpuppeter gains the benefit of a slightly higher Amazon rating, a slightly more positive comment thread, or a slightly more flattering Wikipedia entry. He runs the risk of, at best, ridicule: the combination of Google and negativity bias means that the critic Lee Siegel will always be associated with describing himself as "brave, brilliant, and wittier than [Jon] Stewart will ever be" on the *New Republic's* forum, while the historian Orlando Figes will be the man who used Amazon to describe his own book as "beautiful and necessary" and his rival's as "dense" and "pretentious." At worst, the sockpuppeter will go to jail. Raphael Golb was convicted for online harassment in November 2010, after abusing academics who disagreed with his historian father's views on the origin of the Dead Sea Scrolls.

The biggest concern with online society, however, is not that it bestows a patchy and difficult-to-gauge degree of anonymity but that it destroys privacy. More and more of our pasts are recorded and accessible to everyone, forever. Perhaps, given what we know about the power of scrutiny to promote good behavior, this will bring about a golden age of civility.

Being in public, though, is not the same thing as losing your privacy. Facebook founder Mark Zuckerberg has noted that humans are hard-wired to be interested in people. Yet that wiring evolved in a particular environment. We are well adapted, through culture and biology, to a world of gossip and policing. We understand how to manage these forces and the kinds of demands they place on us. This is why being in public makes us behave better. We are less well adapted to a world of eavesdropping and spying, where it's harder to know what information is on display and what isn't, and where it's more difficult to manage our reputations. Like songbirds, we will send our messages without knowing who might be listening from the undergrowth. And like birdsong, we will need to account for the effects of eavesdropping in the message. People are already adapting: they tell fewer lies when using permanent and easily forwarded e-mail, for example, than they do when conversing face-to-face or by telephone or instant messenger.[8]

In some situations, a reduction in anonymity can work wonders: commercial fleets that put "How's my driving?" stickers on their vehicles, together with a phone number where other road users can comment on the driver, see accidents drop by roughly half. Inspired by such examples, Lior Strahilevitz, a law professor at the University of Chicago, has argued that technology can "transform loose-knit environments, where reputation often fails to constrain antisocial behavior, into close-knit environments, where reputation constrains misbehavior more effectively."[9]

Strahilevitz advocates applying this to everybody and everything, envisaging smartphones evolving into wearable computers that carry a whuffie-like record of our behavior and transmit it to others nearby. This, he suggests, will counter statistical discrimination (otherwise known as stereotyping), where groups are disadvantaged because their members carry higher average risks for certain kinds of behavior. He gives the example of African Americans' difficulties in getting doctors to prescribe painkillers, because medics risk prosecution and prison if the drugs end up on the black market. Electronic reputation, Strahilevitz suggests, will make it easier to see people as individuals and treat them fairly and harder for conmen to escape their reputations.

The combined power of camera phones and the Web to expose bad behavior has already led to sites such as Ihollaback.org, which posts photos and reports of men who harass women in the street. Dontdatehimgirl.com and iparklikeanidiot.com are self-explanatory. Yet as well as bringing benefits, monitoring behavior in this way has its limits and pitfalls. There's the possibility that people will try to inflate their ratings or that such systems will be used maliciously. As long as no one makes the mistake of giving his or her system a Sims-style hub of hate, though, it can be designed to defend against weaponized feedback, by throwing away extreme ratings, for example. The human complications are harder to fix.

For a start, the person exposed needs to actually feel shame at what he or she has done. The Hollaback movement against street harassment began in New York in 2005, when Thao Nguyen, a twenty-two-year-old Web designer, photographed a man masturbating across from her in a subway car and posted it to *Laundromatic*, a feminist webzine. The image spread around the Web and onto the front page of the *Daily News*. The flasher turned out to be Dan Hoyt, a raw-food chef and restaurateur with a previous conviction for lewd display. He was arrested for the latest offense and given two years' probation, but he seemed unabashed, telling *New York* magazine that "I've met women who enjoy it," and that if Nguyen had met him under different circumstances, "she'd probably want to go out with me."[10]

Sites like Hollaback let women connect, communicate, and publicize issues; let men know what women have to deal with; and give women a sense of control and the power to punish. Online gossip, like its real-world counterpart, is a useful weapon against those who abuse their physical, financial, or political power, be they sexual harassers, violent police, unethical corporations, or hypocritical politicians. The potential for exposure is growing all the time. Google is working on incorporating face-recognition software into its image searches, so that once you've snapped the man who flashed you on the bus, you can work out who he is, find his Facebook page, and inform his friends.

At least at present, though, it's more doubtful whether the punishment actually reaches the culprits and shames them into reforming. Cyberfeminists and sexual harassers probably have little in the way of shared social connections and norms—some men would probably regard an appearance on a harassers' website as a badge of honor. So it's hard for social pressure and reputation to spread from one group to the other. It's been suggested that by making it easy for like-minded folk to find one another, online society balkanizes social groups. Raw-food eater speaks only unto raw-food eater, creating an echo chamber where people tell one another what they want to hear and in the process become intolerant of any other viewpoint. At school, at work, and in our neighborhoods, in contrast, we are thrown together with people and have to make some effort into getting along with them, even if they're not exactly like us, helping us become more tolerant.

There are other problems with relying on online social connections to channel reputation. Few of us view public masturbation as a delicate question of etiquette, but most of us would acknowledge that there are many social situations where right and wrong can't be judged, to borrow from eBay feedback, as $+1$ or -1. The evidence from reputation systems in online societies is that electronic communication and monitoring are most effective and fair when they aim to regulate behavior in limited, narrow circumstances, where acts, not people, are being judged and the definition of good behavior is obvious and universally accepted. At present, the same goes for using technology as a reputation delivery system to regulate offline behavior. Dangerous driving is a good example of such a situation, because everyone knows what it looks like, and it's difficult to excuse. Others might be less common than they first appear—when I came across Howsmynanny.com, I was glad that I don't have a "How's my parenting?" telephone number on my back allowing bystanders to expose my short-fused and butter-fingered moments. The more complicated and subjective the social situation, the more problematic online feedback becomes: users of online dating sites report that they are more likely than any other group to find embarrassing or inaccurate things about themselves online.

Just because online reputation works best when tightly focused, this doesn't mean that's how people will use it. Social networking sites actually make it harder to compartmentalize your life, because they create links between groups, such as family, friends, and colleagues, that had little previous overlap. Online anonymity also makes people judgmental and aggressive, and there are multiple instances of people whose small crimes—plagiarizing a term paper or stealing a mobile phone—have brought down a torrent of online vitriol on their heads. Get caught on YouTube doing something silly, and you're in for a tsunami of snark, such as Ghyslain Raza, aka the Star Wars Kid, who videoed himself wielding a golf-ball retriever as if it were a light saber. Raza's schoolmates put the video online, where it has since been viewed more than 900 million times. He changed schools and needed psychiatric help.[11]

Privacy is more like an amenity than a right. It's something we can build into our lives if we have the inclination and the technology (that is, a house with walls and separate rooms). It also depends on how much other people want to pry into our lives, and how they judge our attempts to reveal or conceal what we are up to. Various societies around the world have very different attitudes toward the acceptability of privacy. As the language researcher John Locke has noted, there are many groups where anybody not in view is assumed to be up to no good. He quotes the anthropologist Gillian Feeley-Harnik's study of the Sakalava people of Madagascar: "To stay alone in the house is considered a sure sign of evil intent. . . . Secrecy and separation indicate at best a lack of generosity, a suspiciously anti-social striving for distinction."[12]

In the West, online society is reshaping our norms, creating tensions and trade-offs between free speech and privacy, social connection and autonomy, and self-expression and good manners. Webster's word of 2008 was "overshare," inspired by what looks like people's eagerness to throw their privacy away before anyone has a chance to wrench it from them.

What might appear to be excessive self-disclosure isn't necessarily a misjudgment. For young men in particular, recklessness can be strategic. A group of French researchers asked more than twelve thousand Internet users what type of photo they would put up on their profiles. They found that young men were more likely to pick a picture that featured some combination of nudity, theatricality, physical activity or risk, drunkenness, and so on.[13] At least some young men seem to use their social networking profiles in the same way that they use fast cars and illegal file-sharing—as costly signals of physical and mental strength, of having resources so great that they can be abused. Evolutionary biologists call this the handicap principle, the idea being that the signaler shows that he is in great shape by doing dumb things and getting away with it. Using mock profiles, another team of researchers found that when they put comments about drunken antics on a man's Facebook wall— "WOW were you ever trashed last night!"—he became better looking in observers' eyes.[14] For women, the reverse was true, showing that the medium has changed, but the sexual double standard remains the same.

Youthful oversharing isn't just about getting laid. Young people are establishing their identities, forming alliances that will last a lifetime, and competing for status. We share information about ourselves and others, so that the people we share it with will like and trust us, and we gather information about others so that we can decide whether to befriend or belittle them. To tell someone a secret is to give that person something valuable and to put yourself in his or her power.

Besides the release from inhibitions caused by the sense of anonymity, another reason that people overshare online is, I think, because social information is relatively less powerful there than it is in face-to-face relationships. In the real world, simply being with someone is a sign of your commitment to that relationship. The other person knows you value him or her before you say anything. Online, we lack that element of relationship building, so we overcome it by accelerating the exchange of information, building a bond by offering more intimate details. One study found that "A-list" bloggers, with more than a hundred inbound links from other blogs, tend to reveal more about themselves than the average blogger does.[15] Another found that the more information you gave about yourself on Facebook, the more friends you had, because people were able to work out that you had similar backgrounds or liked the same sort of things.[16] The same relative weakness of online social links might partly explain why online criticism tends to be so vituperative. We don't have anything but words with which to punish those we disapprove of, so we escalate our verbal attacks.

Hiding too much is as socially damaging as revealing too much — but what constitutes too much is always changing. It may also be that people are learning to manage their reputations not by hiding their embarrassments but by revealing them and so, by taking control of the story, reducing the incident's gossip value and capacity to inflict damage. If you put something out there yourself, it's harder for others to turn it against you. The increasing difficulty of keeping secrets has already caused some corporations to opt for "radical transparency," where they use tactics such as employee blogs to reveal the details of decision-making and the missteps along the way. Individuals are going the same way.

The flexibility of human attitudes toward privacy and our ability to adapt to new social conditions make me relatively relaxed about the effect that online interaction and exposure will have on our social lives. Some people will be more skilled than others, and some will get hurt, but that has always been true. As we know more about one another, our judgments will change, because certain kinds of information will no longer be distinguishing or useful. As British MPs and investment bankers have shown, if everybody in a group is doing a thing and knows it, it becomes normal, not shaming. People are learning how to shape their communication to protect their reputations—by orienting their Facebook profiles toward activities that will impress university admission tutors, rather than peers, for example.[17] A survey conducted by the Pew Internet and American Life Project, published in May 2010, found that those whom they called millennials, ages eighteen to twenty-nine, were more likely than any other age group to have posted things online that they regret and more likely to have found something embarrassing or inaccurate about themselves.[18] Yet they were also the most careful curators of their online personae, more likely to have asked someone else to remove information about them, more likely to customize the privacy settings on social networking sites, and least trusting of the companies that run the sites.

The threat comes, not from revealing ourselves to one another and the gossip and flaming that might result—Ghyslain Raza made it to law school—but from revealing ourselves to corporations and governments who know more about us than we know about them. Already, 35 percent of U.S. employers admit to rejecting a job applicant after looking at his or her social networking site.[19] Companies are providing profiles summarizing a person's online activity, and revealing yourself on one site can allow you to be identified on another, even if you've been using it anonymously. One might hope for legal changes, so that, as with our medical records, certain areas of our lives become off-limits to the powerful, but this seems unlikely to happen and hard to enforce. More probable is a technological and behavioral arms race between individuals and institutions about what traces we leave online.

Arthur C. Clarke is usually seen as a technological visionary, but he also had some thoughts about evolution. In his 1953 novel

Childhood's End, the world's children lose their individuality and become part of a pan-galactic entity called the Overmind. Speaking as someone whose teenage years are recorded in half a dozen reels of film, and who can remember waiting for Web pages to load on the Mosaic browser, it seems that we are currently living through a mild version of this. To quote the writer Susan Maushart, media use has become "pervasive, invisible, shrink-wrapped around pretty much everything kids do and say and think."[20] Digital natives are always plugged into the network and into one another, and the distinction between online and offline society gets less meaningful by the moment.

In Clarke's novel, the leap to complete social interconnection leads to humanity's extinction and the Earth's destruction, but it often looks as if we're achieving this quite nicely with our current, nongalactic version of sociality. Our species faces problems of collective action and tragedies of the commons that threaten to undo the work of millennia of cooperation. Reputation has helped tackle these problems within our groups. Can it work for the world?

CHAPTER 12

Us and Them

W hen Richard Alexander was growing up on a farm in Illinois, decades before he began to think about evolution, human behavior, and indirect reciprocity, his mother would take the family to a small church in, he says, a "town that disappeared." Each week, the preacher finished his prayers by asking God to bless all of those present and all of those in the congregation who were too ill to attend. "I used to sit there as a little kid," Alexander says, "and think, Wow, he sure is limiting things."

That priest was handing down a lesson about human nature. People are sociable and cooperative—but not to everyone. We are nicer to members of our own tribe, faith, or nation than to outsiders. Cheating or persecuting a member of your own group tends to be a consequence of desperation or psychopathy. Yet when groups come into conflict, over land, food, water, mineral resources, or religion, altruistic humans will treat one another savagely, provided they believe their victims are from a different group. Before people try to destroy one another, they label them outsiders.

The urge to favor members of our own group is so deep-seated that it doesn't need shared interests or ideals or history. It can kick in any time people are divided into groups on any basis, however slight. The study of our instinct to discriminate was pioneered by the psychologist Henri Tajfel, a Polish-born Jew, most of whose family was murdered by the Nazis. In a classic paper published in 1971, Tajfel and his colleagues describe their experiments with what have since become known as minimal groups.[1] Tajfel asked a classroom of British schoolboys, around fifteen years of age, to make an arbitrary judgment. In one experiment, he asked them to guess the number of dots flashed up on a screen. Then he split the boys into overestimators and underestimators. In another, Tajfel showed them paintings by Paul Klee and Wassily Kandinsky and created groups of Klee fans and Kandinsky lovers. In fact, both experiments ignored the boys' decisions and assigned them to groups at random.

Minimal groups seem ridiculous. Their members never meet. They don't know who else is in their group. The group lasts only as long as the experiment, and membership offers no benefits or drawbacks. But for Tajfel, that was the point—minimal groups allowed him to separate the fact of group membership from everything else that influences how we treat one another.

Once the minimal groups had been created, each boy was sent into a room on his own and asked to divide up some money between two other boys who were identified only by numbers. When a boy was dividing money between two members of the same group, be it his own or the other, he tended to divide the cash as fairly as possible. But when asked to divide the money between someone in his own group and a member of the other group, the boys chose the distribution that maximized the difference between the two groups, thus putting their own—anonymous, arbitrary, and evanescent—team as far ahead of the other as they could.

People, Tajfel concluded, define themselves as both "I" and "we," as both individuals and as members of various groups. This sense of social identity, as he christened it, drives us to make comparisons and create differences between our own group and others and to promote our group's interests at outsiders' expense. Because our group holds part of our identity, treating it well or treating other groups badly makes us feel better. Here, perhaps, is the seed of prejudice that in the wrong social and political environment can bear horrific fruit.

Since then, many other studies have replicated Tajfel's finding that people prefer their own group, even when that group is minimal.

Yet to say that people want to feel good about their groups is like saying that people want self-esteem because it feels nice or want to eat chocolate cake because it tastes good. What do we gain from targeting our altruism toward a member of our own group? The answer, once again, seems to be reputation.

Toshio Yamagashi, a psychologist at the University of Hokkaido in Japan, has done many studies on minimal groups, typically dividing people using Tajfel's Kandinsky versus Klee test and getting similar results. He can also make this bias disappear.

Yamagishi and his colleagues do this by manipulating what people know about one another's identity. For example, in some experiments each player had to choose what proportion of 100 yen to give to her partner. The experimenters doubled the money en route, so two trusting players who handed over all of their money each got 200 yen, but there was also the temptation to sit tight and exploit the other person, in the hope of ending up with 300 yen.

When both players knew they belonged to the same minimal group, the average contribution was about 30 yen. When they both knew they belonged to different groups, this dropped to 20 yen. However, when a player was told that she and her partner were in the same group but that her own group identity would remain a secret, she became much less generous and parted with an average of 24 yen, which was statistically indistinguishable from the result for different groups.[2]

If people favor their own groups because they feel warmly toward them and want them to do well, this shouldn't have happened. It shouldn't matter who knows which group you belong to. Instead, Yamagishi and his colleagues believe that people favor members of their own groups because the group is an arena where favors can be traded by direct and indirect reciprocity. "[G]roup categories are simply containers of various forms of social interactions; what matters is what is inside the container, not the empty container per se," they wrote.[3] Behaving altruistically toward group members is the price of entry into the container, but if no one else inside can see your ticket, there's no point in paying for it. Your group identity evaporates, taking its effects and consequences with it. Similarly, Manfred Milinski and his colleagues have found that if you create connections rather than sever them, and tell people in a group how a new member behaved towards his previous group, then reputation promotes cooperation just as it does within a group.[4] These experiments show how information can overcome prejudice, but the researchers also worked hard to make all other things equal. Outside the lab, other things are not equal, and people's groups are far from minimal. Prejudices are rooted in history, culture, and gossip. A stereotype is a form of reputation; like an individual's reputation, it serves the people who hold it more than the people it is attached to, and it can bear little relation to actual behavior.

In Tajfel's original experiment, the boys dividing up the cash didn't know who was rewarding them, but they still showed favoritism. This, Yamagishi believes, is because in-group favoritism gets activated any time a person knows he is in a group, and it takes conscious effort and definite information to override this behavior. Group living and reciprocity are such ancient, universal, and essential aspects of human life that unless you're told otherwise, being biased in favor of the people in your group is the best rule of thumb. It's much safer to assume you are in a cooperative but judgmental group and so treat its members well than it is to risk being kicked out of that group for not paying your dues. By having the boys pass money among themselves, Tajfel created an illusion of group life. In other experiments, however, Yamagishi's team has found that in-group bias disappears if you remove reciprocity and interdependence. If you pay people a flat fee for taking part in an experiment, for example, rather than tying their earnings to how other subjects behave, they become group-blind.

Another experiment by Yamagishi and his colleagues shows how easy it is to activate the sense of being held accountable by your group.[5] The researchers divided subjects into Klee and Kandinsky groups and then had them play a computerized dictator game, dividing 900 yen with an unseen partner who did not know which group the dictator belonged to. In anonymity, dictators treated in- and out-group members the same and kept hold of most of the money. This changed, however, if there was an eyespot picture on the computer desktop—in this case, a menacing glare wearing the tigerlike makeup used by actors in the kabuki theater (borrowed from a crime-prevention poster used by the Tokyo Metropolitan Government). The eyespots were enough to trigger in-group bias: dictators were still unwilling to share with a member of another group, but they became significantly more generous toward a member of their own group. Those eyes seem to have triggered a sense that the rest of the group was watching and judging.

We favor our own groups, in other words, because those are the people we depend on and answer to, so those are the people we need to think well of us. Two people lacking social connections care much less about each other's opinions and fates. One thing that drives people to exploit other groups is the freedom from reputation. If you meet a member of another group and treat him or her well, people in your group will not reward you, because they will not come to hear of it, and those in the beneficiary's group will not reward you, because they will not get the chance. If your groups are in conflict, your own group might view the exported altruism as treachery. Your reputation stops at the edge of your group, which is why, like anonymous benefactors, those who help members of other groups can seem especially noble. The point of the parable of the Good Samaritan is that the Samaritan's charity crossed group lines, aiding a Jew despite the animosity between their peoples.

Should Michael Bay ever film the New Testament, he can give this scene more oomph, while still preserving its essence, by having the Samaritan arrive on the scene earlier and beat up the robbers. That's because punishment, like cooperation, also struggles to cross the group divide. In another experiment that combined the dictator game with an opportunity to pay for punishment, Yamagishi found that punishers directed their fire inward, investing more in punishing uncooperative members of their own group than they did in punishing cheaters in another group.[6] Punishers also felt a greater sense of anger and injustice toward cheaters from close to home than toward those from a different group.

• • •

A team of researchers led by the economist Ernst Fehr, whose work on altruistic punishment and strong reciprocity we encountered in chapter 6, carried out a similar experiment in the mountains of Papua New Guinea, where many different tribes live in various states of tolerance and hostility.[7] The experimental subjects came from two groups, the Wolimbka and the Ngenika, which were neutral toward each other—not at war but not in close contact. Again, they played a third-party punishment game. Two people played the dictator game—that is, one player decided whether to split some money with the other—and then a bystsander was given the chance to punish.

When all three players came from the same group, punishers were hard on unfair dictators. But if the dictator and the punisher came from one group and the recipient the other—so that, say, a Wolimbkan's decision was whether to penalize, at his own expense, another Wolimbkan for treating a Ngenikan unfairly—dictators gave less and punishers punished less. Dictators suspected correctly that a member of their own group would spend less on fining them for maltreating a member of another group. Likewise, if a Wolimbkan was placed in judgment over two Ngenikans—so that his decision was whether to spend money on doing another group's policing—he spent less on punishment, because why should he care if members of the other group treat one another unfairly? As social distance increases, the probability declines that other people's behavior will affect us, and so does our willingness to do something about it. A mugging in your neighborhood might shake you more than a massacre in a faraway country. The limit of your group is the point at which what you do stops being anyone else's business and the point at which what other people do stops being your business.

The logic of prioritizing members of your own group for punishment is clear enough. Punishment is costly, so to make it worthwhile you need to get something back, such as a reputation as a public-spirited avenger or better behavior from the punished person. Yet without having regular contact with the person you've punished or with the audience that saw you do it, you'll get neither.

Both Yamagishi's and Fehr's studies of punishment also threw up some surprises, though. In Yamagishi's, the players who gave least to their own group spent the most on punishing the other group. This could be, the researchers suggest, because these selfish players were driven not by moral outrage but by competitiveness and wanted to increase the income gap between themselves and others, a bit like the schoolboys in Tajfel's original experiment. In support of this idea, when punishment could not be used as a means to create inequality—that is, when its cost equaled its impact, so that each yen spent on punishment deprived the target of just one yen—such out-group punishment almost vanished.

This result suggests how societies might enhance the power of punishment. Punishments, it seems, will be most effective not when they are harshest or most humiliating, but when they seem to come from within an offender's own community, from the people he is closest to. The Australian criminologist John Braithwaite has contrasted "reintegrative shaming," which strengthens the ties between the offender and society and so encourages him back into the fold, with "stigmatic shaming," which severs those ties and pushes him further beyond the group. This idea underpins what's called restorative justice, where offenders confront the consequences of crime by meeting their victims, thus building social connections—even just making eye contact—with those they have harmed. Offenders in such schemes also talk about how their actions affect their own families and friends, thus emphasizing their existing social connections. This approach seems to be a particularly effective way of reducing recidivism. On the other hand, a potential weak point of shaming punishments, such as making thieves stand outside shops they have robbed wearing sandwich boards advertising their crimes or making prison work parties wear garish clothing, is that they are stigmatizing and are usually administered from on high by people with no connections to their target. The object of such punishment might feel more attacked than ashamed.

It's easy to forget that the best reason to invest in punishment is to change behavior, not to make wrongdoers suffer or gratify the law-abiding (Thomas Aquinas believed that one perk of heaven was the chance to watch the damned suffer). It seems obvious, yet it's often not the way we use punishment. We'd be better off if criminals felt as if they were a part of everyday life, not of the criminal underworld, or if classroom troublemakers felt common cause with the good kids, not with the other naughty kids. Yet when we deal with people who make our lives difficult, we tend to emphasize their differences from the rest of us. Reputation research suggests this is often exactly the wrong decision. Ostracism—which is what prison or expulsion is— should be a last resort, because to cast someone off is also to cut him loose. Once a person (or a group or a country) goes beyond the pale, with no connections to others who have different standards and with no chance of redemption, self-interest gives him or it no reason to do anything other than behave selfishly.

The experiment in Papua New Guinea also uncovered an unexpected enthusiasm for punishing members of other groups. Fehr and his colleagues expected little punishment when the dictator was from one group and the recipient and the punisher from the other. In this situation, the dictator is not violating any norm by being mean, because people aren't expected to be generous across the group divide. Yet in fact, punishers treated meanness in this situation even more severely than they did when all three players belonged to the same group. This pattern of punishment is hard to explain in terms of either individual benefit to the punisher or the kind of group effects predicted by strong reciprocity. Perhaps, the researchers mused, by coming down hard on an outsider who wrongs a member of your own group, the punishers were seeking to deter attacks from outside. If this was the case, these Papua New Guineans' behavior fell neatly within several millennia of thinking about how deterrence works.

Adam Smith understood the links between social contact, reputation, and behavior well. In his *Lecture on the Influence of Commerce on Manners*, he wrote,

> Where people seldom deal with one another, we find that they
> are somewhat disposed to cheat, because they can gain more
> by a smart trick than they can lose by the injury which it does
> their character. They whom we call politicians are not the

most remarkable men in the world for probity and punctuality. Ambassadors from different nations are still less so: they are praised for any little advantage they can take, and pique themselves a good deal on this degree of refinement. The reason for this is that nations treat with one another not above once or thrice a century, and they may gain more by one piece of fraud than lose by having a bad character.[8]

One trait, though, that countries have always strived to display to one another is resolve. For as long as we have records, groups have worried that if they back down in the current confrontation, their other enemies will take note, think them weak, and be more likely to attack. In his *History of the Peloponnesian War*, written in the fifth century BC, the historian Thucydides wrote that his fellow Athenians conquered the Melians partly to avoid appearing weak to others who might challenge their empire. America's involvement in Cold War conflicts was often driven by concerns for its reputation. "We lost thirty thousand dead in Korea, to save face for the United States and the United Nations, not to save South Korea for the South Koreans," wrote the economist Thomas Schelling in 1966, "and it was undoubtedly worth it."[9] A year earlier, John McNaughton, an academic whom Schelling had recommended as an adviser to the U.S. Defense Department, had written a memo to secretary of defense Robert McNamara stating that the main motivation for U.S. military involvement in South Vietnam was "to avoid a humiliating U.S. defeat (to our reputation as guarantor)."[10]

More recently, President Bill Clinton argued that military intervention in the Balkans would deter ethnic cleansers elsewhere, and in 2006 President George W. Bush argued that withdrawal from Iraq would "embolden the terrorists and help them find new recruits."[11]

Individuals value honor and resolve in situations where they must defend themselves without help from the wider community. A nation can't rely on any other country's coming to its aid when attacked, and there is no international police force to enforce norms and punish transgressions. The principal features of international relations are often said to be anarchy and self-interest. That sounds a lot like a culture of honor, so it's not surprising that states have always placed such a value on appearing resolute.

Since the Cold War ended, however, scholars have become much more skeptical about whether deterrence actually works. Some, such as Jonathan Mercer of the University of Washington, have argued that when two states find themselves in conflict, the concerns of the present—namely, how strong each party is, and how much they value what is at stake—take precedence over each party's previous record.[12] Mercer analyzed a series of confrontations between European powers in the years leading up to World War I and found that during each crisis, the past had little bearing on the present. International confrontations, in effect, become one-shot games. The past teaches nothing, and the glare of the moment destroys the shadow of the future, because if you make the wrong move, you might not have a future. Nations are consequently more likely to break their international commitments when most is at stake.

Some studies go even further and seem to turn the entire logic of deterrence on its head. Toward the end of 2003, Mark Crescenzi, who studies international relations at the University of North Carolina, was trying to get hold of a *Toy Story* DVD as a Christmas present for his son. The only place it seemed available was on eBay, which at the time was still a new and unusual place to shop. Dipping his toe into the online marketplace, Crescenzi was interested to see that each seller had a feedback rating summarizing his or her previous behavior. At the time, Crescenzi was trying to work out how mathematical models might be used to analyze how history influenced nations' dealings with one another. Mathematical modeling has been used in political science since the 1930s, but models have usually dealt with interactions between two states at one point in time, because the alternative—working out who's watching who and what they make of it—is so complex, it's difficult to know where to start. Crescenzi thought that if he could devise some version of eBay feedback for countries, he might be able to open the picture outward and actually measure the effect of reputation in international relations.

Crescenzi was fortunate in that his colleagues had already collected the data on which such scores could be based. Since the 1960s, several large databases have been developed that seek to collect information on international interactions in a numerical form. The Correlates of War Project, for example, founded in 1963, seeks to render every "militarized interstate dispute" since 1816 (just after Napoleon left the stage) in a numerical form, giving it a ranking of 0 for an incident resolved without any military activity through to 5 for a full-blown war, with troop maneuvers, warning shots, and similar skirmishes ranking somewhere in between.

Crescenzi and his colleagues built a model that took every possible two-state interaction between 1817 and 2000 and, using the data on militarized disputes, analyzed what made war more likely.[13] Sharing a border increased the chances of armed hostility, as did a previous history of conflict between two states. Less intuitively, however, the model showed that when two countries square up, war is more likely if either has a history of fighting other nations. Reputation does seem to matter, but not in the way predicted by the conventional view of deterrence. If a country shows a willingness to fight, its international audience sees it not as resolute but as aggressive, and thus treats it with greater hostility and distrust. It chimes with the view revealed in experiments on individuals and tribes that punitive action from beyond the group is seen not as punishment but as attack and thus provokes a different emotional response. In some senses, this isn't surprising: if you go around starting fights, Crescenzi's study says, you'll get into more fights. It does suggest, though, that whatever nations gain by fighting, it isn't deterrence.

At least, that's what the numbers say. Crescenzi's models reveal a statistical trend that suggests that reputation is a factor in the background of how countries deal with one another, one of many things that together push two nations into or away from a fight. Direct historical evidence of a particular war triggered or prevented by reputation is hard to come by—leaders are keen to trumpet their own countries' reputations for resolve but seldom invoke another nation's reputation as a reason for their policy toward it. Crescenzi does believe, however, that writings from the early 1950s show that U.S. policy toward the Soviet Union in the early years of the cold war was motivated by diplomats' observations of how Stalin's regime oppressed its own citizens.[14]

In some areas of international life, reputation works exactly how you'd expect it to. The economist David Tomz analyzed government borrowing on international bond markets between the mid-eighteenth and early twentieth centuries. He found that countries that defaulted on their debts (such as Greece) had to pay higher interest on future borrowing, and those that kept up payments even in bad times—such as during the global depression of the 1930s—were rewarded with lower rates.[15] The leaderless, self-interested lenders in the international bond market can do little to force states to honor their debts, but reputation gives them immense power.

Since Adam Smith's time, people, money, goods, and information have become ever more mobile. The international connections that this mobility creates have made international reputation a more powerful force. In 1990, the international relations expert Joseph Nye emphasized the growing importance of what he called *soft power* to describe a nation's ability to wield influence through attraction, giving people an example to follow and things they value, in contrast to the military hard power that states have always used to get their way. Hard and soft power correspond exactly to the concepts of dominance and prestige that we've encountered repeatedly throughout this book.

Yet states and other players on the world stage, such as multinationals, are much less willing than individuals to treat others in one area based on how they behave in another. Tomz, for example, found that nations rarely, if ever, used punishment, in the form of military force or trade sanctions, to help their creditors collect from foreign governments. Rather, countries have many reputations, both in terms of how other countries see them—what the United States does looks different depending on whether you're viewing it from the United Kingdom or from North Korea—and in terms of the various aspects of their behavior.[16] In Chile during the 1970s, the military dictatorship of Augusto Pinochet overturned a democratically elected government and abducted, tortured, and murdered its opponents. But the country's reputation for abusing human rights had little impact on international investors. They were more concerned with its reputation for economic stability, which the junta enhanced by returning assets that the previous regime had nationalized.[17] How Chileans treated one another was of small concern to self-interested members of other groups, and in general, the international community seems not that bothered about how a country treats its own citizens or environment, as long as it is a trustworthy and rewarding partner in direct inter-actions such as trade. It looks as if a nation has got to do something glaringly unjust, on a par with apartheid in South Africa, before its reputations start to bleed into one another.

This apparent lack of crosstalk between different aspects of reputa-tion is reminiscent of how reputation behaves in online society. As on the Web, international dealings create relationships and dilemmas that the social tools provided by biology and culture have never had to deal with before, ones in which the broad sweep of friendship is replaced with a set of nonoverlapping interests and interactions—for eBay, Amazon, and World of Warcraft, you could read trade agree-ments, human rights, and arms-control treaties. In such a situation, we can't expect reputation to work in the same way that it does between neighbors.

This is bad news for anyone hoping to address the international issues, such as fisheries and climate change, that most resemble a public-goods game and in which a tragedy of the commons looms. Manfred Milinski's experiments and similar theoretical work have shown that for individuals, reputation points a way out of these dilemmas by translating public virtue into private benefits. Those who work for the common good are rewarded, and those who cheat or free ride are punished. Yet countries are unwilling to punish one another for free riding and do little to reward one another's virtue.

Combine this with the facts that free riding becomes easier in larger groups, that people who belong to different groups are less likely to cooperate, that humanity confronts climate change without the benefit of a threatening out-group to drive us together, and that rich countries are being asked to change their behavior not to fix a stark and present wrong—as was the case, for example, with the movement to abolish slavery—but to benefit unborn people in distant countries, and you can see why international climate negotiations are such a shambles. Yet the repeated failure of negotiations is a perverse testament to the power of international agreements—if they were meaningless, countries would sign up and then break them with impunity. Countries tend not to sign treaties they don't intend to honor, and most of them honor most of their commitments most of the time. In a world of anarchy and self-interest, this is hard to explain, but reputation seems to be a big part of why nations keep their promises. The more trustworthy they appear now, the more others will trust them in the future. Mark Crescenzi, for example, has found that countries that honor their current alliances find it easier to attract future allies, and vice versa.[18]

To bring our better natures to bear on the problem of building global cooperation, we need to repeat the trick that language and the Web achieved, of increasing the spread and longevity of social forces such as reputation. Online, despite the problems of anonymity and unaccountability, people have been ingenious about harnessing different aspects of reputation to create trust, altruism, and cooperation. Climate change is a good test case for whether reputation can work on a global scale, because it is difficult and pressing and because it is so similar to the well-studied public goods game, with free riding and cheating threatening a common good.

Evolutionary theorists spend their days trying to work out how cooperation might arise in a world of cheats, and how it might persist despite the short-term advantages of cheating. Never in their models does this happen by a mass conversion to altruism—which is essentially what, for example, the 2009 Copenhagen negotiations were seeking. Instead, cooperators appear in small numbers and manage to find one another. Stable environments where your neighbors remain the same help this process because it's easier for cooperators to build long-term relationships.

As far as climate change goes, the seed of cooperation is already present, in the form of the many who care about the problem and are willing to do something about it. There's some evidence that reputation can help spread and reward this norm. Milinski did an experiment where he alternated a public-goods game, in which players contributed to a common pot, with an indirect reciprocity game, in which players could pass money to one another. This setup should be familiar, except that in this case the common pot was not divided among the players: it was used to buy an advertisement in the *Hamburger Abendblatt* newspaper warning of the dangers of climate change and the importance of reducing fossil-fuel consumption. Milinski found that players donated more to the common pot when donations were public, and that generous players were rewarded in the intervening rounds of private business.[19]

In most laboratory public-goods games, the common resource is the group pot of money. It's easy to see why players reward those who contribute to this, because the generous ones are sharing money with other group members. Milinski's experiment shows that public-spirited behavior improves your reputation even when you contribute to a far more diffuse and distant common resource, in the form of the atmosphere. This is perhaps not so surprising: if you are an environmentally concerned and active citizen, chances are that you already reward similar people and businesses with your friendship and patronage. What was most remarkable in Milinski's experiment, though, was that players who didn't pay into the climate fund rewarded players who did. People seemed willing to reward public-spirited deeds that they didn't themselves support.

Perhaps this is because public generosity was seen as a costly signal, a general demonstration of wealth, intelligence, and social conscience, so other players curried favor with the generous even if they didn't care about climate change. This competitive side of altruism is particularly useful in the case of climate change, because it gives altruists benefits even in a world of free riders. Environmentally friendly products are costly signals—there's some evidence that such products are more popular precisely because they are more expensive and less effective than the conventional alternatives. Vladas Griskevicius, a professor of marketing at the University of Minnesota, and his colleagues found that undergraduates' consumer choices became greener when they were primed to care about status, when they imagined shopping in public, and when the environmentally friendly option was more expensive. This, they suggest, might be why Toyota sold more Priuses when it put the price up.

Costly signaling isn't foolproof. British engineers have criticized "eco-bling," in the form of expensive and ostentatious wind turbines and solar panels that, while being an accurate signal of wealth, don't do much to reduce a household's emissions. When consumption is the problem, conspicuous consumption, even of eco-friendly products, isn't the solution. The problem is that the key word is *costly*—the point is the expense, not the result. This makes costly signaling vulnerable to changing norms and economics: a few hundred years ago, being fat was a sign of wealth and status. Now, calories are cheap, and people spend their time and money on trying to get thin. Unfortunately for any appeal to costly signaling, the most environmentally friendly option, of not sending the signal—not taking the flight, not buying the car—is often taken as a sign of low status.

Even so, costly signaling, by leaders anxious to show both their virtue and their wealth, could also be a potent force on the international stage. The European Union, Japan, and Canada were all motivated partly by concern for their reputations to sign up to the Kyoto Protocol on carbon emissions and, in doing so, sent a signal to the rest of the world.[20] In any cooperative endeavor, if you wait for everyone to join in before starting, you'll wait forever. That's just reiterating what we understand about how cooperation spreads. Yet if, for example, one country in Western Europe (the most likely candidate) could begin to reshape its economy in a low-carbon direction, envy and shame might drag much of the rest of the European Union in a similar direction. If this led to the European Union collectively agreeing to meaningful reductions in carbon emissions, its leaders would get colossal bragging rights at world gatherings. Because the EU is a clique, where nations deal more with one another than with outsiders, member states would be interacting with other cooperators more than with free riders, limiting their losses. I have a fantasy of a global environmental potlatch, where the world's leaders demonstrate their might through the depth of their generosity. It's possible that this isn't a complete pipe dream: cities are increasingly competing with one another on a global scale to be pleasant, vibrant, and hip places to live and visit, via costly signals such as Frank Gehry buildings and Olympic bids. Just as the bourgeoisie are most concerned about how their behavior affects their standing in society, however, reputation matters most for the countries in the middle, who want to maintain or improve their standing. At either end of the scale, reputation isn't so influential. Somalia and the Democratic Republic of Congo have enough trouble coping with the present, and China and the United States can expect to wield influence no matter how they behave.

Sometimes, though, what looks like a costly signal turns out to be just cheap talk: many companies plant a few trees somewhere obvious while carrying on destructive business as usual elsewhere. And countries' grand promises made at summits can slip into free riding once the spotlight moves on, as shown by the failure of many rich nations to meet their Kyoto targets and aid pledges. The gap between words and deeds revealed by national backsliding and corporate greenwash is the perfect environment for cynicism, which, by dismissing appearances and assuming bad intentions, devalues reputation. Public commitments are useful hostages to reputation, but it seems that at present the hostages aren't valued enough.

All of the evidence for individuals suggests that the power of reciprocity needs to be backed up with punishment if nations and corporations are to pay their reputational ransoms. For individuals, to quote the evolutionary psychologist Geoffrey Miller, poking gentle fun at your conspicuously consuming neighbors is your public duty. For groups, the picture is more problematic. As Miller points out, the weapons of human social behavior, such as shaming and ostracism, are useless against faceless, mindless institutions run by people with no social connections to those who would hold them to account.[21] The legal scholar Joel Bakan has said that the behavior of corporations can appear psychopathic (although consumer "brands" tend to care deeply about their images, even if they're part of a larger corporation).[22] The same goes for governments, but this probably isn't because governments or corporations are run by psychopaths. It's because the conditions that breed cooperation are missing—indeed, giving a company a legal obligation to maximize returns to its shareholders, come what may, practically builds psychopathy into the system.

On top of this, nations are unwilling to inflict material punish-ments on international cheats and free riders for fear of damaging their own interests. Like online reputation, international reputation seems to work best in a targeted, limited sense and to be most influential with regard to issues, such as economics and the environment, that aren't matters of immediate life and death.[23] Perhaps this is the best we can hope for when trying to use reputation in new and unnatu-ral situations. Groups regard external punishment as an act of aggres-sion, rather than as censure, and may, at least in the short term, be more likely to retreat into a siege mentality than to reform. Yet per-haps there's a place for cheap social rewards and punishments that yield a high return in pride or shame. Sports, as one of the few things that everybody in the world seems to pay attention to, is an ideal vehicle for this. In the early 1970s, the United States improved relations with China by sending table tennis players there to get thrashed. This gave Chinese pride a great boost and did little or no damage to America's self esteem. Similarly, one of the most obvious signs of South Africa's pariah status was its ostracism from international cricket and rugby. Perhaps every time the Canadian ice-hockey team leaves its Kyoto-reneging, tar sand–mining homeland to play abroad, it should skate out onto a rink awash with several inches of symbolic slush.

Sporting punishments also have the advantage that individuals and teams from different nations interact with one another on more or less equal terms. If one team doesn't show up, it doesn't matter how good the other is. In most international interactions, in contrast, the various players wield hugely varying clout. Powerful nations work to preserve their advantage, which rarely involves giving less powerful nations the means to hold them to account. Thucydides's observation still holds: that "right, as the world goes, is only in question between equals in power, while the strong do what they can and the weak suffer what they must."[24]

The prospect of using social punishments to create international altruism is not entirely hopeless. Powerful nations don't like to be exposed as hypocrites. For example, once the U.S. government put pressure on Bayer to lower the price of its antibiotic Cipro follow-ing the anthrax attacks of 2001, it was hard for the country to go on opposing cheap retrovirals being used to treat HIV in the developing world. A deal duly followed. Yet this "shaming and taming," as the political scientists Kelly Greenhill and Joshua Busby call it, requires a particular set of circumstances.[25] One of these is public commitments by leaders that can then be used against them. Another, even more important, is public engagement. Leaders are more worried about their image at home than abroad, because these are the people with most power over them. So international action is unlikely without domestic pressure, backed up with the threat that failure to contribute to the public good will be punished at the ballot box. On climate change, this pressure is lacking, giving leaders another reason to do nothing.

Above all, international cooperation needs international connections along which to spread. The more contact people have, the more cooperative with one another they become. The more isolated a nation, the more likely that its leaders' concern for their in-group reputation will trump any consideration of their international reputation. The more hostile to outsiders a nation's citizens feel, the less kindly they will view a leader who seems to give too much away to foreigners. The most isolated nations are the least concerned for their international reputations, the least cooperative, and the least trustworthy. One value of international institutions, such as NATO or the World Trade Organization, is that they are social gatherings where the community of nations can gossip, observe one another, develop norms, and enter into the long-term relationships where reputation and reciprocity flourish.[26] Activists and nongovernmental organizations are similarly forming a web of international networks that has been dubbed global civil society. Yet none of this will gain any traction without a more general sense that we all belong to the same group.

The Web, of course, is fantastic at connecting people, and there's excitement about online society's power to catalyze collective action such as the revolutions of the Arab Spring. The role of social networking sites in social change is still unclear, however, and it's probable that for a network to become a movement, with the courage and sacrifice that this entails, it still requires tight, face-to-face bonds between people.

There's also some tentative but hopeful experimental evidence that things might be moving in this direction. The economist Nancy Buchan and her colleagues looked at the effects of globalization on cooperation.[27] The researchers got people living in six cities on five continents to play the public goods game. Each player had three options: keep the money for herself, put it into a pot that was doubled and divided among three other players from the same place, or put it into an international account that was tripled and divided among twelve players from around the world. The global account thus offered the highest potential returns, as long as everyone put in the same amount, but it also required the most trust, because the common resource was spread so much more thinly.

Buchan found that people from the most globalized countries, measured by factors such as foreign trade, migration and tourism, Internet access, and diplomatic contacts, contributed the most to the global pot. (From the most globalized city to the least, this was Columbus, Ohio; Milan, Italy; Kazan, Russia; Buenos Aires, Argentina; Johannesburg, South Africa; and Tehran, Iran.) Within a country, the most globalized individuals, measured by factors such as whether they watched foreign movies, whether they made international phone calls, and whether they worked for multinational companies (putting aside the objection that multinationals might be the enemies of global public goods in many other regards), were the most willing to trust people in other countries and put their money in the international account.

Admittedly, these suggestions and positive signs look wishy-washy, more like a list of reasons we will fail to preserve the planet's public goods than any kind of a playbook for helping the project along. Almost everything we need to do goes against the forces that make people more likely to pick the altruistic option. We need to get a vast group, which is itself divided into different groups with competing interests and wildly unequal starting points, to agree to pay a cost now to benefit people in distant places and generations who cannot thank them or punish them. Here, in contrast, is what's pushing in cooperation's favor: an attachment to virtuous showing off and a wish not to be cursed by our grandchildren. So we need to make cooperation's forces work as hard as we can.

In his book *The Biology of Moral Systems*, written when nuclear war seemed like the biggest threat to civilization, Richard Alexander pondered how to achieve détente and disarmament. His words apply equally well to all of the current and future threats to our societies. "The problem," he wrote, "is one of inducing between and among societies the same processes of moralizing pressure and democratization that have developed so intricately within them." To put it another way: not so long ago, Alexander was driving through Michigan and passed a small country church much like the one he used to attend as a boy—except outside was a notice board reading, "God bless everyone: no exceptions." That's the gap we need to cross, he thought—from blessing everyone in our group to blessing everyone. Reputation is the human power to bless and curse. It lets us aid and control one another in ways that no other species can and so has helped us achieve things that no other species has. We need to find ways to broaden reputation's reach still further.

ACKNOWLEDGMENTS

One thing that researching and writing this book has brought home is that people generally achieve things not because they defeat their competitors but because they have help. My work is no different.

I began thinking about a book on reputation in the autumn of 2007 while visiting the Santa Fe Institute. It is the most beautiful and intellectually luxurious place I've ever been lucky enough to work in, and I shall always be in debt to the people who work there for their hospitality and ideas, especially professor Geoffrey West, who invited me.

I would also be unable to do what I do without researchers' willingness to take the time to explain their thinking to a stranger. I am grateful to all who responded to e-mails or granted interviews, and especially to those who read and commented on draft chapters: Quentin Atkinson, Mark Crescenzi, Daniel Fessler, Nicole Hess, Kevin Laland, Hassan Masum, Peter McGregor, Manfred Milinski, Karl Sigmund, Daniel Silverman, Eric Smith, and Jessica Tracy.

My agent, Jim Levine at Levine Greenberg, and editor, Eric Nelson at Wiley, both put a lot of work into the book at various stages, and it is better for their efforts. It is a pleasure to work with both of them.

I am fortunate enough to receive large quantities of kin-selected altruism from my mother and father. Science has yet to explain why my wife, Sara, is so nice to me, but her love and support makes writing books and all other things possible.

NOTES

Introduction

1. Cohen, A., *The Perfect Store: Inside EBay* (Boston: Little, Brown and Company: 2003).
2. "Feedback," eBay.co.uk, http://pages.ebay.co.uk/services/forum/feedback-foundersnote.html.
3. Smith, A., "Lecture on the Influence of Commerce on Manners," reprinted in Klein, D. B., ed., *Reputation: Studies in the Voluntary Elicitation of Good Conduct* (Ann Arbor: University of Michigan Press, 1997), 17–20.
4. Craik, K. H., *Reputation: A Network Interpretation* (New York: Oxford University Press, 2009).

1. Follow the Leader

1. Coolen, I., Y. V. Bergen, R. L. Day, and K. N. Laland, Species difference in adaptive use of public information in sticklebacks, *Proceedings of the Royal Society of London*, Series B: Biological Sciences 270, 2413–2419 (2003).
2. Valone, T. J., From eavesdropping on performance to copying the behavior of others: A review of public information use, *Behavioral Ecology and Sociobiology* 62, 1–14 (2007).
3. Coolen, I., O. Dangles, and J. Casas, Social learning in noncolonial insects? *Current Biology* 15, 1931–1935 (2005).
4. Dugatkin, L. A., and J. J. Godin, Reversal of female mate choice by copying in the guppy (Poecilia reticulata), *Proceedings of the Royal Society of London*, Series B: Biological Sciences 249, 179–184 (1992).
5. Uller, T., and L. C. Johansson, Human mate choice and the wedding ring effect, *Human Nature* 14, 267–276 (2003).

221

6. Jones, B. C., L. M. DeBruine, A. C. Little, R. P. Burriss, and D. R. Feinberg, Social transmission of face preferences among humans, *Proceedings of the Royal Society of London*, Series B: Biological Sciences 274, 899–903 (2007).

7. Place, S. S., P. M. Todd, L. Penke, and J. B. Asendorpf, Humans show mate copying after observing real mate choices, *Evolution and Human Behavior* 31, 320–325 (2010).

8. Gilbert, D. T., M. A. Killingsworth, R. N. Eyre, and T. D. Wilson, The surprising power of neighborly advice, *Science* 323, 1617–1619 (2009).

9. Olsson, A., and E. A. Phelps, Social learning of fear, *Nature Neuroscience* 10, 1095–1102 (2007).

10. Henrich, J., and F. J. Gil-White, The evolution of prestige: Freely conferred deference as a mechanism for enhancing the benefits of cultural transmission, *Evolution and Human Behavior* 22, 165–196 (2001).

11. Rendell, L., et al., Why copy others? Insights from the social learning strategies tournament, *Science* 328, 208–213 (2010).

12. Giraldeau, L., T. J. Valone, and J. J. Templeton, Potential disadvantages of using socially acquired information, *Philosophical Transactions of the Royal Society of London: Series B: Biological Sciences* 357, 1559–1566 (2002).

13. Coolen, I., A. J. Ward, P. J. Hart, and K. N. Laland, Foraging nine-spined sticklebacks prefer to rely on public information over simpler social cues, *Behavioral Ecology* 16, 865–870.

14. Van Bergen, Y., I. Coolen, and K. N. Laland, Nine-spined sticklebacks exploit the most reliable source when public and private information conflict, *Proceedings of the Royal Society of London*, Series B: Biological Sciences 271, 957–962 (2004).

15. Boulinier, T., K. D. McCoy, N. G. Yoccoz, J. Gasparini, and T. Tveraa, Public information affects breeding dispersal in a colonial bird: Kittiwakes cue on neighbours, *Biology Letters* 4, 538–540 (2008).

16. Dugatkin, L. A., Genes, copying, and female mate choice: Shifting thresholds, *Behavioral Ecology* 9, 323–327 (1998).

17. Duffy, G. A., T. W. Pike, and K. N. Laland, Size-dependent directed social learning in nine-spined sticklebacks, *Animal Behaviour* 78, 371–375 (2009).

18. Horner, V., D. Proctor, K. E. Bonnie, A. Whiten, and F. B. M. de Waal, Prestige Affects Cultural Learning in Chimpanzees, *PLoS ONE* 5, e10625 (2010).

19. Amlacher, J., and L. A. Dugatkin, Preference for older over younger models during mate-choice copying in young guppies, *Ethology Ecology & Evolution* 17, 161 (2005).

20. Yorzkinski, J. L., and M. L. Platt, Same-sex gaze attraction influences mate-choice copying in humans, *PLoS ONE* 5, e9115 (2010); Waynforth, D., Mate choice copying in humans, *Human Nature* 18, 264–271 (2007).

21. Walther, J.B., B. Van Der Heide, S. Kim, D. Westerman, and S.T. Tong. The role of friends' appearance and behavior on evaluations of individuals on Facebook: Are we known by the company we keep? *Human Communication Research* 34, 28–49 (2008).

22. Ryckman, R. M., W. C. Rodda, and M. F. Sherman, Locus of control and expertise relevance as determinants of changes in opinion about student activism, *Journal of Social Psychology*, 88, 107–114 (1972).
23. Bauer, G. P., R. S. Schlottmann, J. V. Bates, and M. A. Masters, Effect of state and trait anxiety and prestige of model on imitation, *Psychological Reports* 52, 375–382 (1983).
24. Plath, M., S. Richter, R. Tiedemann, and I. Schlupp, Male fish deceive competitors about mating preferences, *Current Biology* 18, 1138–1141 (2008); Bierbach, D., et al., Male fish use prior knowledge about rivals to adjust their mate choice, *Biology Letters* (2010), doi:10.1098/rsbl.2010.0982.

2. An Introductory Offer

1. Smith, E.A., R. B. Bird, and D. W. Bird, The benefits of costly signaling: Meriam turtle hunters, *Behavioral Ecology* 14, 116–126 (2003).
2. Sell, A., et al., Adaptations in humans for assessing physical strength from the voice, *Proceedings of the Royal Society of London*, Series B: Biological Sciences, doi:10.1098/rspb.2010.0769.
3. Lyle, H. F., and R. J. Sullivan, Competitive status signaling in peer-to-peer file-sharing networks, *Evolutionary Psychology* 5, 363–382 (2007).
4. Sylwester, K., and G. Roberts, Cooperators benefit through reputation-based partner choice in economic games, *Biology Letters* 6, 659–662 (2010).
5. Raihani, N. J., and T. Hart, Free-riders promote free-riding in a real-world setting, *Oikos* 119, 1391–1393 (2010).
6. Van Vugt, M., and C. L. Hardy, Cooperation for reputation: Wasteful contributions as costly signals in public goods, *Group Processes & Intergroup Relations* 13, 101–111 (2010).
7. Lyle, H. F., E. A. Smith, and R. J. Sullivan, Blood donations as costly signals of donor quality, *Journal of Evolutionary Psychology* 7, 263–286 (2009).
8. Burkitt, L., "Companies' Good Deeds Resonate with Consumers," Forbes.com (2010), www.forbes.com/2010/05/26/microsoft-google-apple-ford-cmo-network-most-inspiring-companies.html.
9. Barclay, P., and R. Willer, Partner choice creates competitive altruism in humans. *Proceedings of the Royal Society of London*, Series B: Biological Sciences 274, 749–753 (2007).
10. Boehm, C. *Hierarchy in the Forest: The Evolution of Egalitarian Behavior* (Cambridge, MA: Harvard University Press: 2001).

3. You Scratch His Back, and I'll Scratch Yours

1. Warneken, F., and M. Tomasello, Varieties of altruism in children and chimpanzees, *Trends in Cognitive Sciences* 13, 397–402 (2009).
2. Oates, K., and M. Wilson, Nominal kinship cues facilitate altruism, *Proceedings of the Royal Society of London*, Series B: Biological Sciences 269, 105–109 (2002); and Krupp, D. B., L. M. Debruine, and P. Barclay, A cue of kinship

promotes cooperation for the public good, *Evolution and Human Behavior* 29, 49–55 (2008).

3. Trivers, R. L., The evolution of reciprocal altruism, *Quarterly Review of Biology* 46, 35–57 (1971).

4. Hammerstein, P., *Genetic and Cultural Evolution of Cooperation* (Cambridge, MA: MIT Press, 2003).

5. Alexander, R. D., Ostracism and indirect reciprocity: The reproductive significance of humor, *Ethology and Sociobiology* 7, 253–270 (1986).

6. Alexander, R. D., *The Biology of Moral Systems* (New York: Aldine de Gruyter, 1987).

7. Boyd, R., and P. J. Richerson, The evolution of indirect reciprocity, *Social Networks* 11, 213–236 (1989).

8. Pollock, G., and L. A. Dugatkin, Reciprocity and the emergence of reputation, *Journal of Theoretical Biology* 159, 25–37 (1992).

9. Nowak, M. A., and K. Sigmund, Evolution of indirect reciprocity by image scoring, *Nature* 393, 573–577 (1998).

10. Wedekind, C., and M. Milinski, Cooperation through image scoring in humans, *Science* 288, 850–852 (2000).

11. Olson, K. R., and E. S. Spelke, Foundations of cooperation in young children, *Cognition* 108, 222–231 (2008).

12. Hamlin, J. K., K. Wynn, and P. Bloom, Social evaluation by preverbal infants, *Nature* 450, 557–559 (2007).

13. Leimar, O., and P. Hammerstein, Evolution of cooperation through indirect reciprocity, *Proceedings of the Royal Society of London*, Series B: Biological Sciences 268, 745–753 (2001).

14. See www.youtube.com/watch?v=E3h-T3KQNxU.

15. "Three Teenage Suspects Held Over Homophobic Murder in London," *Guardian*, October 16, 2009, at www.guardian.co.uk/uk/2009/oct/16/teenagers-arrested-homophobic-murder. (Two of the three were later convicted of manslaughter, the third of affray.)

16. The economist Robert Sugden pioneered the use of game theory to analyze these sorts of strategies; see his book *The Economics of Rights, Co-operation and Welfare* (London: Palgrave Macmillan, 2004).

17. Ohtsuki, H., and Y. Iwasa, The leading eight: Social norms that can maintain cooperation by indirect reciprocity, *Journal of Theoretical Biology* 239, 435–444 (2006). Such rules, however, while good at preserving cooperation where it is already present, are less good at promoting cooperation when it is rare, because it is impossible to tell a defector from a punisher. See Panchanathan, K., Two wrongs don't make a right: The initial viability of different assessment rules in the evolution of indirect reciprocity, *Journal of Theoretical Biology* 277, 48–54 (2011).

18. Milinski, M., D. Semmann, T. C. Bakker, and H. J. Krambeck, Cooperation through indirect reciprocity: Image scoring or standing strategy? *Proceedings of the Royal Society of London*, Series B: Biological Sciences 268, 2495–2501 (2001).

19. Bloom, P., "The Moral Life of Babies," *New York Times*, May 5, 2010, http://www.nytimes.com/2010/05/09/magazine/09babies-t.html.

20. Milinski, M., D. Semmann, and H. Krambeck, Reputation helps solve the "tragedy of the commons," *Nature* 415, 424–426 (2002). For a theoretical version of the same idea, see Panchanathan, K., and R. Boyd, Indirect reciprocity can stabilize cooperation without the second-order free rider problem, *Nature* 432, 499–502 (2004).

21. Semmann, D., H. Krambeck, and M. Milinski, Strategic investment in reputation, *Behavioral Ecology and Sociobiology* 56, 248–252 (2004).

22. Jacquet, J., C. Hauert, A. Traulsen, and M. Milinski, Shame and honour drive cooperation, *Biology Letters*, doi: 10.1098/rsbl.2011.0367 (2011).

23. Milinski, M., D. Semmann, and H. Krambeck, Donors to charity gain in both indirect reciprocity and political reputation, *Proceedings of the Royal Society of London*, Series B: Biological Sciences 269, 881–883 (2002).

4. Casting a Shadow

1. Moore, H. T., Further data concerning sex differences, *Journal of Abnormal Psychology and Social Psychology* 17, 210–214 (1922). (Of the forty-two pieces of gossip that Moore quotes, about half could be said to concern others who were absent.)

2. Wert, S. R., and P. Salovey, A social comparison account of gossip, *Review of General Psychology* 8, 122–137 (2004).

3. Dunbar, P. R., *Grooming, Gossip and the Evolution of Language* (London: Faber and Faber, 2004).

4. Nowak, M. A., Generosity: A winner's advice, *Nature* 456, 579 (2008).

5. Sommerfeld, R. D., H. Krambeck, D. Semmann, and M. Milinski, Gossip as an alternative for direct observation in games of indirect reciprocity, *Proceedings of the National Academy of Sciences* 104, 17435–17440 (2007).

6. Mesoudi, A., A. Whiten, and R. Dunbar, A bias for social information in human cultural transmission, *British Journal of Psychology* 97, 405–423 (2006).

7. Cosmides, L., and J. Tooby, "Cognitive Adaptations for Social Exchange," , in Barkow, J. H., L. Cosmides, and J. Tooby, eds., *The Adapted Mind: Evolutionary Psychology and the Generation of Culture* (New York: Oxford University Press, 1992), 163–228.

8. Gross, A., *Lincoln's Own Stories* (New York: New York Garden City Publishing Co., 1862).

9. Christakis, N. A., and J. H. Fowler, *Connected: The Amazing Power of Social Networks and How They Shape Our Lives.* (London: HarperPress, 2010).

10. Nowak, M. A., Five rules for the evolution of cooperation, *Science* 314, 1560–1563 (2006).

11. Richman, B. D., Community enforcement of informal contracts: Jewish diamond merchants in New York, at http://works.bepress.com/barak_richman/12/.

12. Burt, R. S., "Closure and Stability—Persistent Reputation and Enduring Relations among Bankers and Analysts," in Rauch, J. E., ed., *The Missing Links: Formation and Decay of Economic Networks* (New York: Russell Sage Foundation, 2007), 100–141.

13. Anderson, C., and A. Shirako, Are individuals' reputations related to their history of behavior? *Journal of Personality and Social Psychology* 94, 320–333 (2008).

14. Burt, R. Gossip and reputation, Globalisation Seminar Series, Queen Mary University of London, author's notes, February 13, 2008.

15. Higgins, E. T., Achieving "shared reality" in the communication game: A social action that creates meaning, *Journal of Language and Social Psychology* 11, 107–131 (1992).

16. Gilovich, T, Secondhand information and social judgment, *Journal of Experimental Social Psychology* 23, 59–74 (1987).

17. Burt, R.S, *Brokerage and Closure: An Introduction to Social Capital* (New York: Oxford University Press, 2007).

5. Saving Face

1. Leary, M., Sociometer theory and the pursuit of relational value: Getting to the root of self-esteem, *European Journal of Social Psychology* 16, 75–111 (2005).

2. Hazlitt, W. *An Essay on the Principles of Human Action* (London: J. Johnson, 1805), 3.

3. Chiu, P., et al., Self responses along cingulate cortex reveal quantitative neural phenotype for high-functioning autism, *Neuron* 57, 463–473 (2008); Frith, C., and U. Frith, The self and its reputation in autism, *Neuron* 57, 331–332 (2008).

4. Humphrey, N. K., "The Social Function of Intellect," in P. P. G. Bateson and R. A. Hinde, eds., *Growing Points in Ethology* (Cambridge, UK: Cambridge University Press, 1976), 303–317.

5. Byrne, R. W., A. Whiten, *Machiavellian Intelligence: Social Expertise and the Evolution of Intellect in Monkeys, Apes, and Humans* (New York: Oxford University Press, 1988).

6. Dickerson, S. S., T. L. Gruenewald, and M. E. Kemeny, When the social self is threatened: Shame, physiology, and health, *Journal of Personality* 72, 1191–1216 (2004).

7. Tracy, J. L., R. W. Robins, and J. P. Tangney, eds., *The Self-Conscious Emotions: Theory and Research.* (New York: Guilford Press, 2007).

8. Keltner, D., and A. Anderson, Saving face for Darwin: The functions and uses of embarrassment, *Current Directions in Psychological Science* 9, 187–192 (2000); Harris, C., Embarrassment: A form of social pain, *American Scientist* 94, 524–533 (2006).

9. Fessler, D. M. T., Shame in two cultures: Implications for evolutionary approaches, *Journal of Cognition and Culture* 4, 207–262 (2004).

10. Tracy, J. L., and R. W. Robins, The nonverbal expression of pride: Evidence for cross-cultural recognition, *Journal of Personality and Social Psychology* 94, 516–530 (2008).

11. Semin, G. R., and A. S. R. Manstead, The social implications of embarrassment displays and restitution behaviour, *European Journal of Social Psychology* 12, 367–377 (1982).

12. De Jong, P. J., M. L. Peters, and D. De Cremer, Blushing may signify guilt: Revealing effects of blushing in ambiguous social situations, *Motivation and Emotion* 27, 225–249 (2003).

13. Levin, J., and A. Arluke, Embarrassment and helping behavior, *Psychological Reports* 51, 999–1002 (1982).

14. Apsler, R., Effects of embarrassment on behavior toward others, *Journal of Personality and Social Psychology* 32, 145–153 (1975).

15. Tracy, J. L., and D. Matsumoto, The spontaneous expression of pride and shame: Evidence for biologically innate nonverbal displays, *Proceedings of the National Academy of Sciences* 105, 11655–11660 (2008).

16. Tracy, J. L., Shariff, A. F., and J. T. Cheng, A naturalist's view of pride, *Emotion Review* 2, 163–177 (2010).

17. Fessler, Shame in two cultures.

18. Cheng, J. T., J. L.Tracy, and J. Henrich, Pride, personality, and the evolutionary foundations of human social status, *Evolution and Human Behavior* 31, 334–347 (2010).

19. Fessler, D. M. T., "From Appeasement to Conformity: Evolutionary and Cultural Perspectives on Shame, Competition and Cooperation," in Tracy, J. L., R. W. Robins, and J. P. Tangney, eds., *The Self-Conscious Emotions: Theory and Research* (New York: Guilford Press, 2007), 174–193.

6. Just to Get a Rep

1. Texas Crime Rates 1960–2009, http://www.disastercenter.com/crime/txcrime.htm; Massachusetts Crime Rates 1960–2009, http://www.disastercenter.com/crime/macrime.htm.

2. Cohen, D., R. E. Nisbett, B. F. Bowdle, and N. Schwarz, Insult, aggression, and the Southern culture of honor: An "experimental ethnography," *Journal of Personal and Social Psychology* 70, 945–959 (1996).

3. Nisbett, R. E., and D. Cohen, *Culture of Honor: The Psychology of Violence in the South* (Boulder, CO: Westview Press, 1996).

4. Henrich, J., et al., In search of Homo Economicus: Behavioral experiments in 15 small-scale societies, *American Economic Review* 91, 73–78 (2001); Henrich, J., et al., Costly punishment across human societies, *Science* 312, 1767–1770 (2006).

5. Cameron, L. A., Raising the stakes in the ultimatum game: Experimental evidence from Indonesia, *Economic Inquiry* 37, 47–59 (1999).

6. Fehr, E., and U. Fischbacher, The nature of human altruism, *Nature* 425, 785–791 (2003).

7. Bloom, P., "The Moral Life of Babies," *New York Times*, May 5, 2010, http://www.nytimes.com/2010/05/09/magazine/09babies-t.html.

8. Fehr, E., and U. Fischbacher, Third-party punishment and social norms, *Evolution and Human Behavior* 25, 63–87 (2004).

9. Fehr, E., S. Gachter, Altruistic punishment in humans, *Nature* 415, 137–140 (2002).

10. Gürerk, Ö., B. Irlenbusch, and B. Rockenbach, The competitive advantage of sanctioning institutions, *Science* 312, 108–111 (2006).

11. Kurzban, R., P. Descioli, and E. Obrien, Audience effects on moralistic punishment, *Evolution and Human Behavior* 28, 75–84 (2007).

12. Barclay, P., Reputational benefits for altruistic punishment, *Evolution and Human Behavior* 27, 325–344 (2006).

13. Fehr, E., and S. Gachter, Altruistic punishment in humans, *Nature* 415, 137–140 (2002).

14. Kümmerli, R., M. N. Burton-Chellew, A. Ross-Gillespie, and S. A. West, Resistance to extreme strategies, rather than prosocial preferences, can explain human cooperation in public goods games, *Proceedings of the National Academy of Sciences*, doi:10.1073/pnas.1000829107 (2010).

15. Gintis, H., Strong reciprocity and human sociality, *Journal of Theoretical Biology* 206, 169–179 (2000).

16. Figueredo, A. J., I .R. Tal, P. McNeil, and A. Guillén, Farmers, herders, and fishers: The ecology of revenge, *Evolution and Human Behavior* 25, 336–353 (2004).

17. Bourgois, P. I., *In Search of Respect: Selling Crack in El Barrio* (Cambridge, UK: Cambridge University Press, 2003).

18. Hattenstone, Simon, "Jay-Z: The Boy from the Hood Who Turned Out Good," *Guardian*, November 20, 2010, http://www.guardian.co.uk/music/2010/nov/20/jay-z-interview-simon-hattenstone.

19. Silverman, D., Street crime and street culture, *International Economic Review* 45, 761–786 (2004).

20. Shackelford, T. K., An evolutionary psychological perspective on cultures of honor, *Evolutionary Psychology* 3, 381–391 (2005).

21. Akman, H., Honour, feuding and national fragmentation in Kurdistan, in Aase, T., ed., *Tournaments of Power: Honor and Revenge in the Contemporary World* (Farnham, UK: Ashgate, 2002), 101–114.

22. Spacks, P. M., *Gossip* (New York: Knopf, 1985).

23. Rose, J., "A Piece of White Silk," *London Review of Books* 31, 5–8 (November 5, 2009).

24. Felson, R. B., Impression management and the escalation of aggression and violence, *Social Psychology Quarterly* 45, 245–254 (1982).

25. Johnstone, R. A., and R. Bshary, Evolution of spite through indirect reciprocity, *Proceedings of the Royal Society of London*, Series B: Biological Sciences 271, 1917–1922 (2004).

26. Jones, B. C., L. M. DeBruine, A. C. Little, C. D. Watkins, and D. R. Feinberg, "Eavesdropping" and perceived male dominance rank in humans, *Animal Behaviour* 81, 1203–1208 (2011).
27. Milgrom, P., and J. Roberts, Predation, reputation, and entry deterrence, *Journal of Economic Theory* 27, 280–312 (1982).
28. Gilligan, J. *Violence: Our Deadly Epidemic and its Causes* (New York: G. P. Putnam, 1996).
29. Machiavelli, N., *The Prince*, translated by G. Bull (London: Penguin, 1961).
30. Ibid.
31. Dur, R., *Status-Seeking in Criminal Subcultures and the Double Dividend of Zero-Tolerance*, CESIFO Working Paper no. 1762 (July 2006), www.cesifo.de/DocCIDL/cesifo1_wp1762.pdf.
32. Appiah, K. A., *The Honor Code: How Moral Revolutions Happen* (New York: W. W. Norton & Company, 2010).

7. Nosy Neighbors

1. Peake, T. M., A. M. Terry, P. K. McGregor, and T. Dabelsteen, Male great tits eavesdrop on simulated male-to-male vocal interactions, *Proceedings of the Royal Society of London*, Series B: Biological Sciences 268, 1183–1187 (2001).
2. Akçay, Ç., V. A. Reed, S. E. Campbell, C. N. Templeton, and M. D. Beecher, Indirect reciprocity: Song sparrows distrust aggressive neighbours based on eavesdropping, *Animal Behaviour* 80, 1041–1047 (2010).
3. Grosenick, L., T. S. Clement, and R. D. Fernald, Fish can infer social rank by observation alone, *Nature* 445, 429–432 (2007).
4. Earley, R. L., and L. A. Dugatkin, Eavesdropping on visual cues in green swordtail (Xiphophorus helleri) fights: A case for networking, *Proceedings of the Royal Society of London*, Series B: Biological Sciences 269, 943–952 (2002).
5. Dabelsteen, T., P. K. McGregor, H. M. Lampe, N. Langmore, and J. Holland, Quiet song in song birds: An overlooked phenomenon, *Bioacoustics* 9, 89–105 (1998).
6. Doutrelant, C., and P. K. McGregor, Eavesdropping and mate choice in female fighting fish, *Behaviour* 137, 1655–1669 (2000).
7. Ophir, A. G., and B. G. Galef, Female Japanese quail that "eavesdrop" on fighting males prefer losers to winners, *Animal Behaviour* 66, 399–407 (2003).
8. Otter, K., et al., Do female great tits (Parus major) assess males by eavesdropping? A field study using interactive song playback, *Proceedings of the Royal Society of London*, Series B: Biological Science 266, 1305–1309 (1999).
9. Mennill, D. J., L. M. Ratcliffe, and P. T. Boag, Female eavesdropping on male song contests in songbirds, *Science* 296, 873 (2002).
10. Heinsohn, R., and C. Packer, Complex cooperative strategies in group-territorial African lions, *Science* 269, 1260–1262 (1995).

11. Angier, N., "Please Say It Isn't So, Simba: The Noble Lion Can Be a Coward," *New York Times*, September 5, 1995, http://www.nytimes.com/1995/09/05/science/please-say-it-isn-t-so-simba-the-noble-lion-can-be-a-coward.html.

12. Doutrelant, C., and R. Covas, Helping has signalling characteristics in a cooperatively breeding bird, *Animal Behaviour* 74, 739–747 (2007).

13. Call, J., and M. Tomasello, Does the chimpanzee have a theory of mind? 30 years later, *Trends in Cognitive Science* 12, 187–192 (2008).

14. De Waal, F. B. M., *Chimpanzee Politics* (Baltimore, MD: Johns Hopkins Univ. Press, 2007).

15. Hare, B., J. Call, and M. Tomasello, Chimpanzees deceive a human competitor by hiding, *Cognition* 101, 495–514 (2006).

16. Slocombe, K. E., and K. Zuberbühler, Chimpanzees modify recruitment screams as a function of audience composition, *Proceedings of the National Academy of Sciences* 104, 17228–17233 (2007).

17. Melis, A. P., B. Hare, and M. Tomasello, Chimpanzees recruit the best collaborators. *Science* 311, 1297–1300 (2006).

18. Russell, Y. I., J. Call, and R. I. M. Dunbar, Image scoring in great apes, *Behavioural Processes*, 78, 108–111 (2008).

19. Subiaul, F., J. Vonk, S. Okamoto-Barth, and J. Barth, Do chimpanzees learn reputation by observation? Evidence from direct and indirect experience with generous and selfish strangers, *Animal Cognition* 11, 611–623 (2008).

20. Melis, A. P., B. Hare, and M. Tomasello, Do chimpanzees reciprocate received favours? *Animal Behaviour* 76, 951–962 (2008).

21. Kundey, S. A. M., A. De Los Reyes, E. Royer, S. Molina, B. Monnier, R. German, and A. Coshun, Reputation-like inference in domestic dogs (*Canis familiaris*), *Animal Cognition* 14, 291–302 (2011); and Marshall-Pescini, S., C. Passalacqua, A. Ferrario, P. Valsecchi, and E. Prato-Previde, Social eavesdropping in the domestic dog, *Animal Behaviour* 81, 1177–1183 (2011).

22. Grutter, A. S., and R. Bshary, Cleaner wrasse prefer client mucus: Support for partner control mechanisms in cleaning interactions, *Proceedings of the Royal Society*, Series B: Biological Sciences 270, S242–S244 (2003).

23. Bshary, R., and A. S. Grutter, Image scoring and cooperation in a cleaner fish mutualism, *Nature* 441, 975–978 (2006).

24. Bshary, R., and A. S. Grutter, Punishment and partner switching cause cooperative behaviour in a cleaning mutualism, *Biology Letters* 1, 396–399 (2005).

25. Bshary, R., Biting cleaner fish use altruism to deceive image-scoring client reef fish, *Proceedings of the Royal Society*, Series B: Biological Sciences 269, 2087–2093 (2002).

8. Panopticon

1. Bateson, M., D. Nettle, and G. Roberts, Cues of being watched enhance cooperation in a real-world setting, *Biology Letters* 2, 412–414 (2006).

2. Ernest-Jones, M., D. Nettle, and M. Bateson, Effects of eye images on everyday cooperative behavior: A field experiment, *Evolution and Human Behavior* 32, 172–178 (2011).

3. Bentham, J., *Writings on the Poor Laws*, ed. M. Quinn (Oxford: Oxford University Press, 2001), 277. See also Bentham, J. *The Panopticon Writings*, ed. M. Bozovic (London: Verso, 1995).

4. Soetevent, A. R., Anonymity in giving in a natural context—a field experiment in 30 churches, *Journal of Public Economics* 89, 2301–2323 (2005).

5. Burnham, T. C., and B. Hare, Engineering human cooperation, *Human Nature* 18, 88–108 (2007); and Haley, K., and D. Fessler, Nobody's watching? Subtle cues affect generosity in an anonymous economic game, *Evolution and Human Behavior* 26, 245–256 (2005).

6. Oda, R., Y. Niwa, A. Honma, K. Hiraishi, An eye-like painting enhances the expectation of a good reputation, *Evolution and Human Behavior* 32, 166–171 (2011).

7. Rigdon, M., K. Ishii, M. Watabe, and S. Kitayama, Minimal social cues in the dictator game, *Journal of Economic Psychology* 30, 358–367 (2009).

8. Fehr, E., and F. Schneider, Eyes are on us, but nobody cares: Are eye cues relevant for strong reciprocity? *Proceedings of the Royal Society of London*, Series B: Biological Sciences 277, 1315–1323 (2010).

9. Diener, E., and M. Wallbom, Effects of self-awareness on antinormative behavior, *Journal of Research in Personality* 10, 107–111 (1976); Diener, E., S. C. Fraser, A. L. Beaman, and R. T. Kelem, Effects of deindividuation variables on stealing among Halloween trick-or-treaters, *Journal of Personality and Social Psychology* 33, 178–183 (1976).

10. Emery, N. J., The eyes have it: The neuroethology, function and evolution of social gaze, *Neuroscience & Biobehavioral Reviews* 24, 581–604 (2000).

11. Farroni, T., G. Csibra, F. Simion, and M. H. Johnson, Eye contact detection in humans from birth, *Proceedings of the National Academy of Sciences of the United States of America* 99, 9602–9605 (2002).

12. Bayliss, A. P., and S. P. Tipper, Predictive gaze cues and personality judgments: Should eye trust you? *Psychological Science* 17, 514–520 (2006).

13. Tomasello, M., B. Hare, H. Lehmann, and J. Call, Reliance on head versus eyes in the gaze following of great apes and human infants: The cooperative eye hypothesis, *Journal of Human Evolution* 52, 314–320 (2007).

14. Kobayashi, H., and S. Kohshima, Unique morphology of the human eye, *Nature* 387, 767–768 (1997).

15. Bering, J. M., K. McLeod, and T. K. Shackelford, Reasoning about dead agents reveals possible adaptive trends, *Human Nature* 16, 360–381 (2005).

16. Shariff, A. F., and A. Norenzayan, God is watching you: Priming God concepts increases prosocial behavior in an anonymous economic game, *Psychological Science* 18, 803–809 (2007).

17. Pettazzoni, R., On the attributes of God, *Numen* 2, 1–27 (1955).

18. Atkinson, Q. D., and P. Bourrat, Beliefs about God, the afterlife and morality support the role of supernatural policing in human cooperation, *Evolution and Human Behavior* 32, 41–49 (2011).
19. Blogowska, J., and V. Saroglou, Religious fundamentalism and limited prosociality as a function of the target, *Journal for the Scientific Study of Religion* 50, 44–60 (2011).
20. Johnson, D. D. P., God's punishment and public goods, *Human Nature* 16, 410–446 (2005).
21. Henrich, J., et al., Markets, religion, community size, and the evolution of fairness and punishment, *Science* 327, 1480–1484 (2010).
22. Johnson, D., and J. Bering, Hand of god, mind of man: Punishment and cognition in the evolution of cooperation, *Evolutionary Psychology* 4, 219–233 (2006).

9. A Tool and a Weapon

1. Kniffin, K. M., and D. S. Wilson, Utilities of gossip across organizational levels, *Human Nature* 16, 278–292 (2005).
2. Landers, A., "Gossip's a Vicious Killer," *Spokane Daily Chronicle*, April 5, 1976, at Google News Archive, http://bit.ly/cT5o4c.
3. Ellickson, R., *Order without Law: How Neighbors Settle Disputes* (Cambridge, MA: Harvard University Press, 1994).
4. Wilson, D. S., C. Wilczynski, A. Wells, and L. Weiser, "Gossip and Other Aspects of Language as Group-Level Adaptations," in Heyes, C. M., and L. Huber, *The Evolution of Cognition* (Cambridge, MA: MIT Press, 2000), 347–365.
5. Kniffin, K. M., and D. S. Wilson, The effect of nonphysical traits on the perception of physical attractiveness: Three naturalistic studies, *Evolution and Human Behavior* 25, 88–101 (2004).
6. Dunbar, R., A. Marriott, and N. Duncan, Human conversational behavior, *Human Nature* 8, 231–246 (1997).
7. Anderson, E., E. H. Siegel, E. Bliss-Moreau, and L. F. Barrett, The visual impact of gossip, *Science*, doi: 10.1126/science.1201574 (2011).
8. Hamlin, J. Kiley, K. Wynn, and P. Bloom, Three-month-olds show a negativity bias in their social evaluations, *Developmental Science* 13, 923–020 (2010).
9. Riskey, D. R., and M. H. Birnbaum, Compensatory effects in moral judgment: Two rights don't make up for a wrong, *Journal of Experimental Psychology* 103, 171–173 (1974).
10. McAndrew, F., E. K. Bell, and C. M. Garcia, Who do we tell and whom do we tell on? Gossip as a strategy for status enhancement, *Journal of Applied Social Psychology* 37, 1562–1577 (2007).
11. Hansen, L. K., A. Arvidsson, F. Å., Nielsen, E. Colleoni, and M. Etter, Good friends, bad news—affect and virality in Twitter, 2011, at http://arxiv.org/abs/1101.0510.

12. Sommerfeld, R. D., H. Krambeck, and M. Milinski, Multiple gossip statements and their effect on reputation and trustworthiness, *Proceedings of the Royal Society of London*, Series B: Biological Sciences 275, 2529–2536 (2008).

13. Sommerfeld, R. D., H. Krambeck, D., Semmann, and M. Milinski, Gossip as an alternative for direct observation in games of indirect reciprocity, *Proceedings of the National Academy of Sciences* 104, 17435–17440 (2007).

14. Hess, N., and E. Hagen, Psychological adaptations for assessing gossip veracity, *Human Nature* 17, 337–354 (2006).

15. McAndrew, F. T., and M. A. Milenkovic, Of tabloids and family secrets: The evolutionary psychology of gossip, *Journal of Applied Social Psychology* 32, 1064–1082 (2002).

16. *OK! Magazine* Celebrity Media Pack 2011, www.ok.co.uk/pdfs/Celebrity factbook.pdf.

17. Hess, N. C., and E. H. Hagen, Informational warfare, http://citeseerx.ist.psu .edu/viewdoc/summary?doi=10.1.1.147.4070.

18. Hess, N., and E. Hagen, Sex differences in indirect aggression: Psychological evidence from young adults, *Evolution and Human Behavior* 27, 231–245 (2006).

19. Hess, N., C. Helfrecht, E. Hagen, A. Sell, and B. Hewlett, Interpersonal aggression among Aka hunter-gatherers of the Central African Republic, *Human Nature* 21, 330–354 (2010).

20. Dunbar, Marriott, and Duncan, Human conversational behavior.

21. Rodseth, L., et al., The human community as a primate society, *Current Anthropology* 32, 221–254 (1991).

22. Campbell, A., Staying alive: Evolution, culture, and women's intrasexual aggression, *Behavioral and Brain Sciences* 22, 203–252 (1999).

23. De Backer, C., *Like Belgian Chocolate for the Universal Mind: Interpersonal and Media Gossip from an Evolutionary Perspective*, PhD thesis, University of Ghent, 2005, http://www.ethesis.net/gossip/gossip_contence.htm.

24. Hyde, J. S., The gender similarities hypothesis, *American Psychologist* 60, 581–592 (2005).

10. Future Discounting

1. Knoch, D., F. Schneider, D. Schunk, M. Hohmann, and E. Fehr, Disrupting the prefrontal cortex diminishes the human ability to build a good reputation, *Proceedings of the National Academy of Sciences* 106, 20895–20899 (2009).

2. Lykken, D. T., *The Antisocial Personalities* (Hillsdale, NJ: Lawrence Erlbaum, 1995).

3. Colman, A. M., and J. C. Wilson, Antisocial personality disorder: An evolutionary game theory analysis, *Legal and Criminological Psychology* 2, 22–34 (1997).

4. Jonason, P. K., and J. Tost, I just cannot control myself: The Dark Triad and self-control, *Personality and Individual Differences* 49, 611–615 (2010); Jonason, P. K., et al., The Dark Triad: Facilitating a short-term mating strategy in men, *European Journal of Personality* 23, 5–18 (2009).

5. Blair, R. J. R., and L. Cipolotti, Impaired social response reversal, *Brain* 123, 1122–1141 (2000); Mendez, M. F., et al., Acquired sociopathy and fronto-temporal dementia, *Dementia and Geriatric Cognitive Disorders* 20, 99–104 (2005).

6. Lykken, The Antisocial Personalities, 118.

7. Book, A. S., and V. L. Quinsey, Psychopaths: Cheaters or warrior-hawks? *Personality and Individual Differences* 36, 33–45 (2004).

8. Mullins-Sweatt, S. N., N. G. Glover, K. J. Derefinko, J. D. Miller, and T. A. Widiger, The search for the successful psychopath, *Journal of Research in Personality* 44, 554–558 (2010).

9. Mealey, L., The sociobiology of sociopathy: An integrated evolutionary model, *Behavioral and Brain Sciences* 18, 523–541 (1995).

10. Alencar, A., J. Deoliveirasiqueira, and M. Yamamoto, Does group size matter? Cheating and cooperation in Brazilian school children, *Evolution and Human Behavior* 29, 42–48 (2008).

11. Putnam, R. D., *Bowling Alone: The Collapse and Revival of American Community* (New York: Simon & Schuster, 2001).

12. "Duck Island MP 'feels humiliated'," BBC News, May 23, 2009, http://news .bbc.co.uk/1/hi/england/hampshire/8065083.stm.

13. "Talk to the Times: Andrew Ross Sorkin," *New York Times*, October 19, 2009, www.nytimes.com/2009/10/19/business/media/19askthetimes.html.

14. Merry, S. E., "Rethinking Gossip and Scandal," in Klein, D., ed., *Reputation: Studies in the Voluntary Elicitation of Good Conduct* (Ann Arbor: University of Michigan Press, 1997), 47–74.

15. Hutton, W., "I've Watched the Economy for 30 Years. Now I'm Truly Scared, *Observer*, September 28, 2008, www.guardian.co.uk/commentisfree/2008/ sep/28/globaleconomy.creditcrunch.

16. Marx, K. "The Power of Money," www.marxists.org/archive/marx/works/1844/ manuscripts/power.htm.

17. Wilkinson, R., and K. Pickett, *The Spirit Level: Why Equality Is Better for Everyone* (London: Penguin Group, 2010).

18. Yassukovich, S., "Whatever Happened to Shame?" *Spectator*, March 12, 2005, 34–37.

19. Elleray, K., and M. Morley, "Big Brother's Watching You—and Your Rubbish," *Stockport Express*, November 21, 2007, http://menmedia.co.uk/stockportexpress/ news/s/1025209_big_brothers_watching_you__and_your_rubbish.

11. Panopticon 2.0

1. Resnick, P., R. Zeckhauser, J. Swanson, and K. Lockwood, The value of reputation on eBay: A controlled experiment, *Experimental Economics* 9, 79–101 (2006).

2. Brown, J., and J. Morgan, Reputation in online auctions: The market for trust, *California Management Review* 49, 61–81 (2006).

3. Farmer, F. R., and B. Glass, *Building Web Reputation Systems* (Sebastopol: O'Reilly Media, Inc., 2010).

4. "Trying to Predict the Present: An Interview with Cory Doctorow," http://sites .duke.edu/writingthefuture/2010/04/26/trying-to-predict-the-present-an-interview-with-cory-doctorow/.

5. Martin, A., "As a Hiring Filter, Credit Checks Draw Questions," *New York Times*, April 10, 2010, http://www.nytimes.com/2010/04/10/business/10credit.html.

6. Utz, S., "Egoboo" vs. altruism: The role of reputation in online consumer communities, *New Media & Society* 11, 357–374 (2009); Baytiyeh, H., and J. Pfaffman, Open source software: A community of altruists, *Computers in Human Behavior* 26, 1345–1354 (2010).

7. Manjoo, F., "Why Digg's MrBabyMan Is the King of All Social Media," *Slate*, February 3, 2009, www.slate.com/id/2210365/.

8. Hancock, J. T., J. Thom-Santelli, and T. Ritchie, Deception and design: The impact of communication technology on lying behavior, *Proceedings of the SIGCHI Conference on Human Factors in Computing Systems* 129–134 (2004), doi:10.1145/985692.985709.

9. Strahilevitz, J. J., "How's my driving?" for everyone (and everything), *NYU Law Review* 81, 1699–1765 (2006).

10. Smith, R. S., "Onan the Vegetarian—a Raw-food Guru Turns 'Subway Perv,'" *New York*, April 2, 2006, http://nymag.com/news/features/16576/.

11. Solove, D. J. *The Future of Reputation: Gossip, Rumor, and Privacy on the Internet* (New Haven: Yale University Press, 2007).

12. Locke, J. L., "Looking for, Looking At: Social Control, Honest Signals and Intimate Experience in Human Evolution and History, in McGregor, P. K., ed., *Animal Communication Networks.* (Cambridge, UK: Cambridge University Press, 2005), 416–441.

13. Aguiton, C., et al., "Does Showing Off Help to Make Friends? Experimenting a Sociological Game on Self-Exhibition and Social Networks," Third International AAAI Conference on Weblogs and Social Media (2009), http:// www.aaai.org/ocs/index.php/ICWSM/09/paper/viewPaper/178.

14. Walther, J. B., B. Van Der Heide, S. Kim, D. Westerman, and S. T. Tong, The role of friends' appearance and behavior on evaluations of individuals on Facebook: Are we known by the company we keep? *Human Communication Research* 34, 28–49 (2008).

15. Trammell, K. D., and A. Keshelashvili, A. Examining the new influencers: A self-presentation study of A-list blogs, *Journalism and Mass Communication Quarterly* 82, 968–982 (2005).

16. Lampe, C. A. C., N. Ellison, and C. Steinfield, A familiar face(book): Profile elements as signals in an online social network, *Proceedings of the SIGCHI Conference on Human Factors in Computing Systems* 435–444 (2007), doi:10.1145/1240624.1240695.

17. Adee, S., Keeping up e-ppearances, *New Scientist*, February 19, 2011, 47–49.

18. Madden, M., and A. Smith, "Reputation Management and Social Media," http://www.pewinternet.org/Reports/2010/Reputation-Management.aspx.

19. Eaton, K., "If You're Applying for a Job, Censor Your Facebook Page," August 19, 2009, http://www.fastcompany.com/blog/kit-eaton/technomix/if-youre-applying-job-censor-your-facebook-page.

20. Maushart, S., *The Winter of Our Disconnect: How Three Totally Wired Teenagers (and a Mother Who Sleeps with Her iPhone) Pulled the Plug on Their Technology and Lived to Tell/Text/Tweet the Tale* (London: Profile Books Limited, 2011).

12. Us and Them

1. Tajfel, H., M. G. Billig, R. P. Bundy, and C. Flament, Social categorization and intergroup behaviour, *European Journal of Social Psychology* 1, 149–178 (1971).

2. Yamagishi, T., J. Nobuhito, and T. Kiyonari, Bounded generalized reciprocity: Ingroup boasting and ingroup favoritism, *Advances in Group Processes* 16, 161–197 (1999).

3. Yamagishi, T., and N. Mifune, Does shared group membership promote altruism? *Rationality and Society* 20, 5–30 (2008).

4. Semmann, D., H. Krambeck, and M. Milinski, Reputation is valuable within and outside one's own social group, *Behavioral Ecology and Sociobiology* 57, 611–616 (2005).

5. Mifune, N., H. Hashimoto, and T. Yamagishi, Altruism toward in-group members as a reputation mechanism, *Evolution and Human Behavior* 31, 109–117 (2010).

6. Shinada, M., T. Yamagishi, and Y. Ohmura, False friends are worse than bitter enemies: "Altruistic" punishment of in-group members, *Evolution and Human Behavior* 25, 379–393 (2004).

7. Bernhard, H., U. Fischbacher, and E. Fehr, Parochial altruism in humans, *Nature* 442, 912–915 (2006).

8. Smith, A., "Lecture on the Influence of Commerce on Manners," reprinted in Klein, D. B., ed., *Reputation: Studies in the Voluntary Elicitation of Good Conduct* (Ann Arbor: University of Michigan Press, 1997).

9. Schelling, T. C., *Arms and Influence* (New Haven: Yale University Press, 1966).

10. Sheehan, N., *The Pentagon Papers* (New York: Bantam, 1971).

11. Fletcher, M. A., Bush Attacks Party of 'Cut and Run'," *Washington Post*, September 29, 2006, http://www.washingtonpost.com/wp-dyn/content/article/2006/09/28/AR2006092801844.html.

12. Mercer, J., *Reputation and International Politics* (Ithaca, NY: Cornell University Press, 2009).

13. Crescenzi, M. J., J. D. Kathman, and S. B. Long, Reputation, history, and war, *Journal of Peace Research* 44, 651–667 (2007).

14. See, for example, Kennan, G. F., "America and the Russian Future," *Foreign Affairs* 3, 351–370 (1951).

15. Tomz, M., *Reputation and International Cooperation: Sovereign Debt across Three Centuries* (Princeton, NJ: Princeton University Press, 2007).
16. Downs, G. W., and M. A. Jones, Reputation, compliance, and international law, *Journal of Legal Studies* 31, S95–S114 (2002).
17. Guzman, A. T., *Reputation and International Law*, UC Berkeley Public Law Research Paper no. 1112064 (2008), http://papers.ssrn.com/sol3/papers.cfm?abstract_id=1112064.
18. Crescenzi, M. J. C., J. D. Kathman, K. B. Kleinberg, and R. M. Wood, "Reliability, Reputation, and Alliance Formation," SSRN eLibrary (2009), http://papers.ssrn.com/Sol3/papers.cfm?abstract_id=1450539.
19. Milinski, M., D. Semmann, H. Krambeck, and J. Marotzke, Stabilizing the Earth's climate is not a losing game: Supporting evidence from public goods experiments, *Proceedings of the National Academy of Sciences* 103, 3994–3998 (2006).
20. Busby, J., "The Hardest Problem in the World: Leadership in the Climate Regime," in Brem, S., and K. W. Stiles, *Cooperating without America: Theories and Case Studies of Non-Hegemonic Regimes* (London: Routledge, 2009), 64–82.
21. Miller, G., *Spent: Sex, Evolution, and Consumer Behavior* (New York: Penguin Group USA, 2010).
22. Bakan, J., *The Corporation: The Pathological Pursuit of Profit and Power* (New York: Free Press, 2005).
23. Guzman, A. T., A compliance-based theory of international law, *California Law Review* 90, 1823–1887 (2002).
24. Thucydides, *The Peloponnesian War* (London: J. M. Dent, 1910), http://www.perseus.tufts.edu/hopper/text?doc=Perseus:text:1999.01.0200:book=5:chapter=89:section=1.
25. Greenhill, K., and J. Busby, "Ain't That a Shame? Hypocrisy, Punishment, and Weak Actor Influence in International Politics," paper presented at the 2011 International Studies Association Annual Convention, www.allacademic.com/meta/p502454_index.html.
26. Keohane, R. O., *After Hegemony: Cooperation and Discord in the World Political Economy* (Princeton, NJ: Princeton University Press, 2005).
27. Buchan, N. R., et al., Globalization and human cooperation, *Proceedings of the National Academy of Sciences* 106, 4138–4142 (2009).

INDEX